LANCHESTER LIBRARY

3 8001 00143 8377

KU-304-787

WITHDRAWN

LANCHESTER LIBRARY, Coventry University
Gosford Street, Coventry CV1 5DD Telephone 024 7688 7555

This book is due to be returned not later than the date and
time stamped above. Fines are charged on overdue books

The Characteristics of Aphasia

Brain Damage, Behaviour and Cognition
Developments in Clinical Neuropsychology

Series editors: Chris Code, Scraptoft Campus, Leicester Polytechnic, and Dave Muller, Suffolk College of Higher and Further Education

Brain Damage, Behaviour and Cognition
Developments in Clinical Neuropsychology

The Characteristics of Aphasia

Edited by Chris Code
Leicester Polytechnic

LAWRENCE ERLBAUM ASSOCIATES, PUBLISHERS
Hove and London (UK)   Hillsdale (USA)

Coventry University

Copyright © 1991 by Lawrence Erlbaum Associates Ltd.
   All rights reserved. No part of this book may be reproduced in any
   form, by photostat, microform, retrieval system, or any other
   means without the prior written permission of the publisher.

First published by Taylor & Francis 1989
Reprinted 1991

Lawrence Erlbaum Associates Ltd., Publishers
27 Palmeira Mansions
Church Road
Hove
East Sussex, BN3 2FA
U.K.

British Library Cataloguing in Publication Data

The Characteristics of aphasia.
   1. Aphasia
   I. Code, Christopher, *1942*– II. Series
   616.85'52

   ISBN 0-86377-185-8 (Hbk)
   ISBN 0-86377-186-6 (Pbk)   *lo 4267*

Phototypeset by Input Typesetting Ltd, London
and printed in Great Britain by
Page Bros (Norwich) Ltd.
Mile Cross Lane, Norwich, NR6 6SA.

Contents

For Gabby and Billy who do love to see their names in print, and for Chris, who couldn't care less.

Series Preface

From being an area primarily on the periphery of mainstream behavioural and cognitive science, neuropsychology has developed in recent years into an area of central concern for a range of disciplines. We are witnessing not only a revolution in the way in which brain–behaviour–cognition relationships are viewed, but a widening of interest concerning developments in neuropsychology on the part of a range of workers in a variety of fields. Major advances in brain-imaging techniques and the cognitive modelling of the impairments following brain damage promise a wider understanding of the nature of the representation of cognition and behaviour in the damaged and undamaged brain.

Neuropsychology is now centrally important for those working with brain-damaged people, but the very rate of expansion in the area makes it difficult to keep up with findings from current research. The aim of the *Brain Damage, Behaviour and Cognition* series is to publish a wide range of books which present comprehensive and up-to-date overviews of current developments in specific areas of interest.

These books will be of particular interest to those working with the brain-damaged. It is the editors' intention that undergraduates, postgraduates, clinicians and researchers in psychology, speech pathology and medicine will find this series a useful source of information on important current developments. The authors and editors of the books in this series are experts in their respective fields, working at the forefront of contemporary research. They have produced texts which are accessible and scholarly. We thank them for their contribution and their hard work in fulfilling the aims of the series.

CC and DJM
Leicester and Ipswich
Series editors

Preface

Aphasia has been a topic of intense argument since at least the mid 1860s when Broca conducted his famous studies, and the impairments of language processing which characterize aphasia have always been central in neuropsychology. The interest in aphasia, as well as the intensity of argument, have increased in recent years and now form the spearhead of the general expansion of activity in the cognitive and neurosciences. Aphasia can be approached from several directions, reflecting the range of interdisciplinary interest, and each approach has its own story to tell. The neurological, the cognitive, the mainly clinical or purely theoretical viewpoint can be accessed easily in a range of good books.

So, why another book on aphasia? The aim of this book is to present an introductory but comprehensive account of the major characteristics, or symptoms, of aphasia. Thus, for example, there are chapters on paraphasia, on auditory verbal comprehension impairment, on fluency and on agrammatism and paragrammatism. A problem which arises is trying to decide what to include and what to leave out of a book which aims to discuss the major symptomatology of aphasia. Should it include apraxia of speech, reading impairments, writing impairments? Should it not also have a chapter on gestural impairment? Apraxia of speech and reading and writing impairments are included as they have not only been central in discussion for many years, and many aphasic individuals present with such problems, but developments in these areas impinge very significantly on discussion of other characteristics. Gesture could have been included, as might other chapters on 'nonverbal' aspects of communication. But the major characteristics of aphasia were therefore considered to be those which impair core linguistic aspects of communication.

Each chapter concerns itself with one of the major characteristics of aphasia, and each chapter attempts an overview of contemporary issues pertinent to the topic of the chapter. There is no set format to the individual chapters and some authors have paid more attention to linguistic or neurological or clinical issues, for instance, depending upon their relevance to discussion. Thus, Chapter 5 on Agrammatism and Paragrammatism, Chapter 6 on Phonological

Paraphasia and Chapter 7 on Jargonaphasia spend more time on psycholinguistic issues than other chapters. Chapter 8 on Apraxia of Speech examines the contribution of speech production modelling while Chapter 10 on Acquired Disorders of Reading and Spelling concentrates on recent developments in the cognitive neuropsychology of reading and writing impairment.

Aphasia is a complex topic and is becoming more so as research advances, especially perhaps in psycholinguistic research which has seen revolutionary development in recent years. So, while each chapter can be read individually, some of the inevitably more technical chapters may require some prior knowledge, and readers new to aphasia may prefer to read Chapter 1 first which presents an introduction to the historical and contemporary issues in aphasiology and highlights their relevance to discussion of aphasic symptomatology in other parts of the book.

The book should be of interest to advanced undergraduates, postgraduates and clinicians in speech pathology and neuropsychology. Those responsible for teaching and training may find that individual chapters make useful sources of course and seminar material.

I am grateful, as often, to the red pen of Dave Muller and for the patience and cooperation of contributors who were always willing for me to take liberties with their hard work.

Chris Code
Leicester

Contributors

Christopher Barry

Department of Applied Psychology
University College of Cardiff
University of Wales
Park Place
Cardiff, UK

Hugh W. Buckingham

Interdepartmental Linguistics Program
College of Arts and Sciences
Louisiana State University
Baton Rouge
Louisiana 70803, USA

Sara Dale Brandt

Hearing and Speech Department
Kansas University Medical Center
Kansas City
Kansas, USA

Sarah S. Christman

Department of Speech Communication, Theatre,
   and Communication Disorders
College of Arts and Sciences
Louisiana State University
Baton Rouge
Louisiana 70803, USA

Chris Code

School of Speech Pathology
Leicester Polytechnic
Scraptoft Campus
Scraptoft
Leicester LE7 9SU, UK

Robert Goldfarb   Speech and Hearing Center
                          The City University of New York
                          Bedford Park Boulevard
                          Bronx
                          New York 104-1589, USA

Harvey Halpern   Department of Communication Arts and Science
                          Queen's College
                          The City University of New York
                          Bedford Park Boulevard
                          Bronx
                          New York 104-1587, USA

Marjorie Perlman Lorch   Department of Applied Linguistics
                          Birkbeck College
                          University of London
                          43 Gordon Square
                          London WC1H 0PD, UK

Niklas Miller   Speech Therapy Department
                          Frenchay Hospital
                          Bristol BS16 1LE, UK

Klaus Poeck   Vorstand der Abteilung Neurologie
                              Medizinische
                          Fakultat der Technischen Hochchule
                          5100 Aachen
                          den Goethestrasse 27-29
                          Aachen, FR Germany

Ed Schulte   Department of Speech-Language-Hearing
                              Science
                          University of Kansas
                          369 Hawkworth Hall
                          Lawrence
                          Kansas 66044, USA

Chapter 1

Symptoms, Syndromes, Models: The Nature of Aphasia

Chris Code

Symptoms to syndromes

This book looks at aphasia from the perspective of examining its individual characteristics, or, in traditional medical terminology, its symptoms – the signs by which we know it. We recognize phenomena by their signs or features, by the individual characteristics which separate them from other phenomena. In medicine, illness is recognized by symptoms and symptoms are classified into syndromes. A combination of symptoms allows a physician successfully to identify a disease process and prescribe a treatment. The major feature of a syndrome approach is that it endeavours to relate symptoms one to another. It seeks explanations for the co-occurrence of symptoms, and, in some cases, causal links between symptoms. In aphasia too we find signs, features or symptoms: particular characteristics which enable us to state that an individual has aphasia with some degree of accuracy, and collections of features which theorists have used to attempt classification of aphasia into syndromes or types.

Aphasia is the property of no particular specialty. It can be examined from a number of perspectives, reflecting the interest paid to it by a range of disciplinary approaches. In the early years it was neurology that had a monopoly on the topic, but the coming together of neurology and psychology to form the beginnings of neuropsychology in the second half of the last century meant that new paradigms and approaches to research in the area were developed. As the systematic and scientific study of language gave rise to the development of linguistic description and explanation, then other disciplines – linguistics and psycholinguistics – brought different ideas and methodology to the breakdown of language as represented by aphasia. Aphasia therapy is perhaps the best developed area of neuropsychological rehabilitation, and speech pathology has developed foundations for assessment and treatment over the years derived to a large extent from theoretical and empirical progress.

The area is fraught with controversy and has been during the entirety of its history. Over 130 years of study has resulted in a massive literature on aphasia and currently it is coming in for intense investigation from several scientific directions. As with all phenomena, there are a number of ways of looking at aphasia. Also as with other phenomena, the way something is looked at, the perspective that is taken, in itself not only increases our understanding of phenomena, but can also limit it. Having one window on something brings some details into sharper focus but often obscures an alternative or complementary view.

One way to approach aphasia is to adopt the general assumption that it results from impairment in the use of those features of human language which can be characterized through a formal unit-and-rule generative linguistic model. In aphasia the patient has problems which can be described in terms of the representational linguistic levels of phonology, morphology, syntax and lexical semantics. But while there may be good reasons to assume that aphasia represents pure linguistic breakdown, there are acquired communication impairments where it is less clear whether the underlying disorder is specifically linguistic in nature. It may often be convenient to think in general about aphasic symptomatology as being reserved for pure aphasic individuals who have no other deficits at all, but in reality people present with impairments in language use which are clinically indistinguishable from aphasic symptoms, and probably only the mildly aphasic individual who has no other cognitive impairments can be considered 'pure'. For instance, in both dementia (Au, Albert and Obler 1988; and Ch. 3 below) and schizophrenia (Ch. 3 below) patients can present with impairments of language which are clinically indistinguishable from aphasia, suggesting that it is the same processes which are compromised in all cases. In both dementia and schizophrenia individuals can present with a *jargonaphasia* (see Ch. 7 below), for instance, which makes differential diagnosis between them and aphasia difficult purely on the basis of language use.

Apraxia of speech (see Ch. 8 below) also presents problems for assuming aphasia to be simply a 'linguistic' disorder. Interesting and important discussion and disagreement surrounds the linguistic status of apraxia of speech (see Ch. 8 below). Although usually included in discussion of aphasia (as it is in this book), there is controversy over whether it constitutes a linguistic (i.e. phonological) impairment, or a phonetic (i.e. motor-speech programming) disorder. Because many individuals with apraxia of speech will also present with aphasia, and because differentiation of apraxic errors of speech and aphasic errors of speech has not been possible through linguistic analysis, then it will continue to be included in general discussion in aphasia. In addition, because apraxia of speech may represent an impairment at a level intermediate between the abstract phonological level and the concrete phonetic realization level (Code and Ball 1988), and articulatory problems of an apraxic nature are often associated with *agrammatism* (Goodglass 1976; see Ch. 5 below), then it belongs in any comprehensive discussion of aphasia.

Nevertheless, many aphasic patients, perhaps most save the very mildly impaired, are not simply aphasic. They have impairments in other cognitive and behavioural processes such as the control of action and movement, memory and mood (Benson and Geschwind 1975; Starkstein and Robinson 1988). The problem, which is simple to state, is that it is by no means clear which is the primary cause of an observed language problem. One view would encourage us in the belief that in disease processes where there is often language impairment, such as dementia and schizophrenia, the language difficulties are *secondary*, whereas in aphasia they are *primary*. In other words, aphasia is a condition which results in impaired language processing, and its symptoms are individual characteristics of impaired language use. Such a position holds that language is autonomous: it enjoys an existence which is independent of perception, memory and action.

Another problem concerning the nature of aphasic symptoms is to what extent we can consider some symptoms *indirect* in the sense that they are the result of attempts at compensation by the individual and the brain. Thus, some explanations for agrammatism (see Ch. 5 below) suggest that it emerges as a consequence of the speaker's adaptive reaction to grammatical or motor impairment. The nub of this argument is that the symptom does not represent a simple loss of some component of language, but that it is the end result of some complex cognitive process of compensation.

A major theme in the development of aphasiology has been the attempt to classify aphasic individuals into types on the basis of presenting symptoms. But we know that there are significant individual differences between patients who may, on the face of it, present with the same constellation of symptoms. If symptoms change over time and aphasia types evolve one into another, as they appear to (Kertesz 1979), then it is clearly pointless to consider aphasic classification rigidly. Although symptoms may emerge and dissipate over time from onset of brain damage, it may be possible to discern pattern in their evolution which is true for many patients.

Theoretical aphasiology is going through an important transition period where researchers are moving towards detailed experimental fractionation of impaired psycholinguistic processes in individual patients, with a reduction of interest in the conventional comparison of classified groups of subjects. That there are individual differences between patients who present with, say, agrammatism or jargon, is not a new finding, as illustrated in the chapters of this book. What is controversial right now is to what extent we can group individuals with agrammatism or jargon.

So major questions for aphasiology concern which symptoms are primary, which are secondary, and what is the relationship between symptoms and to what extent symptoms are shared by different aphasic individuals. The notion of 'syndrome' is not a complex one; a syndrome is simply the more-or-less regular co-occurrence of symptoms. The relationship of symptoms, one to another, is what is of interest and what is controversial in aphasia. Is it the case, for instance, that *paraphasia* (Chs 6 and 7 below) and *comprehension deficit* (Ch. 4 below) invariably co-occur because there is a causal link? The individual has paraphasic speech because there is a failure in feedback at an internal abstract level or at an external self-monitoring stage.

In this book we hope to present a comprehensive introduction to the nature of aphasia by examining the characteristics by which we know it. This first chapter aims to provide a brief introduction to the modern history and contemporary issues of aphasia and to guide the reader to the detailed discussion presented in the individual chapters of the book. A range of theories have emerged in the past 150 years or so which have sought to identify the impairments in processing which underlie the characteristics of aphasia. In this chapter we will present a brief overview which seeks to introduce the characteristic features of aphasia and see how they have been related to one another over the years.

Syndromes to models

The classical tradition

To understand what is happening in aphasia today it is necessary to know something of the past. The history of aphasia is long and complex, and we must content ourselves with a brief sketch of the main landmarks. An excellent up-to-date survey of the past and present history of aphasia, drawn on in what follows, is Caplan's (1987) recent book which is very much recommended.

In 1861 Paul Broca examined the speech impairment of the 57-year-old patient Leborgne who was very ill following infection of his paralysed right leg. Broca was interested in the patient because he saw it as a test for the phrenological claim, dominant at that time, that the faculty of language was localized in the frontal lobes. At the time of Broca's examination Leborgne had been virtually mute for twenty-one years, able to produce only the *recurring utterance* 'tan' (see Ch. 9 below), although the patient's comprehension was described as intact. At autopsy, three days after Broca's examination, Leborgne's brain was found to have a lesion in the 3rd frontal convolution of the left hemisphere caused by a cyst. Broca proposed that this circumscribed area of the left frontal lobe (now called Broca's area) was the centre for the 'faculty of articulate language'. In 1865 Broca presented a second paper which drew attention to the fact that he had observed eight consecutive cases of aphasia following left hemisphere damage, and he concluded that it was lesions of the *left* frontal lobe which produced the impairment in articulate language.

The presentation of these famous cases to the scientific community constitutes the traditional birth of modern aphasiology and the beginnings of neuropsychology. In fact, Broca was not the first to suggest that aphasia followed only left hemisphere damage. Among several others (see Lecours, Nespoulous and Pioger 1987; Caplan 1987), Dax (1836, but not published until 1865) had made the same observation. Notwithstanding, it is with Broca's famous cases that the modern history of aphasia traditionally begins, and it is with this discovery that the doctrine of cerebral (left-hemisphere) dominance began. Before this there was a long history of general support for duality of brain function (Bogen 1969). The concentration on the significant disabilities which follow left-hemisphere damage, meant that it was not until the 1960s that researchers began to realize that impairments in language could indeed result from right hemisphere lesions (Code 1987).

In 1874 the 26-year-old Carl Wernicke described two patients with impairments in the comprehension of spoken language resulting from damage to the posterior two-thirds of the superior temporal lobe. In contrast to Leborgne, the speech of these patients was produced fluently, although characterized by sound production errors, now called paraphasias (Ch. 6 below), that were sometimes so severe that the impression on the examiner was of hearing jargon (Ch. 7 below) and words which were apparently unrelated to any known words. With this observation, Wernicke proposed a model of language production and comprehension that accounted for the expressive nonfluent (see Ch. 2 below) form of aphasia with intact comprehension described by Broca and the fluent aphasic syndrome described by Wernicke. It also predicted at that time undiscovered forms of aphasia and still provides the basis for much standard neurolinguistic research. Wernicke's 'connectionist' model, as it is sometimes called, is best appreciated by considering its development by Lichtheim (1885) who proposed what is now known as the Wernicke–Lichtheim model of the representation of language in the brain (Figure 1.1).

Figure 1. shows Lichtheim's more elaborated second model. 'A', 'M' and 'B' represent what Lichtheim called the 'centre for auditory images' (Wernicke's area), the 'centre for motor images' (Broca's area) and 'the part where concepts are elaborated' respectively. 'O' is a centre for visual representations (reading) and 'E' a motor writing centre. The letters 'a' and 'm' represent the primary auditory area and peripheral speech organs respectively (Lichtheim 1885: pp. 435–6). The various features of aphasia result from damage or interference to centres or pathways between centres, and Lichtheim describes seven syndromes predicted by the model.

On the model damage to 'M' produces the first type, Broca's aphasia, where there is loss of volitional speech and writing, repetition, reading aloud and writing to dictation. Wernicke's aphasia is the second type resulting from

Figure 1.1 The 'Wernicke-Lichtheim house'; Lichtheim's second diagram

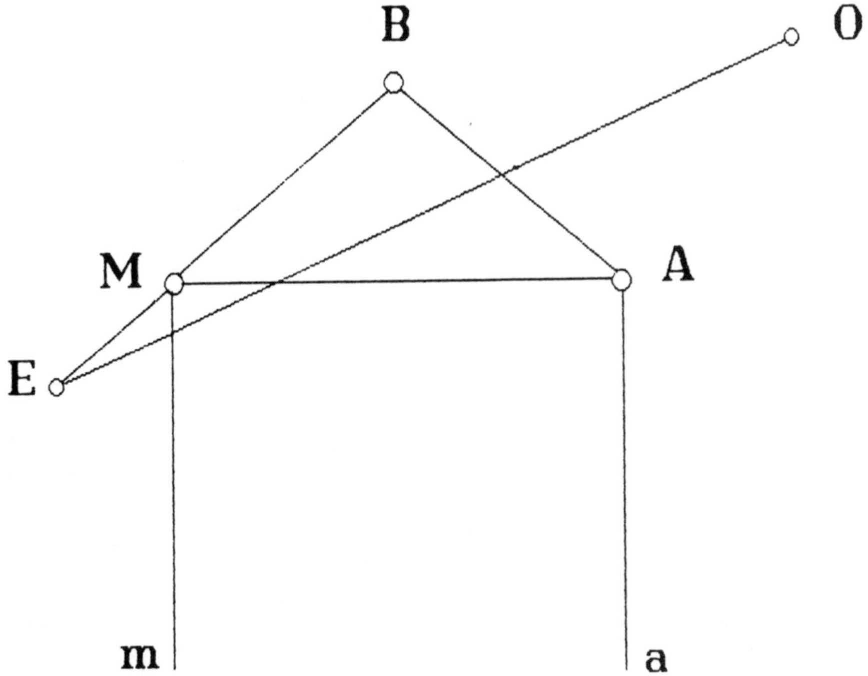

Source: Adapted with permission from L. Lichtheim (1885) On aphasia. *Brain* **7**, 433–84.

disruption to 'A'. Here there is impairment in the understanding of spoken and written language – producing paraphasia – and problems with repetition, writing to dictation and reading aloud. Interruption in the pathway connecting 'A' and 'M' produces the third type, now called Conduction aphasia, where there are mainly disturbances of repetition, reading aloud and writing to dictation, while auditory and written comprehension and volitional speech and writing are largely intact. Disruption to the pathway between Broca's area (M) and the conceptual area (B) leads to the fourth condition, where there is impairment of volitional speech and writing with preserved understanding of speech and writing, repetition, writing to dictation and reading aloud. This condition is now recognized as transcortical motor aphasia. The fifth type predicted by Lichtheim's model is what most people now call apraxia of speech, which results from damage to the pathway between 'M' (Broca's area) and 'm' (the organs of speech). Here there is loss of volitional speech, repetition and reading aloud while understanding of speech and writing are preserved. It is distinguished from Broca's aphasia through intact volitional writing and writing to dictation. A lesion to the pathway between Wernicke's area (A) and the higher conceptual centre (B) is predicted to result in Lichtheim's sixth type, transcortical sensory aphasia. Here there is a loss of understanding of speech and written language with preserved volitional speech and writing, repetition, reading aloud and writing to dictation. Lastly, damage to the pathway between Wernicke's area and the primary auditory reception area 'a', produces the seventh condition, what Lichtheim called 'isolated speech-deafness' (p. 460) and what is today called pure word-deafness. The diagram describes impaired auditory comprehension, repetition and writing to dictation. Volitional speech, writing and reading are intact, suggesting, as Lichtheim notes, that the condition is not a 'true' aphasia at all. It can be seen that the model is primarily subductive: aphasia is seen in terms of a simple *loss* of function. Types are recognized through a combination of loss and preservation of language functions.

Figure 1.2 is a schematic diagram of the left hemisphere and shows the major neocortical anatomical landmarks associated with aphasia on the classical model.

Levels of representation

The 'classical' approach to the explanation of aphasia flourished from the turn of the century until the 1920s. Not everybody was happy with it and Henry Head (1926) represented these feelings when he dubbed researchers in this tradition 'the diagram makers'. A different, more comprehensive, perspective on the neurological representation of language in the nervous system was being proposed by Hughlings Jackson in the late 1800s (1866, 1879; see Taylor 1958, for selected writings, and Caplan 1987, for detailed introductory discussion), and Head did much to promote Jackson's views. Jackson's ideas still form the essential bedrock of the standard model of neurological organization, and have attracted renewed interest in recent years with developments in neural imaging which allow detailed examination of subcortical and right hemisphere involvement in aphasia. The general model also finds expression

Figure 1.2 Schematic representation of the left hemisphere showing the main areas associated with language. See text for full discussion

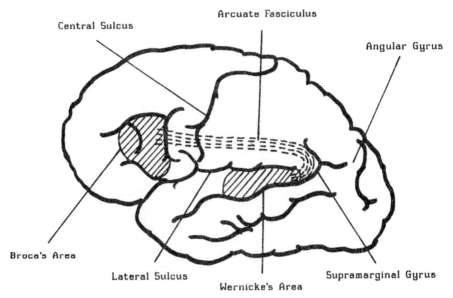

and expansion in Jason Brown's (Brown 1975, 1979, 1988) contemporary microgenic model of aphasia.

Both Jackson's and, to an even greater extent, Brown's neurolinguistic model, attach great importance to the evolutionary and developmental substrate of language, emphasizing that human language has emerged with evolution of the central nervous system from primitive to sophisticated, from simple to more complex. The architecture of the neocortex itself is the product of relatively recent evolutionary processes and appears to reflect a structural differentiation resulting in specialization for higher, human, cognitive activities (Galaburda 1982). The symptoms we observe in aphasic individuals are the result of lesions to different neural levels which are responsible for different levels of language representation in the brain.

Jackson's ideas were much influenced by the work of the highly influential Victorian philosopher and psychologist Herbert Spencer (1820–1903) who introduced the notion of hierarchical organization in the nervous system, where each evolutionary stage added a new level of brain and consequently a new level of neurological and cognitive complexity. Hierarchy is the fundamental feature of the standard neurological model. It provides powerful explanatory force and forms the essential basis to our understanding of how the nervous system functions. The opposing forces of inhibition and facilitation or excitation are understood to operate in an hierarchically organized fashion at different anatomical, developmental and phylogenic levels. On this Jacksonian concept of *levels of representation*, language is represented at different anatomico-structural levels, where expression by levels lower down the hierarchy is inhibited by controlling mechanisms higher up the hierarchy in the normally functioning nervous system. Stages which are 'earlier' in the sense that they are ontogenically (in terms of individual development) and phylogenically (in terms of evolution) earlier stages of language are represented at the lower levels, and more complex and developmentally later features represented higher up. At the 'top', as it were, in the left neocortex, are represented those aspects of language which can be characterized in formal unit-and-rule linguistic models, while at the bottom, more automatically and holistically mediated language is processed. A lower level of neural organization can be released or disinhibited following damage to a higher controlling level and the symptomatology represents a regression to more primitive levels of behaviour and neural organization. The model therefore links the evolution of the central nervous system and the development of the system in the individual with language development, and predicts certain patterns of disruption to language processing with brain damage.

Although Brown's (1975, 1979) complex microgenic theory is in the tradition of Jackson, explanation for the emergence of aphasic (and other) symptomatology differs somewhat (Brown 1988). For Jackson earlier stages in development and evolution are released (or disinhibited) from the control of higher levels following damage, but for Brown inhibition appears to have a lesser role. An observed behaviour represents, not simply the released, lower-level, more primitive behaviour, but a natural part of the unfolding of a behavioural process. For example, pathological laughing and/or crying are common symptoms of pseudobulbar palsy caused by an upper motor neurone lesion, where the individual breaks into uncontrollable laughter or weeping following exposure to a relatively mild emotional stimulus (e.g. a picture of a baby). On the Jacksonian model the laughing or crying are disinhibited primitive reactions out of control of higher centres damaged by the lesion. Microgenic theory appears to propose that the evolutionarily more primitive reaction is a characteristic which is shaped into a more differentiated expression by later stages in the unfolding of the mental representation. An almost simultaneous action process takes place:

> The basic assumption of microgenisis is that mental representations (perceptions, ideas), as well as actions and effects, have a prehistory that forms the major part of their structure. There is an unfolding in microtime – in seconds or in a fraction of a second – leading to an action or an idea. This unfolding process is concealed from the individual, who is only aware of events in consciousness. The surface events that articulate consciousness – limb movements, utterances, objects and mental images – are like the tip of an iceberg in cognitive structure. They are the outcome of a more or less instantaneous development, a process which is reiterated in the occurrence of every representation (Brown 1988: p. 3).

For Brown symptoms are *errors* but they are not *deficits*, as they are viewed on the classical model. They reflect normal processing mediated by the damaged area which is revealed by pathology. The errors are viewed as achievements of the patient's cognitive processing following damage; an essential part of the normal process. Support for this view that symptoms are revelations of part of the normal cognitive process comes from the observation that aphasic symptoms can be seen in 'normal' non-asphasic language use, as in sleep-talking for instance. Slips of the tongue, word-finding difficulty, failures of comprehension and nonfluency occur for us all occasionally.

One view of the *telegraphic* speech of some agrammatic patients (Ch. 5) is that it reflects a style of speech which can be observed in normal speakers and is in most respects grammatically well-formed (Heeschen and Kolk 1988). A form of this sublanguage is used in situations like talking to young children or non-native speakers, where the situation makes expression of some elements of the sentence dispensable.

A further contribution of Jackson to aphasiology is his notion of a continuum of *propositionality* in language and the repercussions of this for aphasic symptomatology. This is discussed in detail in Chapter 9. The theoretical status of hierarchy in speech production, and alternative models is discussed in Miller's chapter on apraxia of speech (Ch. 8).

Neo-classicism

There was a renaissance of the 'classical' model of aphasia with the development by Norman Geschwind of his 'disconnection' model (Geschwind 1965a, 1965b; Benson and Geschwind 1971) – sometimes referred to as the Wernicke–Geschwind model, which laid the foundation for an explosion of research in the 1960s, centring mainly on the work of Harold Goodglass and his associates working at the Boston Aphasia Research Center. It stems directly from Broca, Wernicke and Lichtheim and emphasizes that aphasic characteristics result from damage to 'centres' themselves or connecting pathways between centres. The strong version of the model, like its antecedent, claims that aphasia can be classified in an individual patient through determining the presence vs. absence and relative severity of characteristics.

The brain may be organized in many complex systems, but one well-established foundation block of the standard neurological model, and an essential feature of the classical and neoclassical model of aphasia, is that the anterior half of the brain, in front of the central sulcus, is responsible for programming motor activity, while the posterior portion is responsible for sensory processing (see Figure 1.2). This led aphasiologists to the conclusion that an anterior lesion would produce a 'motor' aphasia while a posterior lesion would result in a 'sensory' aphasia. This has also led to the fluency dichotomy (see Ch. 2 below), where anterior lesions cause a nonfluent form of aphasia and posterior ones a fluent form. On Geschwind's disconnection model a diagnosis of Broca's aphasia is made if the patient is nonfluent (impaired prosody, reduced speaking rate and phrase length, increased pauses), has repetition difficulties, reduced articulatory agility, telegraphic or agrammatic speech and related reading and writing problems (see Ch. 10 below). Comprehension (see Ch. 4 below) is said to be relatively intact. The speech of the Wernicke's aphasic patient, in contrast, is fluent and grammatically intact, and may even be abnormally fluent and verbose; speech is characterized by semantic paraphasias (e.g. naming a 'table' a 'chair') (see Ch. 3 below) which may be so abundant that it results in jargon and the patient has severe problems of auditory verbal comprehension. There are also accompanying reading and writing difficulties. A patient with conduction aphasia will have speech which is fluent for the most part, and in short bursts, with phonemic paraphasias (e.g. naming a 'table' a 'pable') poor repetition and good comprehension. The lesion on the model is in the *arcuate fasciculus,* a band of fibres which runs between Wernicke's auditory association area and Broca's motor speech area, themselves undamaged. The patient has more problems with repetition than with speech production and comprehension because for speech information to be repeated it must proceed from the secondary auditory association area of Wernicke to Broca's area for reproduction. On the model, because there is damage to the pathway between the two (arcuate fasciculus), there will be difficulties in repetition.

The other major type of aphasia on the model is Anomia (see Ch. 3 below). An impairment of word-finding is a significant feature of aphasia, and according to some theorists one of *the* core characteristics which manifests itself in all aphasic individuals, and, along with reduced auditory verbal retention span constitutes 'pure', or 'simple' aphasia (Schuell, Jenkins and Jimenez-Pabon 1964). All aphasic patients have naming problems or word-finding difficulties of some kind, but an individual with Anomia is said only to have word-finding difficulty. Fluency, comprehension and reading are said to be intact and writing will reflect only the word-finding difficulty. While a variety of impairments indicate difficulty with finding words in aphasia, for this group speech is devoid of substantive words like nouns and verbs. The grammatical words (conjunctions, prepositions, etc.) are unaffected and the patient's speech consequently sounds empty. The patient often uses anaphors like 'thing' and 'whatsit' in place of an object name. On Geschwind's model the lesion responsible for Anomia is in the supramarginal and angular gyri in the inferior parietal lobe where fibres from visual, auditory and somaesthetic association areas converge. For Geschwind naming constitutes the most fundamental act in language, and it is the inferior parietal lobe which is unique to the human brain and from which other aspects of language have developed.

In addition to these major aphasia types, the classical model includes two *transcortical* aphasias – transcortical motor aphasia (TMA) and transcortical sensory aphasia (TSA) (Damasio 1981; Rubens and Kertesz 1983). These types have been controversial since Lichtheim (1885) first proposed them, and are most often not considered real aphasias at all. Apart from the 'non-linguistic' nature of some of the symptoms, the lesions which cause them are outside the classical peri-Sylvian language cortex of the brain. The motor variety is characterized by an apparent lack of will to speak, where spontaneous speech is much reduced in quantity and quality. The major difference between this form of aphasia and Broca's aphasia is that the patient usually has good repetition and, sometimes, echolalia (see Ch. 9 below), with relatively good comprehension. Despite this being due to a lesion sometimes deep in the frontal lobe and anterior or superior to Broca's area, the patient is not nonfluent and usually has good articulation and makes few grammatical errors. Comprehension is also good. On the model, this form of aphasia is due to a disconnection between mechanisms in the frontal lobe responsible for intentions and the actual mechanism – Broca's motor speech area – responsible for carrying out the intentions. The patient with TSA is fluent and paraphasic, with word-finding difficulties, auditory verbal comprehension difficulties and reading and writing impairments. The lesion is considered to be one which effectively cuts off the cortical language area from the cognitive system.

Geschwind's 'disconnection' rebirth of the classical connectionist model provided more detail and developed specific hypotheses concerning the organization and representation of language in the brain (Caplan 1987). Geschwind (1965a and b) developed a detailed model of the representation of naming in the brain, and the types *global* – to represent severe aphasia affecting all modalities due to extensive damage to the peri-Sylvian area, and *the isolation syndrome* (a combination of TSA and TMA) were added to the model (Benson and Geschwind 1971).

The theory has undergone additional change over the years as improved techniques for imaging the brain have been developed. We now know that there is more to the human brain than simply its left neocortex (its 'bark') and more fully appreciate that the right hemisphere (Code 1987) and subcortical structures such as the thalamus (Brown 1979; Crosson 1984) and basal ganglia (Kornhuber 1977; Naeser *et al.* 1982) are also important in the processing of language. The same improvements in technology have found correlations between aphasia type and lesion site for Broca's, Wernicke's, conduction, TMA and global (Naeser and Hayward 1978). Studies have suggested that prediction of lesion site from aphasia type has a success rate of something like 83 per cent using computerized tomography (CT) scanning (Basso *et al.* 1985). This can be interpreted as either a high or low success rate, depending on the theoretical stance adopted.

Despite this, developments in new techniques like positron emission tomography (PET), which allow examination of changes in chemical activity in parts of the brain which on CT scanning are not structurally damaged, are showing that glucose metabolism changes are consistently found in brain regions unaffected by structural damage in aphasic subjects (see Metter 1987, for detailed review).

The syndrome of Broca's aphasia has undergone major revision also in recent years, mainly as a result of the development of improved imaging. This work has identified two separate conditions traditionally included under the term 'Broca's' aphasia (Mohr 1976; Mohr *et al.* 1978). The first is the 'paroxysmal' and temporary disorder caused by a lesion actually confined to the cortical Broca's area itself. The classically defined Broca's aphasia (renamed 'the operculum syndrome' by Mohr 1976), is caused by a much larger lesion involving the area of supply of the upper division of the left middle cerebral artery. This area includes the operculum, Broca's third frontal gyrus, the anterior parietal area and the insula. The condition is characterized by apraxia of speech with mutism or recurring utterance, with the later emergence of agrammatism and severe reading and writing problems. Currently, therefore, the term 'Broca's aphasia' represents a range from the global mute condition to the agrammatic patient.

More recently still, the much maligned 'faculties' and diagrammatic schema of Lichtheim and Wernicke and others have enjoyed their own renaissance in the models of cognitive processing being developed by people working in the contemporary field of *cognitive neuropsychology*. We discuss this approach in a little more detail in a later section.

Luria's processing model

A. R. Luria's model emphasizes a dynamic functional localization which matches aphasic symptoms with damage to particular systems (Luria 1970, 1976). The theory is complex and we can only sketch its significant features, but the introduction by Caplan (1987) is recommended, whereas Kolb and Whishaw (1985) is recommended as an introduction to Luria's general neuro-psychological model.

Luria's model ties language disturbance closely to more general impairments resulting from damage to specific anatomical and functional systems. A *functional system* for Luria is formed by three main components responsible for executing different stages as the function unfolds. Each functional system has a primary, a secondary and a tertiary component through which the mental processes underlying a function unfold. Each of these components is localized at specific anatomical zones. For instance, the auditory analyser is localized in the temporal lobe.

Auditory input proceeds from the primary area (Hescle's gyrus), where pre-categorical processing of auditory sensation takes place, to the secondary zone, where the product of the primary zone goes through a process of categorization and differentiation. In the tertiary zone the information is translated from sensory into symbolic and abstract information and integrated with information from other functional systems via their tertiary zones (e.g. the motor system in the frontal lobes, the visual system in the occipito-parietal lobes and the somatosensory system in the parietal lobes).

The characteristics of aphasia described by Luria differ very little to those described by other workers and a comparison of the classification system proposed by Luria and the Boston system shows significant agreement. Characteristics are described similarly and combine in similar classifications of types, but the underlying causation differs in Luria's model.

The essential features of Luria's major types of aphasia are listed below.

Sensory (Acoustico-gnostic) (damage in the superior temporal area) Disturbed phonemic hearing due to a disturbance of the analysis of speech sounds. Paraphasia and reading and writing impairments reflecting paraphasia (i.e. paralexia and paragraphia).

Acoustic-mnestic (damage to the mid-temporal areas) Naming impaired but phonemic hearing usually remains intact. There may be difficulties in repeating a series of words in their proper order, but repetition of single words is intact. There may be verbal paraphasia and some perseveration.

Semantic (damage to parieto-occipital region) Disturbance of naming and logico-grammatical operations and simultaneous synthesis of words within grammatical structures. In a syntactic context, the meaning of words depends upon their place in a sentence (e.g. the difference in meaning of words *brother* and *father* in 'the brother of my father' and 'the father of my brother'). Impairments in processing such complex logico-grammatical structures containing word meanings which need to be synthesized simultaneously characterize this type of aphasia. This type is similar to anomia on the models we have looked at.

Afferent (kinaesthetic) motor (damage to the lower part of the post-central region) Luria has two forms of motor aphasia. Here there is impairment in fluency due to faulty kinaesthetic feedback where there is difficulty in finding the required movement patterns, whereas transferring from one movement pattern to another is relatively intact. Consequently, individual sound patterns may be impaired but phrases may be unimpaired. Intonation is good. This is conduction aphasia on the neo-classical model.

Efferent (kinetic) motor (damage to Broca's area) This form is characterized by nonfluency due to disturbance of the kinetic structure of the motor speech act. There are said to be two main characteristics 'loss of the inner structure of the speech act with its complex system of dynamic coordination and an increase in the inertia of neurodynamic processes within the motor analyzer' (Luria 1970: p. 187). There may be inertia of motor analysis interfering with rapid transfer from one word pattern to another. Speech loses its automatic character and telegraphic (agrammatic) speech may emerge with recovery. The patient loses the ability to shift smoothly from one articulation to another although individual articulated sounds may be unimpaired. There may be verbal perseveration (see Ch. 9 below), which in severe cases may appear like apraxia of speech. However, Luria acknowledges the contributions of both Vygotsky and Hughlings Jackson when he states that the problems are not simply articulatory because with recovery from the motor speech problems there are language difficulties which 'are associated with the disturbance of inner speech and with disintegration of the dynamic unity of propositions' (p. 188). This type of motor aphasia is equivalent to Broca's aphasia.

Dynamic (frontal) aphasia (damage to frontal lobe anterior to Broca's area) Here there is a disturbance in monologue, a reduction in spontaneous speech, an apparent lack of 'will' to speak. There may be echolalia (see Ch. 9 below). Repeating can be preserved and dialogue is often perfect. Although language is affected, these impairments are non-linguistic. This type is therefore not usually considered a 'true' aphasia and is equivalent to many descriptions of transcortical motor aphasia.

Luria's model of aphasia presents a different and more dynamic characterization of the way language is represented in the brain. It proposes that language has its foundation in the activity of a complex interaction of systems which have responsibility, not simply for language, but also other cognitive functions. It proposes that there is a process of progressive lateralization, where primary sensation areas are seen as the least lateralized (i.e. represented bilaterally), secondary association areas as mostly lateralized to one hemisphere, with tertiary areas being the most specified and lateralized where the subcomponents of the cognitive functions they serve are processed entirely by one hemisphere.

Luria's model is essentially a *process* model in the sense that circumscribed areas of cortex are not seen as responsible for the execution of entire functions (like, for instance, 'naming'), as they are on the classical model, but cognitive functioning is essentially seen as being processed through modular subcomponents. Different forms of naming impairment, for instance, can arise from damage to separate subcomponents. The notions of information processing, modularity and subcomponents of cognition are prominent features of the contemporary approach to aphasia of *cognitive neuropsychology*, which we discuss in the following section.

New perspectives

In recent years there has developed a fundamentally different way of thinking about research into the problems of brain damaged individuals. Cognitive neuropsychology, as this approach has developed into, is having a major impact upon neuropsychology in general and aphasiology in particular and aphasiology may be currently working its way through a paradigm shift. Cognitive neuropsychology has developed as a result of experimental psychologists wishing to test and develop their information processing models of cognition on brain-damaged individuals. Major contributors to this development are working in North America, Japan and Europe, but the approach has had its major impact in the UK, where much of the early development took place. There are some useful recent introductions to cognitive neuropsychology available (see, for example, Coltheart 1984, 1987; Ellis and Young 1988). Attention has been mainly in the area of investigation of the acquired dyslexias and dysgraphias, but naming and comprehension are also under investigation. In this volume Barry (Ch. 10 below) takes a mainly cognitive neuropsychological approach to acquired reading and writing problems. Figure 1.3 shows the essential features of a 'processing' model. Similar models are presented by Barry (Ch. 10 below).

Figure 1.3 A standard information-processing model of the routes (arrows) and modules (boxes) engaged in reading single words aloud and writing them to dictation

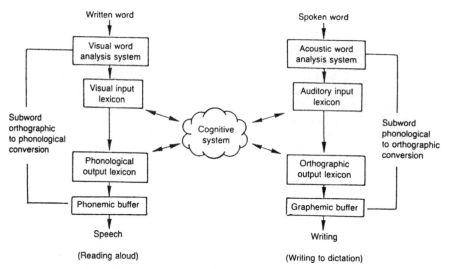

Source: Adapted with permission from R. Lesser (1987) Cognitive neuropsychological influences on aphasia therapy. *Aphasiology* 1, 189–200.

Fundamentally, the view is that a 'theory-driven' approach to the investigation of individual patients is preferable to attempts to compare heterogeneous groups of patients categorized according to the classical syndrome models.

A feeling by many cognitivists is that the syndrome approach to research in neurolinguistics has outlived its usefulness (Caramazza 1984; Schwartz 1984; Ellis 1987). It has been recognized for some time that no two aphasic individuals present with the same pattern of impaired and preserved abilities at a detailed level of analysis, although they have been and are grouped together at a grosser level of appreciation for research (traditionally 'respectable' research employing the comparison of groups of subjects). However, syndromes have intuitive appeal, and even in cognitive neuropsychology there have been attempts to retain the 'syndrome' approach to the acquired dyslexias. Coltheart (1987) suggests that classification of dyslexia and dysgraphia into syndromes has 'allowed considerable progress to be made in our understanding of normal and abnormal processes in reading and spelling'. He adds, however, that 'it has also become clear that the syndrome approach is basically a ground-clearing exercise that needs to be supplanted once initial progress has been made' (p. 2; Coltheart 1987). Others have argued that it can no longer be defended (Caramazza 1984; Schwartz 1984; Ellis 1987; see Ch. 10 below). Marshall and Newcombe (1966, 1973), in their seminal work on acquired dyslexia, suggest that there could be thousands of different forms of dyslexia resulting from different combinations of impairment to the information processing 'flow', rather than half a dozen or so recognizable dyslexic 'syndromes'.

It is argued that we will learn more about the impairments of the brain damaged if we abandon the paradigms of the clinical neurological approach to neuropsychology and adopt the information processing one. Localizing damage in patients, or attempting to map brain structure to cognitive function, are declared to be insignificant concerns for cognitive neuropsychology. Attempts to match structure to function are premature because we still do not know how to delimit a 'function'. To take the common example, the failure by a patient to name a picture of an object could be due to a whole range of impairments including visual or perceptual deficits, attentional deficits, failure to initialize phonetic programming, failure to access phonological specifications or lexical specifications. Talk of localizing 'the naming function', therefore, becomes meaningless. The apparently simple act of naming must involve activity at a number of processing stages and engage a variety of sub-systems and the relationships between sub-systems, depending on the conditions of the naming task.

The view held by many cognitivists is that the neural structures engaged in language are formally dissimilar to those utilized in other cognitive processes such as motor and sensory activity, and that the psychological operations involved in the production and comprehension of speech are unconscious processes which are unique to language (Caplan 1982). Other, as it were, 'extrinsic' features of linguistic structures, such as phrase length, are seen as reflecting such psychological factors as constraints on memory. Thus, there is thought to exist an independent language-specific cognitive system which is unlike other cognitive systems.

The information processing model is the core framework of the cognitive neuropsychology approach for the interpretation of deficits in brain damaged individuals. Cognitive neuropsychology views the brain as a special-purpose computer and assumes that components of cognition, for instance language processing, facial perception, memory, are organized and represented in the brain in a **modular** fashion (Fodor 1983). These modules are seen as domain specific (in the sense that computations performed by a module are specific to that module only), associated with circumscribed neural structures, genetically determined and computationally autonomous, being independent of other cognitive processes. Through experiments with individual subjects, the components and sub-components which are involved in the realization of particular cognitive functions can be mapped in terms of an information processing schema made up of units and input-output routes between units. Diagrammatic versions (Figure 1.3) depict units as boxes and routes as arrows. Much of the current research is directed at determining whether a fairly circumscribed deficit is due to a failure in access to a module via some input/output route (an arrow) or is due to impairment in the module itself (a box). Examples of processing models as applied to normal reading and writing and to acquired dyslexia and dysgraphia are described by Barry (Ch. 10 below).

The evidence for a modular architecture underlying the organization of cognition comes from examination of a range of individual cases, cases which are often very rare. If there is a modular organization to language in the brain then we would expect to observe patients with deficits which affect very specific components and sub-components of the language system. There are reports of patients who have very individual, and rare, forms of impairment. Apart from the now well known cases of acquired dyslexia that have been described (Coltheart *et al.* 1980; Patterson *et al.* 1986), a range of rare category-specific forms of anomia have been reported where the patient has anomia for just one or two semantic categories, such as fruit and vegetables, which cannot be explained away in terms of perceptual or sensory deficits (Hart *et al.* 1985; Benson 1988). This is interpreted to suggest that discreet semantic categories (or some, at least, for some individuals) are represented independently in the brain, demonstrating that modular components underlie cognitive processing. The very fact that these individuals are very rare does not allow us to apply the data to the population in general.

There are a range of views on exactly what may be modular and precisely how independent such modules might be. Analysis entails using the boxes and arrows of a processing model to represent the stages and routes involved in such activities as reading single words aloud, writing single words to dictation and naming objects. A model can be built specifying what is impaired and what is retained by detailed hypothesis-driven assessment of individual patterns of deficit. Examination of reading aloud, for instance, might involve comparing performance on high-frequency and low-frequency words, regularly spelt and irregularly spelt words, concrete and abstract words, real words and non- (but 'possible') words, function words and content words. Through such a process of fractionation, it is suggested, we can gain detailed knowledge of the patient's specific problems in terms of impaired functioning of interconnecting processing routes. An attraction of the approach, perhaps unlike the classical approaches, is that it comes with a promising model for assessment and treatment. Its impact on British aphasia therapy has already been significant (Howard and Hatfield 1987; Lesser 1987). The reader interested application of this approach to aphasia therapy is referred to H Patterson (In press) who make a detailed case for its adoption in treatment. They describe the three broad strategies for therapy which they suggest logically flow from cognitive neuropsychological research: (1) reteaching of the missing information, missing rules or procedures based on a detailed hypothesis testing approach to assessment; (2) teaching a different way to do the same task; (3) facilitating the use of defective access routes. There are promising signs that patient-specific and deficit-specific treatment can improve performance in patients which cannot be accounted for in terms of spontaneous recovery or non-specific effects like attention or novelty (Howard and Hatfield 1987).

Cognitive neuropsychology is now well established, but its development has been controversial. An alternative view, discussed above in relation to microgenic theory, emphasizes the phylogenic and ontogenic origins of motor-sensory processes which underlie language production and comprehension (Brown 1975, 1979, 1988; Marin, 1982; Schweiger and Brown 1988). Few would disagree with the statement that language utilizes physiological systems and mechanisms for production and comprehension, but the focus of the argument is to what extent language processing is an independent enterprise. The view that language is dependent upon other psychological operations was reflected in terminology used in a range of classification systems. Thus the terms *amnesic, amnestic, motor, sensory*, reflect a conception of aphasia which envisages language processing as highly dependent upon pre-existing psychological systems.

However, the uniqueness of language lies, not in the mode of its expression or comprehension, but in its ability to transmit symbolic meaning (Marin 1982). Communication in humans, after all, evolved to meet the needs of the organism. Critics submit (e.g. Marin 1982; Schweiger and Brown 1988; Searle 1984) that the 'logical' computer metaphor, although a useful device which allows a clarity of description, cannot build into an explanatory theory for human cognition because the human brain and brain processing are the result of biological and evolutionary development and operate like computers in only the most superficial of ways. Marin (1982) discusses the brain as a general-purpose computer, where functions are not localized in the hardware, as with a man-made computer, but the hardware is arranged in such a way that it processes information under the control of the software. That is to say, operations performed by the brain are not unique to the cognitive processes using the operations. Doubts are also expressed concerning the validity of developing a model based on the findings of psycholinguistic experiments with normal groups of subjects, the results of which are often unreliable and open to interpretation (Schweiger and Brown 1988).

Despite the view that cognitive neuropsychology does not have a model which can cope with the complexity of human language, it contributes to aphasiology a single-case-study approach to research, a detailed investigation of impairments through psycholinguistically controlled tests, and explanation of underlying patterns of deficit in terms of information processing. These are significant and important contributions, and the approach is still in the early stages of development.

Marin (1982) reminds us that there is so much of human behaviour which cannot be characterized in a scientifically formal manner:

> whereas linguistic description is primarily a theoretical and logical description of an almost idealized system of representations, rules of relations, and combinations, the organism and its brain are neither theoretical nor logical, but are overwhelmingly practical, self-centred, compelled by continuous internal urges, and not always parsimonious or precise . . . parsimony and abstract categorical logic may not be the governing, or even primary, style of brain organization (p. 62).

The characteristics of aphasia reflect impairment to the complex process involved in expressing and comprehending meaning. Marin (1982) states further, 'whereas theory emphasizes the governing rules of syntax and phonology, the organism, healthy or diseased, strives to express primarily its semantic cognitive levels' (p. 62). Such biological considerations emphasize the need for a semantically based linguistics, a model where meaning is primary.

Some of the gaps in our understanding of the complexity of the relationships between brain and language, of the processing of meaning, might be seen as a special form of the mind–body problem. How is it that mental life, consciousness, the abstract and ethereal 'mind', emerges from the activity of neural mechanisms and processes? How is it that the abstract symbolic code of 'meaning' is transduced from or into syntactic, morphological, lexical and phonological unit-and-rule processes? Searle (1987) suggests that we can come to grips with the causal links between mind and body by employing the common distinction made in physics between micro- and macro-properties of systems. A river is composed of micro-particles which are represented at the molecular and subatomic levels; but the river also has the macro-property of liquidity expressed at the surface of the physical system. The macro-property (liquidity) is *caused* by the behaviour of elements at the micro-level and *realized* in the system of micro-elements as a physical property. Surface phenomena *just are* features of systems and they are physical features. Applying this analogy to the relationship between language form and meaning, the causal relationship between the micro-structure (language form) and the macro-structure (semantic meaning) is one where meaning is caused by the activity at the level of language form.

Meaning in language is *caused by*, is *realized in*, the behaviour of the formal symbolic elements of language. In the same way that the micro-elements of the river are not liquid themselves, or the neurones of a brain structure are not conscious themselves, so also the units-and-rules of language have no meaning themselves. However, where liquidity may be an incidental result of the activity of micro-elements in the river, meaning is the *intention* of any *propositional* activity in language. So the meaning realized in a proposition must be specified *before* the form of an utterance. Meaning can, therefore, be understood as an emergent property of the behaviour of the units and rules of the language code in the sense that emergent properties of a system of elements can be explained by the behaviour of individual elements (e.g.

phonemes, syntactic units) but which are not properties of the individual elements themselves (i.e. a phoneme carries no semantic meaning itself).

Conclusion

In this brief discussion I have sought to show that there is a range of explanations for the mechanisms underlying aphasic symptomatology. We have examined a variety of views on the nature of aphasia and have seen that over the past 150 years or so of investigation and debate there has been an evolution from classical models to processing models, from static to dynamic, from 'types' to individuals, from simple to complex. Models have had to become more sophisticated to deal with our improved knowledge base, and they have utilized the general scientific paradigms of their time. The characteristics of aphasia constitute our database for research, and these have not changed; but, as the chapters of this book demonstrate, we know so much more about them. The improvement in our knowledge comes from advances in techniques of investigation, with an associated development of perspectives, insightful models which attempt to explain the nature of aphasia and the relationship of language form and process to brain structure and mechanism. The future development in our understanding of aphasia depends upon the perspectives we adopt to view the characteristics of aphasia.

References

Alajouanine, T. (1956) Verbal realization in aphasia. *Brain* **79**, 1–28.

Au, R., Albert, M. L. and Obler, L. K. (1988) The relation of aphasia to dementia. *Aphasiology* **2**, 161–73.

Basso, A., Lecours, A. R., Moraschini, S. and Vanier, M. (1985) Anatomoclinical correlations of the aphasias as defined through computerized tomography: exceptions. *Brain and Language* **26**, 201–9.

Benson, D. F. (1988) Anomia in aphasia. *Aphasiology* **2**, 229–36.

Benson, D. F. and Geschwind, N. (1971) Aphasia and related cortical disturbances. In A. B. and L. H. Baker (eds), *Clinical Neurology*. New York: Harper & Row.

Benson, D. F. and Geschwind, N. (1975) Psychiatric conditions associated with focal lesions of the central nervous system. In M. F. Reiser (ed.) *Handbook of Psychiatry*, Vol. IV. New York: Basic Books.

Bogen, J. E. (1969) The other side of the brain II: an appositional mind. *Bulletin of the Los Angeles Neurological Societies* **34**, 135–62.

Broca, P. (1861) Remarques sur la siège de la faculté de la parole articulée, suivies d'une observation d'aphemie (perte de parole). *Bulletin de la Société d'Anatomie* (Paris) **36**, 330–57.

Broca, P. (1865) Sur la siège de la faculté du langage articule. *Bulletin d'Anthropologie* **6**, 177–93.

Brown, J. W. (1975) On the neural organization of language: thalamic and cortical relationships. *Brain and Language* **2**, 18–30.

Brown, J. W. (1979) Language representation in the brain. In H. Steklis and M. Raleigh (eds), *Neurobiology of Social Communication in Primates*. New York: Academic Press.

Brown, J. W. (1988) *The Life of the Mind*. Hillsdale, New Jersey: Lawrence Erlbaum Associates.

Caplan, D. (1982) Reconciling the categories-representation in neurology and in linguistics. In M. A. Arbib, D. Caplan and J. C. Marshall (eds), *Neural Models of Language Processes*. New York: Academic Press.

Caplan, D. (1987) *Neurolinguistics and Linguistic Aphasiology*. Cambridge: Cambridge University Press.

Caramazza, A. (1984) The logic of neuropsychological research and the problem of patient classification in aphasia. *Brain and Language* 21, 9–20.

Code, C. (1987) *Language, Aphasia and the Right Hemisphere*. Chichester: John Wiley.

Code, C. and Ball, M. J. (1988) Apraxia of speech: the case for a cognitive phonetics. In M. J. Ball (ed.), *Theoretical Linguistics and Disordered Language*. London: Croom Helm.

Coltheart, M. (1984) Editorial. *Cognitive Neuropsychology* 1, 1–8.

Coltheart, M. (1987) Functional architecture of the language-processing system. In M. Coltheart, G. Sartori and R. Job (eds), *The Cognitive Neuropsychology of Language*. London: Lawrence Erlbaum Associates.

Coltheart, M., Patterson, K. and Marshall, J. C. (eds) (1980) *Deep Dyslexia*. London: Routledge & Kegan Paul.

Crosson, B. (1984) Role of the dominant thalamus in language: a review. *Psychological Bulletin* 3, 491–517.

Damasio, A. (1981) The nature of aphasia: signs and symptoms. In M. Taylor Sarno (ed.), *Acquired Aphasia*. New York: Academic Press.

Dax, M. (1865) Lesions de la moitié gauche de l'encephale coincident avec l'oubli des signes de la pensée. *Montpelière Gazzette Hebdom* (1836) 11, 259–60.

Ellis, A. (1987) Intimations of modularity, or, the modality of mind: doing cognitive neuropsychology without syndromes. In M. Coltheart, G. Sartori and R. Job (eds), *The Cognitive Neuropsychology of Language*. Hove: Lawrence Erlbaum Associates.

Ellis, A. and Young, A. (1988) *Human Cognitive Neuropsychology*. Hove: Lawrence Erlbaum Associates.

Fodor, J. (1983) *The Modularity of Mind*. Cambridge, Mass.: MIT Press.

Galaburda, A. M. (1982) Histology, architectonics, and asymmetry of language areas. In M. A. Arbib, D. Caplan and J. C. Marshall (eds), *Neural Models of Language Processes*. London: Academic Press.

Geschwind, N. (1965a) Disconnection syndromes in animals and man – Part I. *Brain* 88, 237–94.

Geschwind, N. (1965b) Disconnection syndromes in animals and man – Part II. *Brain* 88, 585–644.

Goodglass, H. (1976) Agrammatism. In H. Whitaker and H. A. Whitaker (eds), *Studies in Neurolinguistics*, Vol. I. New York: Academic Press.

Goodglass, H. and Kaplan, E. (1972) *The Assessment of Aphasia and Related Disorders*. Philadelphia: Lea and Febiger.

Hart, J., Berndt, R. S. and Caramazza, A. (1985) Category-specific naming deficit following cerebral infarction. *Nature* 316, 388.

Head, H. (1926) *Aphasia and Kindred Disorders of Speech*. Cambridge: Cambridge University Press.

Heeschen, C. and Kolk, H. (1988) Agrammatism and paragrammatism. *Aphasiology* 2, 299–302.

Howard, D. and Hatfield, F. M. (1987) *Aphasia Therapy: Historical and Contemporary Issues*. London: Lawrence Erlbaum Associates.

Howard, D. and Patterson, K. (In press) Methodological issues in neuropsychological therapy. In X. Seron and G. Deloche (eds), *Cognitive Approaches in Neuropsychological Rehabilitation*. London: Lawrence Erlbaum Associates.

Jackson, J. H. (1866) Notes on the physiology and pathology of language. In J. Taylor (ed.) (1958) *Selected Writings of John Hughlings Jackson*, Vol. II. London: Staples Press.

Jackson, J. H. (1879) On the affections of speech from diseases of the brain. In J. Taylor (ed.) (1958) *Selected Writings John Hughlings Jackson*, Vol. II. London: Staples Press.

Kertesz, A. (1979) *Aphasia and Associated Disorders*. New York: Grune & Stratton.

Kolb, B. and Whishaw, I. Q. (1985) *Fundamentals of Human Neuropsychology*, 2nd edn. New York: W. H. Freeman & Co.

Kornhuber, H. H. (1977) A reconsideration of the cortical and subcortical mechanisms involved in speech and aphasia. In J. E. Desmedt (ed.), *Language and Hemispheric Specialization in Man: Cerebral ERPs*. Basel: Karger.

Lecours, A. R., Nespoulous, J.-L. and Pioger, D. (1987) Jacques Lordat or the birth of cognitive neuropsychology. In E. Keller and M. Gopnik (eds), *Motor and Sensory Processes of Language*. Hillsdale, New Jersey: Lawrence Erlbaum Associates.

Lesser, R. (1987) Cognitive neuropsychological influences on aphasia therapy. *Aphasiology* **1**, 189–200.

Lichtheim, L. (1885) On aphasia. *Brain* **7**, 433–84.

Luria, A. R. (1970) *Traumatic Aphasia*. The Hague: Mouton.

Luria, A. R. (1976) *Higher Cortical Functions in Man*. London: Tavistock.

Marin, O. S. M. (1982) Brain and language: the rules of the game. In M. A. Arbib, D. Caplan and J. C. Marshall (eds), *Neural Models of Language Processes*. London: Academic Press.

Marshall, J. C. and Newcombe, F. (1966) Syntactic and semantic errors in paralexia. *Neuropsychologia* **24**, 5–24.

Marshall, J. C. and Newcombe, F. (1973) Patterns of paralexia. *Journal of Psycholinguistic Research* **2**, 175–99.

Metter, E. J. (1987) Neuroanatomy and physiology of aphasia: evidence from positron emission tomography. *Aphasiology* **1**, 3–33.

Mohr, J. P. (1976) Broca's area and Broca's aphasia. In H. Whitaker and H. A. Whitaker (eds), *Studies in Neurolinguistics*, Vol. II. New York: Academic Press.

Mohr, J. P., Pessin, M. S., Finkelstein, S., Funkenstein, H. H., Duncan, G. W. and Davis, K. R. (1978) Broca aphasia: pathologic and clinical. *Neurology* **28**, 311–24.

Naeser, M. A., Alexander, M. P., Helm-Estabrook, N., Levine, H. L., Laughlin, S. and Geschwind, N. (1982) Aphasia with predominantly subcortical lesion sites: description of three capsular/putaminal aphasia syndromes. *Archives of Neurology* **39**, 2–14.

Naeser, M. A. and Hayward, R. W. (1978) Lesion localization in aphasia with cranial computed tomography and the Boston diagnostic aphasia examination. *Neurology* **28**, 545–51.

Patterson, K., Marshall, J. C. and Coltheart, M. (eds) (1986) *Surface Dyslexia*. London: Lawrence Erlbaum Associates.

Rubens, A. and Kertesz, A. (1983) The localization of lesions in transcortical aphasias. In A. Kertesz (ed.), *Localization in Neuropsychology*. New York: Academic Press.

Schuell, H., Jenkins, J. and Jimenez-Pabon, E. (1964) *Aphasia in Adults*. New York: Harper and Row.

Schwartz, M. F. (1984) What the classical aphasia categories can't do for us, and why. *Brain and Language* **21**, 3–8.

Schweiger, A. and Brown, J. (1988) Minds, models and modules: reflections on M. Coltheart, G. Sartori and R. Job. (eds), The cognitive neuropsychology of language. *Aphasiology* **2**, 531–43.

Searle, J. (1984) *Minds, Brains and Science*. Cambridge, Mass.: Harvard University Press.

Searle, J. (1987) Minds and brains without programs. In C. Blakemore and S. Green-field (eds), *Mindwaves*. Oxford: Basil Blackwell.

Starkstein, S. E. and Robinson, R. G. (1988) Aphasia and depression. *Aphasiology* **2**, 1–19.

Taylor, J. (ed.) (1958) *Selected Writings of John Hughlings Jackson*, Vol. II. London: Staples Press.

Taylor Sarno, M. (1981) Recovery and rehabilitation in aphasia. In M. Taylor Sarno (ed.), *Acquired Aphasia*. New York: Academic Press.

Wernicke, C. (1874) The aphasic syndrome complex. Trans. in R. S. Cohen and M. W. Warofsky (eds), *Boston Studies in the Philosophy of Science*, Vol. 4. Boston: Reidel.

Chapter 2

Fluency

Klaus Poeck

Development of the concept

As early as in 1868, Hughlings Jackson described a dichotomy in the spontaneous expression of his aphasic patients. He divided these into two 'classes'. One class was 'speechless or nearly so', the other one had 'plenty of words but mistakes in words'. A few years later, Wernicke (1874) distinguished two distinct behaviours in the speech production of aphasic patients, that he termed fluent and nonfluent. He noted that comprehension was frequently impaired in the fluent aphasics, whereas many nonfluent patients appeared to have good comprehension. This observation, again, induced him to introduce the well-known dichotomy, i.e. motor and sensory aphasia.

After almost a century had elapsed, Geschwind and Howes suggested again, this time on the basis of a statistical analysis of certain aspects of spontaneous speech, that the language output of aphasic patients corresponds to two distinct patterns, which were termed fluent and nonfluent (Howes 1964, Howes and Geschwind 1964, Geschwind 1966). While the fluency–nonfluency dimension was being revived, the linguistic description of aphasic speech output was still in its infancy. Thus, Benson (1967) in an influential paper, could state: 'It is a purpose of this paper to demonstrate that different types of aphasic production exist' (p. 374).

In contrast to a purely quantitative distinction according to the amount and speed of words produced, Benson referred to a number of distinctive characteristics of aphasic speech. The variables considered by Benson were: Rate of Speaking, Prosody, Pronunciation (i.e. articulation), Phrase Length, Speech Effort, Pauses, Press of Speech, Word Choice, Paraphasia (phonemic or semantic paraphasias, neologisms) and Verbal Stereotypes, by which he meant Recurring Utterances. Analysis of the occurrence of these ten features yielded a bimodal distribution of the patients. Group A corresponded to nonfluent, group B to fluent aphasia. A localization study by means of radioactive isotope scanning showed that patients in group A had their lesion in general anterior and group B posterior to the Fissure of Rolando.

Because Benson's finding could still have been somewhat influenced by the original concept, Kerschensteiner *et al.* (1972) investigated, by means of modern statistical methods, whether the fluent–nonfluent distinction did, in fact, reflect a naturally occurring dichotomy in the speech production of aphasic patients. Basing their study on the same ten variables as proposed by Benson, they could, indeed, confirm the existence of two distinct clusters showing the well-known characteristics of fluent and nonfluent aphasia. When these authors established a rank order of the variables according to their discriminating power between the two classes, Phrase Length, Pauses, Prosody, Rate of Speaking and Effort contributed most to the distinction.

In a subsequent paper, Poeck *et al.* (1972) investigated language understanding to the extent that it is assessed by the Token Test (TT), in the two groups of fluent and nonfluent aphasia. The comparison between the two groups did not yield a significant difference in TT performance. In spite of gross differences in speech output, TT performance was equally impaired in both subgroups. Nonfluent aphasics were not superior to fluent ones even in the less complex first parts of the TT.

These findings, however, had to be interpreted with caution. They did not necessarily imply that the impairment in the psychological processes underlying performance on the TT was qualitatively identical in the two subgroups of aphasia. One has to consider that the behavioural response called for by the TT depends on a sequence of events that take place between the decoding of the instructions and the carrying out of the action. Even today it is not known with certainty what these events are. However it has become obvious that TT performance does not merely reflect auditory language comprehension (Cohen *et al.* 1976; Poeck and Hartje 1979).

The fluency–nonfluency distinction of aphasic speech production found immediate acceptance in the scientific community. However, with increasing application, the distinction was not based any more on a uniform set of criteria. Some authors referred merely to the quantity of speech output, other authors equated fluency with some (but not all) characteristic features of the speech production of patients with Wernicke's aphasia, in the first place fluent paraphasic speech. Kreindler *et al.* (1980) demonstrated that the speaking rate (number of words per time unit) alone was not sufficient to identify a patient as fluent or nonfluent.

The original studies on fluency in aphasia were conducted assessing various aspects of spontaneous speech production. Recent research (e.g. Deloche *et al.* 1979; Feyereisen *et al.* 1986) has addressed the validity and coherence of the fluency variables under conditions of greater or lesser degrees of freedom. These authors compared two situations, interview and description. As expected, in the interview condition speech rate was higher; however differences in fluency were consistent in the two conditions. Feyereisen *et al.* found furthermore that clinical evaluations of fluency were positively correlated with objective measures (automatic analysis) even though clinical judgements were given in part by speakers of a foreign language.

With regard to type of aphasia it turned out that the two categories were superstructures each of which embraced several of the traditional aphasic syndromes. Even those authors who take a sceptical or, in the extreme, agnostic attitude towards the wisdom of this traditional classification will admit that the ensemble of language performance in various modalities differs greatly across these syndromes.

Among the fluent group are found patients with Wernicke's aphasia, amnesic aphasia, conduction aphasia and transcortical sensory aphasia. In the nonfluent group there are patients with Broca's, with global and with transcortical motor aphasia. Thus, when a neurolinguistic and/or neuropsychological study on the language behaviour of aphasic patients is based on a comparison between fluent and nonfluent aphasics, the comparison is made between rather heterogeneous samples.

Localization

In contrast to the wealth of papers on neurolinguistic features of fluent and nonfluent aphasia (see below) there have been very few studies on problems of differential localization. Benson's radionuclid study (1967) has already been referred to above.

Knopman *et al.* (1983) have examined the anatomic correlates of speech fluency in 54 right-handed aphasic stroke patients by means of CT scan. Persistent nonfluency was found with 'destruction of a critical amount of left-hemisphere rolandic cerebral cortex and underlying frontoparietal white matter'. Damage to Broca's area was not necessary for persistent nonfluency.

An interesting paper by Henderson (1983) gives the data on three personally examined strongly right-handed patients with fluent aphasia following right-hemisphere infarction and seven crossed aphasics published in the literature. For these patients, the author found a relation between fluency and infarct localization similar to that of right-handed aphasics with left-sided lesions. It appeared that right-hemisphere language representation in crossed aphasics mirrors that which is normally present in the language-dominant left hemisphere.

Cappa *et al.* (1983) have investigated the thorny problem of subcortical aphasia that had been discussed earlier in the literature by McFarling, Rothi and Heilmann (1982) for thalamic lesions and by Naeser *et al.* (1982) for putaminal lesions. In Cappa's paper there is extensive reference to work on aphasia associated with lesions in the putamen, the caudate nucleus and the anterior limb of the internal capsule. The authors found some rare cases exhibiting an atypical nonfluent aphasia associated with anterior capsular-putaminal lesions. A mild fluent aphasia was sometimes associated with posterior capsular-putaminal lesions. The authors warned, however, that the significance of these findings must be evaluated with caution.

This warning is fully justified if one considers the data published by Mazziotta and Phelps (1986). There are examples in the literature where on the CT scan a deep thalamic or basal ganglia infarct is visualized whereas metabolic studies show extension of the functional lesion to the entirety of the ipsilateral basal ganglia and a neighbouring zone of cortex. The chapter by Mazziotta and Phelps gives several references. In our personal experience four out of nine patients with ischemic infarction in the lenticular nucleus and basal ganglia had hypometabolism extending to the cortex. Three of these patients were aphasic.

From another angle, Basso *et al.* (1980) have studied factors that influence type and severity of aphasia. They found that both trauma and cerebral neoplasm were associated with fluent aphasia significantly more often than vascular accidents. This observation contrasts impressively with the general experience that roughly two-thirds of patients with ischemic lesions of the speech dominant hemisphere are nonfluent.

Exceptions to the association of nonfluent aphasia with anterior and of fluent aphasia with posterior lesions were published by Basso *et al.* in 1987. These authors found an unexpected high number of patients with fluent aphasia and lesion of the dominant frontal lobe. These patients were remarkably older than those with nonfluent aphasia. It appears that damage to the anterior part of the language area has different clinical consequences depending on the age of the patient. The view that age and type of aphasia might be related had already been voiced by Obler *et al.* (1978). In an earlier paper Basso *et al.* (1985) had also found exceptions in the other direction: Out of a total of 207 patients they found 6 cases with nonfluent aphasia and posterior CT lesions.

Observations on the anatomical basis of fluency in aphasic children are rare. Van Dongen *et al.* (1985) reported the cases of three girls, aged 9–11 years, who developed fluent aphasia, in two cases conduction aphasia, in association with acute brain damage. Localization of lesion was in the posterior part of the left hemisphere encroaching upon Wernicke's area in all cases. These observations were at variance with the commonly held view that acquired aphasia in children is invariably nonfluent and that paraphasias are not observed.

Neuropsychological and neurolinguistic investigations

There are very many papers in the literature where groups of patients with fluent aphasia are compared with nonfluent patients in various performances. In this chapter, a selective overview is intended to illustrate broad topics and some pertinent results.

Memory

Rothi and Hutchinson (1981) have investigated the ability of fluent and nonfluent aphasics to apply rehearsal as a strategy for maintaining verbally coded information in primary memory. The starting point of their study was the report by Warrington and Shallice (1969) and by Warrington, Logue and Pratt (1971) that aphasic individuals with poor repetition had a deficit in memory span. Since rehearsal involves the rapid recirculation of verbal information in primary memory, fluency of verbal abilities might strongly influence performance in a task for primary verbal memory. The authors based their study on the Brown–Peterson paradigm where a distractor task interferes with effective rehearsal of the memoranda. Rothi and Hutchinson found that nonfluent aphasic patients did not rehearse the verbal information. In contrast, fluent aphasic patients did demonstrate rehearsal. Compared with right-brain-damaged patients, both groups of aphasics encoded significantly less material into the memory store.

Perseveration

In continuation of previous studies, Albert and Sandson (1986) have examined perseveration in aphasia. They gave ten fluent and eight nonfluent aphasics the following tests: confrontation naming, drawing objects to command, wordless generation and design generation. Perseveration was negatively correlated with number of items named correctly. On confrontation naming, perseveration was associated with posterior and not with anterior lesions. Surprisingly enough, three out of five aphasic patients not producing any perseveration on confrontation naming had lesions restricted to the frontal lobe. In contrast, only one out of eight aphasic subjects producing three or more perseverations had lesions restricted to the frontal lobe.

In order to explain their findings, the authors entertained the idea that decreased verbal fluency associated with frontal lobe lesions results in decreased output that inhibits both the intended response and perseveration. However there were three exceptions: those aphasic patients with lesions restricted to the left frontal lobe did not perseverate, yet correctly named at least ten items.

Self-correction

Marshall and Tompkins (1982) investigated strategies of verbal self-correction in fluent and nonfluent aphasic patients. They found that most fluent and nonfluent aphasics, regardless of severity level or type of aphasia produced a substantial number of self-corrections. There was no difference between fluent and nonfluent aphasics of equivalent severity. This finding supported the hypothesis that severity rather than type of aphasia is strongly related to verbal self-correction.

Lexical decision

Gerratt and Jones (1987) have compared the performance of fluent and non-fluent aphasic patients in a lexical decision task. They found that fluent and nonfluent aphasics did not show a differential impairment. Rather, words with a high number of meanings and with a high frequency of occurrence were recognized as real words faster than words with few meanings or low frequency of occurrence. The observation that fluent aphasic patients had a performance similar to normal subjects suggested to these authors that the organization of multiple word meaning is preserved in fluent aphasia.

Word retrieval

This was studied in aphasia by Drummond *et al.* (1981). These authors found that in a sentence-completion task fluent aphasics had a significantly greater frequency of correct responses than nonfluent aphasics. They interpreted this finding as indicating that fluent aphasics are facilitated to a greater extent than nonfluent aphasics in their production of selected adjectives by the presence of syntactic context. The authors proposed that the characteristics of language performance referred to as fluency are in part syntactic in nature and can notably be observed in situations where syntactic organization is required.

Naming and classification

Fluent aphasics have been found to produce a pattern of naming responses different from that of nonfluent aphasics. Wayland and Taplin (1982) therefore postulated that the reason for the naming difficulty in each subgroup might be different. The authors referred to a number of papers which suggested that fluent aphasics correspond to a lesser extent than nonfluent aphasics to normals in the structuring of semantic categories. Also, Whitehouse, Caramazza and Zurif (1978) had demonstrated that fluent aphasics have a reduced knowledge of the functional and perceptual features of objects.

Wayland and Taplin examined their patients by means of a nonverbal categorization task. Fluent aphasics showed a significant deficit in performance on this task, as compared to nonfluent aphasics. They demonstrated that the problems of fluent aphasics in a naming task were related to their difficulties in abstracting a prototype for each category and to sort category members in relation to that prototype. They demonstrated similar abnormalities in organizing artificial nonverbal categories than in organizing natural semantic categories. In this respect they performed less well than nonfluent aphasic patients. This subgroup, again, performed close to normal in their organization of sets of features.

A similar superiority of nonfluent aphasics was found by McCleary and Hirst (1986). These authors examined twelve fluent aphasics (Wernicke's, anomic and conduction aphasics) and eight Broca's aphasics. Fluent aphasics had significantly more difficulty in classifying semantically related items regardless of the nature of these items (words or pictures, basic level or superordinate level or functionally related items). Fluent aphasics were remarkably little influenced in their performance by function relations.

Semantic field

In an influential paper, Goodglass and Baker (1976) have investigated some kinds of relation that might contribute to the disorganization of the semantic field in patients with fluent aphasia. They arrived at the distinction between fluent and nonfluent aphasics on the basis of language understanding, equating high comprehenders with nonfluent aphasics and low comprehenders with fluent aphasics (but see Poeck *et al.* 1972). The high comprehenders had little difficulty in recognizing superordinate and same word relations, more difficulty in identifying function and attribute relations. They also produced the greatest number of errors when recognizing same class relations. The low comprehenders made a greater number of errors and did not appreciate function relations. The conclusion proposed by Goodglass and Baker has been referred to quite frequently: nonfluent aphasics may know what an object is, but they do not know much about it.

The significance of the fluency concept today

The problem posed in this heading must be considered under two aspects:

1 What is the heuristic (scientific) and practical value of this classification as compared with other widely used systems of classification?
2 What is the value of classification at all for present-day research on aphasia which is mainly focused on clarifying linguistic and/or cognitive processes.

Historically, the introduction of the fluency/nonfluency classification was a step backwards, a revival of a distinction that had been proposed by Wernicke (1874) long before the seven or eight aphasic syndromes normally described today had been outlined. Limiting the classification of the aphasias to aspects of speech production included the assumption that a meaningful statement on language performance of a patient or a group of patients could be made even though other important language modalities, e.g. auditory or visual comprehension, repetition, written language were neglected. The above given listing of the various standard aphasic syndromes that are embraced by the two superstructures fluent–nonfluent gives this assumption little likelihood. In fact, it has become apparent that the modalities assessed in most Aphasia Test Batteries are too crude to reflect the differential impairment observed in certain aphasic patients. Categories that are treated as unitary in standard aphasia tests should, in fact, become the object of research. The most prominent performance is written language. The problems and preliminary results of research into the varieties of dysgraphia and dyslexia cannot be reviewed here (see Ch. 10). We have been inspired to supplement our standardized Aachen Aphasia Test (AAT, Huber *et al.* 1983) that has been produced also in a Dutch, English and Italian version by a group of tests that should be applied whenever a patient is conspicuous to present with a dissociation of performance not fully assessed by the standard version of the test (Poeck and Göddenhenrich 1988).

Given that there is a need to assess ever more ramifications of the aphasic language disorder the question of the scientific and practical value of this classification as compared with other widely used systems of classification must be answered in the negative.

This is all the more true because the diagnosis of fluent or nonfluent aphasia is made on intuitive judgement and not on psychometric criteria. The ten criteria observed in the papers by Benson (1967); Kerschensteiner *et al.* (1972) and Poeck *et al.* (1972) are not analysed any more. The assumption is that 'everybody knows what fluent and nonfluent speech production is'. This is, in addition to the conceptual step backward, also a methodological step backward.

The relatively basic quantitative measures of fluency have recently been complemented by the introduction of pragmatic considerations. Penn (1983) hypothesized that fluency might be sensitive to components of the communicative event and not only to type and localization of brain damage. A similar relation is observed in the language output of normal speakers that is strongly dependent on 'the semantic and cognitive content of the verbal message and on the nature of the situation and social interaction'. Consequently, she investigated a new aspect, i.e. the *appropriateness* of dysfluencies within the context of interactive discourse. Appropriateness is contrasted with correctness, a notion that appears quite promising also in aphasia research. In this context, measurement and rating of fluency might offer some insight into the mechanisms of normal speech production. As in the paper by Deloche *et al.* (1979) there was no clearcut relation of the fluency dimension with type of aphasia. From Penn's study, again, there arises serious doubt on the utility of the fluency/nonfluency dichotomy.

The issue whether classification as such is a meaningful enterprise partly overlaps with the discussion on the merits of group studies as compared with single case studies. The latter problem, in my view, is a false alternative. The role of single case studies is to explore and identify problems that might be an interesting object of further research. Single case studies are also very well suited to generate hypotheses on neuropsychological processes that might underly pathological phenomena. The general applicability of the hypotheses derived from, and of findings obtained in, single case studies must, in my view, be confirmed in group studies before they are accepted as contributions to deranged and, by implication, normal psychological function of the brain.

The two concepts: classification and group studies vs. phenomenological description in single case studies do, in fact, complement each other. For classification purposes the fluency–nonfluency dimension is too broad to be useful. For single case studies it is dispensable. Also for the design of language therapy programmes a much more refined description of disturbed language performance of a given patient is necessary.

References

Albert, M. L. and J. Sandson (1986) Perseveration in aphasia. *Cortex* **22**, 103–15.

Basso, A., Capitani, E., Laiacona, M. and Luzzatti, C. (1980) Factors influencing type and severity of aphasia. *Cortex* **16**, 361–6.

Basso, A., Roch Lecours, A., Moraschini, S. and Vanier, M. (1985) Anatomo-clinical correlations of the aphasias as defined through computerized tomography: exceptions. *Brain and Language* **26**, 201–29.

Basso, A., Bracchi, M., Capitani, E., Laiacona, M. and Zanobio, M. E. (1987) Age and evolution of language area functions. A study on adult stroke patients. *Cortex* **23**, 475–83.

Benson, D. F. (1967) Fluency in aphasia: Correlation with radioactive scan localization. *Cortex* **3**, 373–94.

Cappa, S. F., Cavallotti, G., Guidotti, M., Papagno, C. and Vignolo, L. A. (1983) Subcortical aphasia. Two clinical-CT scan correlation studies. *Cortex* **19**, 227–41.

Cohen, R., Kelter, S., Engel, D., List, G. and Strohner, H. (1976) Zur Validität des Token-Tests. *Nervenarzt* **47**, 357–61.

Deloche, G., Jean-Louis, J. and Seron, X. (1979) Study of the temporal variables in the spontaneous speech of five aphasic patients in two situations, interview and description. *Brain and Language* **8**, 241–50.

Drummond, S. S., Gallagher, T. M. and Mills, R. H. (1981) Word-retrieval in aphasia: an investigation of semantic complexity. *Cortex* **17**, 63–82.

Feyereisen, P. *et al.* (1986) On fluency measures in aphasic speech, *J. Clin. Exper. Neurophysiol.* **8**, 393–404.

Gerratt, B. R. and Jones, D. (1987) Aphasic performance on a lexical decision task: Multiple meanings and word frequency. *Brain and Language* **30**, 106–15.

Geschwind, N. (1966) Discussion to paper by J. M. Wepman and L. V. Jones in E. C. Carterette (ed.), *Brain Function*, Vol. III. Berkeley and Los Angeles: University Press, pp. 156–71.

Goodglass, H. and Baker, E. (1976) Semantic field, naming and auditory comprehension in aphasia. *Brain and Language* **3**, 359–74.

Henderson, V. W. (1983) Speech fluency in crossed aphasia. *Brain* **106**, 837–57.

Howes, D. (1964) Application of the word-frequency concept to aphasia. In A. V. S. de Reuck and M. O'Connor (eds), *Disorders of Language*. London: J. and A. Churchill.

Howes, D. and Geschwind, N. (1964) Quantitative studies of aphasic language. *Ass. Res. Nerv. Ment. Dis.* **42**, 229–44.

Huber, W., Poeck, K., Weniger, D. and Willmes, K. (1983) *Der Aachener Aphasie Test (AAT)*. Göttingen: Hogrefe.

Jackson, J. H. (1915) On the physiology of language. *Brain* **38**, 59–64.

Kerschensteiner, M., Poeck, K. and Brunner, E. (1972) The fluency–nonfluency dimension in the classification of aphasic speech. *Cortex* **8**, 233–47.

Knopman, D. S., Selnes, O. A., Niccum, N., Rubens, A. B., Yock, D. and Larson, D. (1983) A longitudinal study of speech fluency in aphasia: CT correlates of recovery and persistent nonfluency, *Neurology* **33**, 1170–8.

Kreindler, A., Mihailescu, L. and Fradis, A. (1980) Speech fluency in aphasia. *Brain and Language* **9**, 199–205.

Marshall, R. C. and Tompkins, C. A. (1982) Verbal self-correction behaviors of fluent and nonfluent aphasic subjects. *Brain and Language* **15**, 292–306.

Mazziotta, J. C. and Phelps, M. E. (1986) Positron emission tomography studies of the brain. In M. Phelps, J. Mazziotta, and H. Schelbert (eds), *Positron Emission Tomography and Autoradiography: Principles and Applications for the Brain and Heart*. New York: Raven Press.

McCleary, C. and Hirst, W. (1986) Semantic classification in aphasia: A study of basic, superordinate, and function relations. *Brain and Language* **27**, 199–209.

McFarling, D., Rothi, L. J. and Heilman, K. M. (1982) Transcortical aphasia from ischemic infarcts of the thalamus: a report of two cases, *J. Neurol. Neurosurg. Psychiat.* **45**, 107–12.

Naeser, M. A., Alexander, M. P., Helm, N. A., Levine, H. L., Laughlin, S. A. and Geschwind, N. (1982) Aphasia with predominantly subcortical lesion sites; description of three capsular putaminal aphasia syndromes. *Archives of Neurology* **39**, 1–14.

Obler, L. K., Albert, M. L., Goodglass, H. and Benson, D. F. (1978) Aphasia type and aging. *Brain and Language* **6**, 318–22.

Penn, C. (1983) Fluency and aphasia: a pragmatic reconsideration. *South African J. Commun. Disorders* **30**, 3–8.

Poeck, K. and Hartje, W. (1979) Performance of aphasic patients in visual versus auditory presentation of the Token Test: Demonstration of a supramodal deficit. In

Boller, F. (ed.), *Auditory Comprehension: Clinical and Experimental Studies with the Token Test*. New York and London: Academic Press.

Poeck, K. and Göddenhenrich, S. (1988) Standardized tests for the detection of dissociations in aphasic language performance. *Aphasiology* **2**, 375–80.

Poeck, K., Kerschensteiner, M. and Hartje, W. (1972) A quantitative study on language understanding in fluent and nonfluent aphasia. *Cortex* **8**, 299–304.

Rothi, L. J. and Hutchinson, E. C. (1981) Retention of verbal information by rehearsal in relation to the fluency of verbal output in aphasia. *Brain and Language* **12**, 347–59.

Van Dongen, H. R., Loonen, M. C. B. and Van Dongen, K. J. (1985) Anatomical basis for acquired fluent aphasia in children. *Ann Neurol* **17**, 306–9.

Warrington, E. K. and Shallice, T. (1969) The selective impairment of auditory-verbal short-term memory. *Brain* **92**, 885–96.

Warrington, E. K., Logue, V. and Pratt, R. T. C. (1971) The anatomical localisation of auditory-verbal short-term memory. *Neuropsychologia* **9**, 377–87.

Wayland, S. and Taplin, J. E. (1982) Nonverbal categorization in fluent and nonfluent anomic aphasics. *Brain and Language* **16**, 87–108.

Wernicke, C. (1874) *Der aphasische Symptomencomplex*. Breslau: Cohn und Weigert.

Whitehouse, P., Caramazza, A. and Zurif, E. B. (1978) Naming in aphasia: interacting effects of form and function. *Brain and Language* **6**, 63–74.

Chapter 3

Impairments of Naming and Wo. d-Finding

Robert Goldfarb and Harvey Halpern

A complaint frequently voiced by aphasic patients is, 'I know what I want to say, but I can't say it.' The patient's effortful, and often unsuccessful search for a target word is a source of embarrassment and frustration. The reader's own experiences with a word on 'the tip of the tongue' begin to approximate to those of the aphasic adult with anomia. You may recall the first letter of the word, the number of syllables, even the point of primary stress, but you cannot retrieve the word.

What is anomia? It literally means 'without names' or nouns, but this is too restrictive. We use the term here to refer to all word-finding problems which occur in aphasia and related language disorders. The adjective 'anomic' refers to one of the major subtypes of aphasia, and has been described as an 'amnesic' type of speech disorder as far back as the sixteenth century (Benton 1988). We begin this chapter with a discussion of naming and word-finding impairments in all aphasia subtypes, with some historical and current views on localization. This will be followed by the aphasic condition classified as 'anomia', and theoretical explanations for various forms of naming impairment. Finally, impairments of naming and word finding in language disorders related to aphasia will be addressed, as well as recommendations for clinical intervention.

Naming and word retrieval in aphasia

An early distinction in the study of aphasia was between internal and external speech. Verbal amnesia, considered a residual of sensory aphasia (Marie 1906), was differentiated from Broca's aphasia, which was considered largely a motor disturbance. However, Wernicke (1874) maintained that anomia was a form of transcortical motor aphasia. Until the publication of a paper by Pitres (1898), most aphasiologists focused on identifying separate forms of aphasia to which the visual, auditory, and motor components of anomia might correspond. While 'anomia' is currently regarded as a specific type of aphasia, there is no doubt that word-finding defects are associated with all the aphasia

..romes. As a migratory, rather than a static symbolic language disorder, aphasia in its various forms may be marked by relatively more or less anomia, throughout the stages of recovery. For example, neologistic jargon improves to conduction aphasia, but the latter improves to anomia (Brown 1972).

Descriptions of naming errors in aphasia must clearly differentiate between the narrower sense of naming on confrontation and the broader sense of word finding in the flow of speech. Geschwind (1967) described failures in confrontation naming which are of theoretical and diagnostic significance. There is a classic form of anomia, characterized by difficulty in naming on confrontation, while the patient recognizes the object and usually accepts the correct name. The word-finding difficulty in spontaneous speech is not confined to the names of physical stimuli, but also involves abstract nouns and adjectives, as well as other parts of speech (Wepman *et al.* 1956; Howes 1964). In the classic form, patients have basically the same difficulty in confrontation naming for all types of material and for all sensory modalities. In contrast to the classic type is another more restricted form (Geschwind 1967). The patient can neither produce the name when presented with the stimulus nor choose the correct stimulus when given a name. The difficulty is confined to a single modality, perhaps even to a single class within that modality, and may be confined to a visual half-field or to the hemiparetic side of the body. However spontaneous speech is normal even for the categories which are particularly impaired in confrontation naming.

Localization

Geschwind's interest in the pathoanatomy of language disorders led to his descriptions of localization of lesions producing anomia. For example, a patient with an infarction of the corpus callosum sparing only the splenium had no difficulty naming objects visually and speech was normal. However, when blindfolded, he misnamed objects held in the left hand (Geschwind and Kaplan 1962). In another example, anomia was restricted to a colour-naming deficit in a patient with pure alexia without agraphia (Geschwind and Fusillo 1966). In this case the left visual cortex and the splenium were destroyed. Most cases of anomia may be localized to lesions in the left angular gyrus (for the classic form), and to lesions which isolate certain sensory regions from the left angular gyrus (for the more restricted form). Geschwind's work expands the efforts of neurologists dating from the last century who felt that a lesion in a specific language area of the brain would result in a specific language loss. Early localizationists included Bastian (1887), Broca (1861) and Wernicke (1874). Among the strict localizationists of the twentieth century, Henschen (1926) and Nielson (1946) are foremost. A comprehensive treatise on the contribution of Wernicke and the Breslau School to aphasia has been published by Geschwind (1966).

A second consideration regarding localization is a philosophical one. The early diagram-makers used localization deductively, because they discussed pathologies which were new. They considered it to be the task of subsequent clinical observations to test the validity of relating lesion site to aphasia type. Now that most of these syndromes have been observed, the connectionistic models of the diagram-makers must be used inductively. In other words, localization theory is now used to predict lesion site (Buckingham 1984). The resultant philosophy, known as association psychology, may be adequate to explain slips of the tongue in normals and semantic paraphasias in brain-damaged patients, but is probably inadequate to account for normal or disordered syntax.

The syndrome of anomia

'Word amnesia' or 'amnesic aphasia' was first described in three forms by Pitres (1898), and was defined by Pick (1931; 1973) as the absence or lack of recall for the proper word in the process of object naming or in the course of a sentence. Other early classifications included 'nominal aphasia' (Head 1926) and 'word-muteness' (Kleist 1934).

Anatomically and behaviourally, anomia and Wernicke's aphasia are not sharply differentiated in individual cases, both belonging to the category of fluent aphasia. Some studies discuss anomic and Wernicke's aphasic patients together when the basis of grouping is fluency or a posterior lesion site (Berndt, Caramazza and Zurif 1983). In addition, naming errors have been found following stimulation of a broad area of lateral dominant cortex (Ojemann 1979). However the classic forms of the syndromes are clearly distinct. Anomic aphasia is marked by word-finding difficulty in the presence of preserved syntax and fluency. Phonemic paraphasias (see Ch. 6 below), such as cabbage/garbage, do not usually occur. More common is 'periphrasis' (Brown 1972), which seems to be a form of self-cuing, where patients describe the function or structure of an object rather than its name. In both temporal and parietal types of anomia, the closer the paraphasia to the target word, the less is the awareness of error, according to Brown.

Spontaneous conversation is often marked by circumlocutions, where patients verbally beat around the bush without coming to the point satisfactorily (Darley 1982). In the following example, an anomic patient was asked to describe what he thought of, when presented with a ruler: 'According to what size you get – a long one, and you got narrow ones. You measure the inches and so forth.' The site of lesion for anomia, as for Wernicke's aphasia, is posterior to those encountered in nonfluent, or Broca's aphasia, and usually in the left temporoparietal region. When the injury extends into the angular gyrus, alexia and agraphia may appear. On the other hand, anomia has been shown to be the least reliably localized aphasic syndrome (Goodglass and Kaplan 1983). 'Anomic responses per se have little localizing value; lesions from anywhere in the language zone seem to be able to produce anomia' (Ojemann and Whitaker 1978: p. 242).

In sum, anomia refers to a condition where lexical access is poor, that is, naming vocabulary is impaired, but fluency of speech, precision of articulation, and use of grammar are relatively spared. It is emphasized that reduction of efficiency in lexical access characterizes virtually all adults with aphasia. Ability to access premorbid vocabulary, then, more properly reflects severity of aphasia, regardless of type (Goodglass *et al.* 1976).

The process of word retrieval

If reduced available vocabulary is the surface realization of word-retrieval difficulties, then it behoves us to examine the underlying reduction of efficiency in the retrieval process itself. We have noted (Goldfarb and Halpern 1981) the interrelations between word-retrieval and word-association responses. Schuell *et al.* (1964) considered a word retriever to be a device which transfers information from the permanent memory unit and makes it accessible for further processing. In aphasia one of three adverse conditions occurs. In the most severe the retriever does not work and there is no response. In the second the retriever operates with reduced efficiency, and activates part of the appropriate pattern in the network. This fragment may or may not contain the precise information required. The word may or may not be the one the aphasic patient was searching for, but it will probably be a closely associated one. Under the third condition the retriever works a little better, and the aphasic adult may be able to continue the search, correct a wrong response, produce synonyms, related responses, or longer responses.

Production of a word-association response involves word retrieval, lexical search, and encoding. A part or parts of this process may be impaired in aphasia. The difficulty may lie in the aphasic adult's auditory or visual processing of the stimulus word. While the word may not be understood to the extent that it can be repeated or even recognized in a multiple-choice task, it may retain the 'power of excitement or revivability of associates' (Buckingham 1984: p. 22). That is, the aphasic patient may still be able to perceive the word sufficiently well so that the sphere of meaning to which it belongs is elicited, and the patient may summon up another word belonging to this sphere. Naming difficulty, according to Goldstein (1948), stems from an inability to assume an 'abstract attitude' with regard to the stimulus. Words which could not be produced upon confrontation may appear spontaneously in conversation. Thus word memory may be unimpaired, but may be subject to the condition under which it is evoked. In other words, there is a problem with the word-retrieval mechanism.

An interesting study of the central organization of language processes in word retrieval involved a description of the types of retrieval behaviour employed by aphasic subjects in conversation (Marshall 1976). From a corpus of 740 instances of word retrieval, five behaviours were identified. In *delay* the patient took or requested additional time to produce the word. Hesitation phenomena, such as filled pauses and unfilled pauses, were usually identified. *Semantic association* included production of antonyms (table–chair), in-class associations (Ford–Plymouth), part–whole relationships (branch–tree), and serially related items (one, two, three) (examples are from Marshall 1976). *Phonetic association* involved production which was phonetically similar to the target word, such as a spoonerism. These efforts were not the groping off-target productions associated with apraxia of speech. In *description*, subjects provided semantic features of form and function related to the target word. Finally, *generalization* consisted of generic, or empty words produced in place of a desired word (e.g. 'thing', 'place', 'these'). Only in generalization was it possible to separate associational processes from the word-retrieval phenomenon. Generalization was also the least effective retrieval technique used by the subjects.

Marshall's classification of relative effectiveness of word retrieval behaviour was based on group data; clearly there are single case and individual differences. Furthermore, delay, which was the most successful approach, was used predominantly by higher-level subjects. The most unsuccessful technique, generalization, was used primarily by lower-level subjects. In addition, the strategies used by all subjects, association and description, were far more successful for the higher-level subjects.

Linguistic investigations of word-finding deficits have focused on semantic knowledge, word-initial phonology and response activation, and, in particular, frequency of occurrence of word usage. Wepman *et al.* (1956) hypothesized that 'anomic-like' speech patterns might be produced in either of two ways. First, suppression of lower-frequency words would curtail nouns more than other parts of speech. Second, if nouns were suppressed, a compensatory overuse of high-frequency words would result, but some lower-frequency verbs, modifiers, and pronouns would also be expected to occur. Underuse of lower-frequency words and overuse of high-frequency words occurred in the language of the aphasic subject studied. However, the effect was more severe than the anomia model predicted, suggesting that all words of lower frequency were deficient in her speech. Even when the word-finding deficit is less dramatic, conversational speech of aphasic adults is characterized by fewer different words then normal subjects produce in a sample of any given size (Howes 1964).

Anomia may also reflect a disturbance of the lexical-semantic system. For example, anomic aphasic subjects could not reliably use the perceptual dimensions that defined cup-like objects, nor could they integrate the functional context information in classifying them (Whitehouse *et al.* 1978). Some aphasic adults seemingly fail to recognize or fail to focus on the same semantic relations among words that normals do. An alternative explanation is that aphasic adults have difficulty with certain types of classification; classifying by function may be one example of this type (McCleary 1988). The inability to analyse a context into its constituents impairs the decoding process primarily, while the inability to integrate, or to create a context, adversely affects encoding (Jakobson 1966). On the other hand, the word-finding deficit in aphasia may be restricted to the denotative value of words, as aphasic adults produce words of positive and negative connotation in about the same proportion as do normals (Goldfarb 1987).

Finally, it is well known that type of aphasia and severity of the naming deficit influence the effectiveness of cues (Weidner and Jinks 1983). Initial sound cues tend to elicit a word otherwise unavailable to some aphasic adults. Of particular interest is the finding that adults with Broca's aphasia, whose language production is characterized by confusions of phonological form, benefit from phonological cues to a much greater degree than do those with Wernicke's aphasia, whose articulation is much more intelligible. These findings imply that there may be an inner speech image, with an acoustic pattern of the intended word which can be triggered by the initial sound cue. In addition, aphasic adults with posterior lesions and fluent speech may have a unique deficit in this regard (Wingfield and Wayland 1988: pp. 424–5).

37

Classifications of anomia

Not all word-finding impairments are alike, yet, until recently, there were few attempts to subdivide them. The importance of recognizing different anomic impairments is clear when therapeutic intervention is attempted. To be succinct, what you do about anomia depends upon what you think anomia is. As with the aphasias in general, varying classification systems for anomia can be confusing. This review, therefore, will summarize a single classification system (Benson 1979a; 1988) which lists both aphasic and nonaphasic types (see Table 3.1).

Table 3.1: Clinical varieties of anomia

Type of anomia	*Clinical syndrome*	*Anatomical site*
Word production anomia		
(a) Articulatory initiation anomia	Broca's aphasia	Posterior inferior frontal cortex
	Transcortical motor aphasia	Medial or dorso- lateral frontal cortex
(b) Paraphasic anomia	Conduction aphasia	Arcuate fasciculus
Word selection anomia	Anomic aphasia	Brodmann area 37
Semantic anomia	Transcortical sensory aphasia	Angular gyrus
Disconnection anomia		
(a) Category-specific anomia		Posterior pathways
(b) Modality-specific anomia	Agnosia	Posterior pathways
(c) Callosal disconnection anomia		Corpus callosum

Source: Benson 1988; reprinted with permission.

Word-production anomia

Benson's (1979a) classification divides word-production anomia into motor and paraphasic subtypes. In articulatory initiation anomia, patients struggle to produce a word they claim to know. This struggle behaviour may be characterized by phonemic reapproaches, which are repeated efforts at accurate articulation. The major problem seems to be an inordinate difficulty in initiating phonation. Patients frequently exhibit dysarthria, a motor speech disturbance caused by a weakness or paralysis of the speech musculature. They also have difficulty maintaining the flow of speech from word to word. When prompted with the initial phoneme the target word may emerge. In fact the patient may be able to write the word. There is some doubt about including the motor subtype of word production anomia in the category of word retrieval problems, because the ability to write the word indicates it is available on some level. This doubt is reflected in a lively debate concerning the existence of an aphasic phonological impairment (see, for example, Martin 1974 and Ch. 8 below). We take the position that, for a linguistic behaviour to be considered part of one of the aphasia syndromes, it must occur in the great majority of cases, and it may not occur in the absence of aphasia. One of the present authors (Halpern *et al.* 1976) examined the ability of 30 adult aphasic subjects without apraxia of speech or dysarthria to produce phonemes in single test words and in spontaneous contextual speech. Phonemic errors in the structured test condition involving production of single words occurred on only 2 per cent of the target phonemes, and spontaneous contextual speech was virtually free of phonemic errors (28 of the 30 subjects made no articulation errors). It was therefore suggested that aphasia uncontaminated by dysarthria or apraxia of speech is not characterized by significant breakdown in articulatory performance.

The paraphasic subtype refers primarily to phonemic paraphasias; semantic paraphasias are relatively rare in this type of anomia. However, certain aspects of the target word may be retrieved in the search. These have been called 'tip-of-the-tongue' (TOT) characteristics (Goodglass *et al.* 1976). In the TOT state, identification of the first letter and syllabic length in target words was less than 1 in 10 for anomic subjects, followed by Wernicke's (1 in 8), Broca's (1 in 5), and conduction (1 in 3) aphasic subjects. Paraphasic anomia does, though, include one or more incorrectly produced phonemes. Phonemic cuing by the clinician may be of little help, but the patient's own phonemic reapproaches may result in a closer approximation of the target.

The two types of word-production anomia are readily differentiable; however Benson (1988) noted that some admixture of the two is almost always observed in clinical practice. In addition, the patient's knowledge of the target word often appears intact, even though motoric production of the name is impaired.

Word-selection/word-dictionary anomia

In a rare variety of aphasia, all language functions are preserved except for frequent word-finding pauses, compensatory circumlocutions and outright failures to name (Benson 1988: p. 231). The disorder may be considered a pure anomic aphasia. Patients with this disorder indicate understanding of a word's meaning through their description of semantic features of form and function associated with the word. Spontaneous speech may be fluent, but lacking in substantive words. Although the ability to recognize the target word when presented, and to select the word in a multiple-choice task, appears preserved, the patient will probably not benefit from phonemic cues.

Semantic anomia

Poor auditory comprehension characterizes patients with this disorder. Word retrieval is poor, and the target word may not be produced in an imitative task or be understood when spoken by the clinician. Spontaneous language is fluent and semantically empty. Benson's (1988) analogy that this condition resembles the oral repetition of a word in a foreign language that is not understood speaks to the state in which the word no longer possesses symbolic value.

The following categories may be grouped under the classification of 'disconnection anomia' because the word-finding defect results from separation of a primary sensory or sensory association area from the major language centres. These represent the restricted forms of anomia which we discussed earlier (for clinical examples, see Geschwind and Kaplan 1962; and Geschwind and Fusillo 1966), where lesions isolate certain sensory areas from the left angular gyrus.

Category- and modality-specific anomia

Category-specific anomia is limited to naming in a particular category, and has been most frequently reported in the form of colour anomia. Patients have especial difficulty naming colours on confrontation or pointing to colours when named by others, but other naming features are substantially spared or normal. Other examples of category-specific anomia involve naming of body parts, clothing or fruit and vegetables (Hart *et al.* 1985; Berndt 1988). The key to diagnosis is that naming in one category is distinctly poorer than in others.

Failure to name may be limited to presentation of stimuli within a particular modality, most often visual. According to Brown (1972), patients may be able to name when given a functional description after a perceptual failure. For example, a patient who fails to name a razor following a visual or tactile presentation may succeed when prompted with a description of its use (e.g. what you shave with in the morning). In addition, word production in conversational speech is normal. Benson (1988) considered modality-specific anomia to be relatively rare in pure state, and, while truly representing a word-finding defect, is correctly interpreted as an agnosia.

Callosal disconnection anomia

Patients with this disorder have suffered a separation of the corpus callosum, either surgically or because of anterior artery territory infarction (Benson 1988). Resultant split-brain research (Gazzaniga and Sperry 1967) helped to identify specialized functions of the left and right hemispheres. The following example (Springer and Deutsch 1981: pp. 29–30) illustrates these functions.

A woman, suffering from intractable epilepsy, had received a complete commissurotomy. She was seated in front of a small screen with a small black dot in the centre, and was asked to look directly at the dot. When a picture of a cup was flashed briefly to the right of the dot, she reported that she had seen a cup. After fixing her gaze again on the centred dot, a picture of a spoon was flashed to the left of the dot. She reported she had seen nothing, but was able to reach under the screen and, using her left hand, select from among several items the object corresponding to the picture she had seen. When asked what she was holding, she replied, 'pencil'. The general conclusion (Benson 1988: p. 233) is that the right hemisphere correctly analyses and interprets tactile sensations, but the callosal separation isolates this information from the language area necessary for verbal production of the appropriate name.

Anomias occurring in disorders other than aphasia will be discussed next in this chapter. In general, though, anomia linked to phonological and articulatory deficits seems to be limited to stroke patients, while semantic-memory deficits probably cause anomia in dementia of the Alzheimer's type (Margolin 1988).

Non-aphasic misnaming and word-finding difficulties

The language of dementia

Cortical dementia is indicated by patients having problems in cognition, visuo-spatial abilities, behaviour, and in language. Deficits in cognition usually involve memory loss, time and place disorientation, intellectual decline, and faulty judgement. Personality behaviour can be dull and bland, but can also show emotional incontinence at times. Language problems usually include a restricted vocabulary that is limited to small talk and stereotyped clichés. Perseveration (Gewirth *et al.* 1984; Bayles *et al.* 1985), word-finding difficulty (Bayles 1986; Huff *et al.* 1986), semantic errors (Flicker *et al.* 1987; Grober *et al.* 1985; Huff *et al.* 1986; Kempler *et al.* 1987; Murdoch *et al.* 1987) and naming problems (Bayles 1986) are also present.

Bayles *et al.* (1982) and Obler and Albert (1981: pp. 385–98) have delineated three stages in cortical dementia. During the mild stage, patients sense a decline, become apologetic, and are reluctant to be tested. Frequently they are disoriented to time, and memory for recent events has begun to fail. The patient relies heavily on overlearned situations and stereotypical utterances and often is unable to generate sequences of related ideas. In this stage, the patient might resemble the Wernicke's patient; however the Wernicke's patient cannot repeat, whereas the dementia patient often can.

Bayles *et al.* (1982) point out that the dementia patient, at this stage, begins to exhibit semantic impairment (slightly reduced vocabulary; word-finding difficulties; increased use of automatisms and clichés) and pragmatic impairment (mild loss of desire to communicate; occasional disinhibitions), whereas syntax and phonology are intact.

During the moderate stage, the patient has a more noticeable impairment of memory and orientation to time and place. Patients are more perseverative, non-meaningful, and do not correct errors they produce. Bayles *et al.* (1982) have noted that the dementia patient, in this stage, shows further semantic impairment (significantly reduced vocabulary; naming errors usually semantically and visually related; verbal paraphasias evident in discourse), shows some syntactic impairment (reduction in syntactic complexity and completeness), shows further pragmatic impairment (declining sensitivity to context; diminished eye contact; egocentricity), whereas phonology is generally intact.

Because the patient has difficulty with abstraction, utterances are usually concrete. Repetition begins to break down and the patient shows circumlocutions and anomic difficulties. Eye contact begins to diminish indicating that the pragmatics of communication are inappropriate. Wilson *et al.* (1982) found that dementia patients show a deficit in the retention of facial information. The aphasic patient would probably be adequate in this area.

In the advanced stage, the patients are very much disoriented to time, place and person and fail to recognize family and friends. Unable to carry out the routines of life, they require extensive personal care. Many times they will make spontaneous corrections of syntactic and phonologic errors, but without awareness. They have brief moments when stimuli appear to be comprehended, but for the most part they will not comprehend nor self-correct any errors. Their phonology is generally correct and syntax may be disturbed, but not as disturbed as the semantic aspects of language (Bayles 1986; Bayles and Boone 1982). Referential aspects of language are very disturbed, while the mechanics of speech production are not disturbed unless a sub-cortical degeneration process has taken place. In some cases, patients may only exhibit jargon.

Bayles *et al.* (1982) point out that the dementia patient in the advanced stage shows further semantic impairment (markedly reduced vocabulary; frequent unrelated meanings; jargon), further syntactic impairment (many inappropriate word combinations), further pragmatic impairment (nonadherence to conversational rules; poor eye contact; lack of social awareness; inability to form a purposeful intention), and some impairment of phonology (occasional phonemic paraphasias and neologisms).

Naming in aphasia and dementia

Critchley (1970: pp. 349–51) has stated that in dementia language impairment essentially entails a poverty of language due to inaccessibility of the speaking, writing, and reading vocabulary. With advancing mental inelasticity and memory loss, words used by dementia patients become severely restricted in conversation and, to a somewhat lesser extent, in writing. The difficulty in word-finding differs from the anomia of aphasic patients. The dementia patient does not necessarily show hesitancy in naming objects. However the dementia patient finds it difficult to name, unless the real object is present. The patient lapses into a concrete attitude.

Appell *et al.* (1982) found that Alzheimer's patients showed symptoms that resembled Wernicke's and transcortical sensory aphasia more than they resembled Broca's or transcortical motor aphasia. Obler *et al.* (1982) and Nicholas *et al.* (1985) noted that more neologisms and semantic and phonemic paraphasis existed in Wernicke's aphasia, while the Alzheimer's patient produced more conjunctions (e.g. but, or, so, because) and empty phrases (e.g. 'and so on and so forth').

Benson (1979b: p. 160) stated that anomia in the aphasic patient separates him from the dementia patient. Horner *et al.* (1982) and Obler and Albert (1981: p. 391) have noted that the naming errors of the dementia patient are more likely the result of visual misperceptions than the naming errors of aphasic patients which are mostly of a semantic or phonological nature. On the other hand, Cummings *et al.* (1986) found that reading comprehension problems in Alzheimer's patients are due more to a linguistic deficit than a visuo-perceptual impairment. Bayles and Tomoeda (1983) and Martin and Fedio (1983) have also noted that the naming problem in dementia gets worse as the disease progresses.

It is generally known that speech and language therapy or other treatments will not provide long-term improvement in the patient with generalized intellectual impairment. However, speech and language therapy can help the patient and the family to communicate maximally, within the scope of limited abilities. Specific recommendations appear at the end of this chapter.

The language of confusion

Confused language is a part of a condition where the patient's responsiveness to his environment is impaired. The behaviour indicates that the patient is less able to recognize and understand the environment than in the normal state. Clearness of thinking and accuracy of remembering are impaired. The patient usually manifests a disorientation of time and place, confabulations, inability to follow directions, bizarre and irrelevant responses, and is unaware of the inappropriateness of responses (Darley 1964: pp. 38–9; Halpern *et al.* 1973; Mayo Clinic 1964: p. 234; and Wertz 1978: pp. 1–101).

Geschwind (1967) described the syndrome of 'non-aphasic misnaming' that typically occurs in disorders which diffusely involve the nervous system, especially when the disturbance comes on fairly rapidly. Characteristically the errors tend to 'propagate'. Thus the patient being asked where he is may say, 'In a bus', and may continue by identifying the examiner as the bus driver, those around him as passengers, and his bed as being used by the driver for resting. It is usually obvious once a sequence of questions is asked that ordinary aphasic misnaming is readily ruled out. Thus in aphasic misnaming there is no tendency to 'propagation' although perseveration, i.e. repetition of the same incorrect word, occurs frequently. The connected or propagated character of the errors may show up particularly in relation to the hospital and the patient's illness. He may call the hospital a 'hotel', the doctors 'bell boys', the nurses 'chambermaids', and will not accept correction.

One feature which often characterizes non-aphasic misnaming is that spontaneous speech is usually, but not invariably, normal despite gross errors in naming. In aphasia, errors in confrontation naming are almost always accompanied by a disturbance in spontaneous speech in which word-finding pauses, empty phrases, semantic or adequacy errors and circumlocutions appear.

Stengel (1964) has stated that people in confusional states, when called upon to name objects, do not respond in the same way as aphasic adults who say, 'I know what it is, but I can't find the word'. Confused patients would boldly and sometimes recklessly improvise and produce words on the spur of the moment. These words may show effects of perseveration and of slang and other associations. They may contain references to certain aspects of the correct concept. The words produced may show a creative inventiveness. Occasionally they embody references to the patient's personal problems. The patients show no awareness of error and when told to think again they insist that they are right. These responses, which have been called non-aphasic misnaming, are invariably associated with a more general change in behaviour, whereby perception and motivation are altered. The disturbance of motivation is particularly obvious in relation to the task of naming and definition. These patients do not seem to care whether they obtain an accurate correspondence between the object and its generally accepted verbal representation. They disregard the function of language as a code of behaviour and of communication. They are either incapable of this effort or unwilling to make it.

Among the impaired language skills, the factor of relevance is a key differentiating point. In working with a confused language patient, one of the authors (HH) found the following to be typical examples of irrelevant responses. 'A measure of violence', was given as the definition for 'bargain'. 'Should watch out for mail boxes, should watch out for people, should watch out for papers', was given as three things that every good citizen should do. Additional reviews on aspects of the language of confusion can be found in Drummond (1986), and Daniel *et al.* (1987) have reviewed the neuropsychologic aspects of disorientation.

Therapy for the confused language patient tends to follow the same format as that for the patient with a generalized intellectual impairment. The confused-language patient should have highly structured sessions, given as often as possible.

The language of schizophrenia

There is general agreement that schizophrenia is a disorder that affects the total personality in all aspects of its functioning. Not all patients show the same range in magnitude of disturbance, and even the same patient's symptoms will vary from time to time, but the striking feature of this disorder is that it permeates every aspect of the individual's functioning (Bemporad and Pinsker 1974). Day and Semrad (1978: pp. 199–241) pointed out that most schizophrenia begins in the mid-teens and continues at a high level of incidence until the mid-fifties. More women than men become schizophrenic. Married people are less susceptible than those who are single, separated, or divorced. Schizophrenia may affect the patients' perceptions, thoughts, mood, will, speech, motor control, and social behaviour.

With an eye toward diagnosis, the language of schizophrenia data from the Halpern and McCartin-Clark (1984) study was compared with the language data of subjects with a generalized intellectual impairment, confused language, and apraxia of speech (Halpern *et al.* 1973). This comparison revealed the following: subjects with a generalized intellectual impairment showed more impairment in auditory retention span, naming, and syntax than subjects with the language of schizophrenia. Subjects with confused language will be more impaired in reading comprehension, syntax, naming, relevance, writing words to dictation, and general overall language ability than subjects with the language of schizophrenia. Subjects with apraxia of speech will be more impaired in syntax, be more nonfluent, and be less impaired in relevance than subjects with the language of schizophrenia. It seems that normal naming and syntactic ability of the schizophrenic group differentiates them from the above cerebrally involved groups, except for the apraxic subjects where only syntactic ability differentiated them.

In the Halpern and McCartin-Clark (1984) schizophrenic group, length of institutionalization and speaking (especially adequacy (semantic ability) and naming) were positively correlated, indicating that the longer the institutionalization, the more errors in speaking (especially adequacy and naming) are produced. This finding agrees with Wynne (1963) who stated that schizophrenic language can be influenced by long-term institutionalization.

Many utterances of the schizophrenic patient resemble the adequacy errors of the aphasic patient. Although the end product, an adequacy error, is the same, in the aphasic patient it seems to be part of a word-finding disturbance (a linguistic inaccessibility), whereas in the schizophrenic patient it seems to be due to the underlying thought disorder, a lack of stimulation or socialization, and not caring. It seems that if the thought disorder component takes control, a bizarre response will be produced. If the lack of stimulation or socialization, and the not-caring components take over, an adequacy error is produced. The results of the Halpern *et al.* (1973) and Halpern and McCartin-Clark (1984) studies show that adequacy problems were the most common or least differentiating language symptoms of all the groups tested.

Assessment and treatment of word-retrieval problems in aphasia

Most of the standardized tests for aphasia assess anomia through convergent naming tasks (confrontation naming). The patient is required to name a series of objects or pictures presented by the examiner. Of significant importance, but less likely to appear on formal tests, are divergent naming tests (word fluency). An example would be for the patient to explain proverbs without repeating any of the words in the proverb. 'Convergent' refers to the generation of a logical conclusion; 'divergent' refers to the generation of logical alternatives. Naming and word-finding tasks in three of the most frequently used batteries are discussed below.

The *Minnesota Test for Differential Diagnosis of Aphasia* (Schuell 1965) includes norms for aphasic and normal adults. It is strongest in its comprehensive assessment of strengths and weaknesses in all language modalities as a guide to planning clinical intervention. It takes two to six hours to administer, with an average of three hours. Nonpropositional naming is tested in such serial tasks as counting and reciting days of the week; a sentence completion task is also included. Propositional language tasks include picture naming, answering questions, using words in sentences, picture description, word definitions, and retelling a story.

The Porch Index of Communicative Ability (Porch 1967) has norms for aphasic, normal, right hemisphere and bilaterally brain-damaged adults, and is the most completely standardized aphasia test. It is the only aphasia test which presents the patient with more difficult subtests prior to the easier ones, and is usually completed in one-half to two hours. Subtests refer to ten stimulus items and are scored according to a multidimensional system of 16 scale points reflecting accuracy, responsiveness, completeness, promptness, and efficiency.

Naming ability is assessed in Subtest IV, which requires the subject to say the name of each of ten objects. Subtest IX is a sentence completion task, e.g. 'You cut meat with a . . .' Subtest XII requires the subject to repeat the names of the ten objects after the examiner.

The *Boston Diagnostic Aphasia Examination* (Goodglass and Kaplan 1983), normed for aphasic and normal adults, has an administration time of one to four hours. It is the test currently used most frequently for research. Naming and word finding may be informally assessed in the conversational and expository speech section. These skills are examined more fully in the section on oral expression. Non-propositional language is evaluated in serial tasks, reciting verses memorized premorbidly, and singing. Repetition of phrases and sentences are thoroughly assessed. Word retrieval is examined in single-word responses to questions posed by the examiner. Confrontation naming uses the same visual stimuli as the auditory comprehension section does, permitting comparison of modalities. Finally, divergent word retrieval is tested by having the subject produce as many animal names as possible, based on a norm of 22.5 in sixty seconds. In the *Boston Naming Test* (Kaplan *et al.* 1983), naming vocabulary for 60 pictures is assessed.

Therapy for anomia in aphasia

We present below a brief discussion of therapy for anomia. Fuller discussion can be found in Shewan and Bandur (1986) who have summarized data from many sources and have developed a hierarchy of effectiveness of cues. As noted earlier, type of aphasia and severity of the naming deficit influence the effectiveness of cues. In order of most effective to least effective at eliciting the target word, Shewan and Bandur listed the following: repetition, delay, initial phoneme/initial syllable, sentence completion, semantic association, printed word, description, rhyming word, situational context, spelled word, functional description, superordinate term, and generalization.

The clinician may wish to combine several cues at one time, and gradually fade some of them as the anomic patient improves in word finding ability. We present a sample treatment protocol for a Broca's aphasic patient with a moderate impairment in lexical retrieval. We have selected a sentence-completion task because of its greater redundancy and automatic nature (Goodglass 1967), as compared to confrontation naming. A noun in a sentence context may have less nominal quality than when appearing alone. Providing multiple cues before requesting a response is more effective than the same single cues provided sequentially (Weidner and Jinks 1983).

Task Provide the last word to complete a highly associative open-ended sentence.

Cues Initial phoneme, sentence completion, semantic association, and printed word.

Program Present 25 trials, using all four cues noted above. When the patient achieves a criterion level of 80 per cent correct responses for 25 trials over three consecutive sessions, first the printed word, then the initial phoneme, and finally the semantic association cue will be deleted.

Examples Although a minimum of 25 different sentences are required for each session, we are using only two here as illustrative examples. The program is presented in four levels. Failure to achieve criterion indicates that the clinician should return to a previous level for a particular sentence.

Level I Hold a flash card with 'DOOR' printed in one-inch block letters in front of the patient. About five seconds may be optimal. Say to the patient, 'Someone is knocking at the d____'. Use a similar orthographic cue for 'Wash your hands with soap and w____'.

Level II Present sentences as in Level I, but eliminate the flash cards.

Level III Present sentences as in Level II, but eliminate the phonemic cue. For example, 'The barber will cut your ____', or 'When you're sick, you go to the ____'.

Level IV Present open-ended sentences which do not include semantic associations, such as, 'Please pass the ____', or 'I don't like ____'.

Therapy for anomia in related language disorders

Therapy for generalized intellectual impairment should help orient the patient to time and place in a concrete manner. This can be achieved through the use of visual aids such as calendars (days, months, years); blackboard for large words and simple drawings; and poster cards or large, uncluttered pictures.

Decide on what functions the patient can strengthen through daily activities. This can be done by making grocery shopping lists, putting foods in categories, the location and names of supermarkets; money concepts coupled with simple arithmetic; reading bus schedules (time, destinations); simple cooking activities and measuring tasks; setting clocks and timers; and using the telephone for work on numbers in sequence and memory.

Try to help orient the patient to family placement and relationships by using real family names. Vocabulary should be concrete and centred around everyday activities. Patients should be encouraged to engage in social situations to stimulate mental activity.

Therapy for the confused language patient tends to follow the same format as the therapy described for the patient with a generalized intellectual impairment. Therapy for the confused language patient would have to be quite structured and should be given as often as possible. At each hourly session, work on making the patient aware of the month, day, and year of that particular day; also work on making the patient aware of where therapy is taking place.

Initially, keep the questions and responses as succinct as possible so as not to tax the patient. The next step would be short, simple conversations. Accomplish this task by gradually increasing the complexity of the verbalizations. Each time the patient demonstrates that he understands the particular level of syntactic structure move to the next level and observe the patient's responses.

To prevent or at least to limit the irrelevant verbiage by the patient when a given stimulus requires a specific response, one has several options. Initially, request the patient to stop talking. Use a 'time-out' procedure with the patient each time his response becomes irrelevant and wordy. As a last resort, and only with selected patients, leave the room upon a wordy irrelevant response and re-enter the room only when the patient has placed his trust in the clinician's judgement.

Speech and language therapy for the schizophrenic patient can focus on any co-existing aphasia, dysarthria, stuttering, or voice problem. In addition, therapy can focus on overcoming institutional neurosis, which is characterized by apathy and sometimes a stereotyped posture and gait. It is probably caused by incarceration in an institution for two years or longer, and by the intake of drugs. Some clinicians have noted institutional neurosis in patients residing in non-psychiatric nursing homes. Finally, early detection by the clinician of hyperkinetic dysarthria in schizophrenic patients may play a critical role in the recognition of tardive dyskinesia during its reversible stages (Portnoy 1979), and thus help to prevent the onset of a permanent damage to the central nervous system.

References

Appell, J., Kertesz, A. and Fisman, M. (1982) A study of language functioning in Alzheimer's patients. *Brain and Language* **17**, 73–91.

Basso, A., Lecours, A. R., Moraschini, S. and Vanier, M. (1985) Anatomoclinical correlations of the aphasias as defined through computerized tomography: exceptions. *Brain and Language* **26**, 201–29.

Bastian, C. (1887) On different kinds of aphasia, with special references to their classification and ultimate pathology. *British Medical Journal* **2**, 931–6, 985–90.

Bayles, K. (1986) Management of neurogenic communication disorders associated with dementia. In R. Chapey (ed.), *Language Intervention Strategies in Adult Aphasia* (2nd edn). Baltimore: Williams & Wilkins.

Bayles, K. and Boone, D. (1982) The potential of language tasks for identifying senile dementia. *Journal of Speech and Hearing Disorders* **47**, 210–17.

Bayles, K. and Tomoeda, C. (1983) Confrontation naming impairment in dementia. *Brain and Language* **19**, 98–114.

Bayles, K., Tomoeda, C. and Caffrey, J. (1982) Language and dementia producing diseases. *Communicative Disorders* **7**, 131–46.

Bayles, K., Tomoeda, C., Kasniak, A., Stern, L. and Eagans, K. (1985) Verbal perseveration of dementia patients. *Brain and Language* **25**, 102–16.

Bemporad, J. and Pinsker, H. (1974) Schizophrenia: The manifest symptomatology. In S. Arieti and E. Brody (eds), *American Handbook of Psychiatry*, Vol. 3, pp. 524–50. New York: Basic Books.

Benson, D. F. (1979a) Neurologic coordinates of anomia. In H. Whitaker and H. A. Whitaker (eds), *Studies in neurolinguistics*, Vol. 4, pp. 293–328. New York: Academic Press.

Benson, D. F. (1979b) *Aphasia, Alexia, Agraphia*. New York: Churchill Livingstone.

Benson, D. F. (1988) Anomia in aphasia. *Aphasiology* **2**, 229–35.

Benton, A. (1988) Pitres and amnesic aphasia. *Aphasiology* **2**, 209–14.

Berndt, R. S. (1988) Category-specific deficits in aphasia. *Aphasiology* **2**, 237–40.

Berndt, R. S., Caramazza, A. and Zurif, E. (1983) Language functions: syntax and semantics. In S. J. Segalowitz (ed.), *Language Functions and Brain Organization*. New York: Academic Press, 5–28.

Broca, P. (1861) Remarques sur le siège de la faculté du langage articale suivé d'une observation d'aphemie. *Bulletin Société Anatomique de Paris* **36**, 331.

Brown, J. W. (1972) *Aphasia, Apraxia and Agnosia*. Springfield, Illinois: Thomas.

Buckingham, H. W. (1984) Early development of association theory in psychology as a forerunner to connection theory. *Brain and Cognition* **3**, 19–34.

Critchley, M. (1970) *Aphasiology and Other Aspects of Language*. London: Edward Arnold.

Cummings, J., Houlihan, J. and Hill, M. (1986) The pattern of reading deterioration in dementia of the Alzheimer type: observations and implications: *Brain and Language* **29**, 315–23.

Daniel, W., Crovitz, H. and Weiner, D. (1987) Neuropsychological aspects of disorientation. *Cortex* **23**, 169–87.

Darley, F. (1964) *Diagnosis and Appraisal of Communicative Disorders*. Englewood Cliffs, NJ: Prentice-Hall.

Darley, F. (1982) *Aphasia*. Philadelphia: Saunders.

Day, M. and Semrad, E. (1978) Schizophrenic reactions. In A. Nicholi (ed.), *The Harvard Guide to Modern Psychiatry*, pp. 191–241. Cambridge, MA: Harvard University Press.

Drummond, S. (1986) Characterization of irrelevant speech. *Journal of Communication Disorders* **19**, 175–83.

Flicker, C., Ferris, S., Crock, T. and Bartus, R. (1987) Implications of memory and language dysfunction in the naming deficit of senile dementia. *Brain and Language* **31**, 187–200.

Frued, S. (1891) *Zur auffasung der aphasien*. Trans. E. Stengel (1953), *Freud on Aphasia*. New York: International Universities Press.

Gazzaniga, M. S. and Sperry, R. W. (1967) Language after section of the cerebral commissures. *Brain* **90**, 131–48.

Geschwind, N. (1966) Carl Wernicke, the Breslau school, and the history of aphasia. In E. C. Carterette (ed.), *Brain Function, Vol. III: Speech, Language, and Communication*, pp. 1–16. Berkeley and Los Angeles: University of California Press.

Geschwind, N. (1967) The varieties of naming errors. *Cortex* **3**, 97–112.

Geschwind, N. and Fusillo, M. (1966) Color-naming defects in association with alexia. *A.M.A. Archives of Neurology* **15**, 137–46.

Geschwind, N. and Kaplan, E. (1962) A human cerebral deconnection syndrome. *Neurology* **12**, 675–85.

Gewirth, L., Schindler, A. and Hier, D. (1984) Altered patterns of word associations in dementia and aphasia. *Brain and Language* **21**, 307–17.

Goldfarb, R. (1987) The Pollyanna hypothesis in adult aphasia. *Aphasiology* **1**, 361–67.

Goldfarb, R. and Halpern, H. (1981) Word association of time-altered auditory and visual stimuli in aphasia. *Journal of Speech and Hearing Research* **24**, 233–46.

Goldstein, K. (1948). *Language and Language Disturbances*. New York: Grune & Stratton.

Goodglass, H. (1967) Psycholinguistic aspects of aphasia. Presentation at *Linguistic and Oral Communication Aspects of Rehabilitation of Adults with Aphasia*, New Jersey.

Goodglass, H. and Kaplan, E. (1983) *The Assessment of Aphasia and Related Disorders*, 2nd edn. Philadelphia: Lea & Febiger.

Goodglass, H., Kaplan, E., Weintraub, S. and Ackerman, N. (1976) The 'tip-of-the-tongue' phenomenon in aphasia. *Cortex* **12**, 145–53.

Grober, E., Buschke, H., Kanas, C. and Fuld, P. (1985) Impaired ranking of semantic attributes in dementia. *Brain and Language* **26**, 276–86.

Halpern, H., Darley, F. L. and Brown, J. (1973) Differential language and neurologic characteristics in cerebral involvement. *Journal of Speech and Hearing Disorders* **38**, 162–73.

Halpern, H., Keith, R. L. and Darley, F. L. (1976) Phonemic behavior of aphasic subjects without dysarthria or apraxia of speech. *Cortex* **12**, 365–72.

Halpern, H. and McCartin-Clark, M. (1984) Differential language characteristics in adult aphasic and schizophrenic subjects. *Journal of Communication Disorders* **17**, 289–307.

Hart, J., Berndt, R. S. and Caramazza, A. (1985) Category-specific naming deficit following cerebral infarction. *Nature* **316**, 439–40.

Head, H. (1926) *Aphasia and Kindred Disorders of Speech.* New York: Cambridge University Press and Macmillan.

Henschen, S. (1926) On the function of the right hemisphere of the brain in relation to the left in speech, music, and calculation. *Brain* **49**, 110–23.

Horner, J., Heipman, A., Aker, C., Kanter, J. and Royall, J. (1982) *Misnamings of Alzheimer's Dementia Compared to Misnamings Associated with Left and Right Hemisphere Stroke.* Paper presented to the Academy of Aphasia, Lake Mohonk, NY.

Howes, D. (1964) Application of the word-frequency concept to aphasia. In A. V. S. De Reuck and M. O'Connor (eds), *Disorders of Language*, pp. 47–75. Boston: Little, Brown.

Huff, F., Corkin, S. and Growden, J. (1986) Semantic impairment and anomia in Alzheimer's disease. *Brain and Language* **28**, 235–49.

Jackson, J. H. (1886) Clinical remarks on emotional and intellectual language in some cases of diseases of the nervous system. *Lancet* **6**, 174–6.

Jakobson, R. (1966) Linguistic types of aphasia. In E. C. Carterette (ed.), *Brain Function, Vol. III: Speech, Language, and Communication*, pp. 67–91. Berkeley and Los Angeles: University of California Press.

Kaplan, E., Goodglass, H. and Weintraub, S. (1983) *Boston Naming Test.* Philadelphia: Lea & Febiger.

Kempler, D., Curtiss, S. and Jackson, C. (1987) Syntactic preservation in Alzheimer's disease. *Journal of Speech and Hearing Research* **30**, 343–50.

Kleist, K. (1934) *Gehirnpathologie.* Leipzig: Barth.

Margolin, D. I. (1988). Lexical priming by pictures and words in aging, stroke, and dementia. *Dissertation Abstracts International.* (University Microfilms No. pending).

Marie, P. (1906) Revision de la question de l'aphasie. *Sem. Med.* **21**, 241–7.

Marshall, R. C. (1976) Word retrieval behavior of aphasic adults. *Journal of Speech and Hearing Disorders* **41**, 444–51.

Martin, A. D. (1974) Some objections to the term 'apraxia of speech'. *Journal of Speech and Hearing Disorders* **39**, 53–64.

Martin, A. and Fedio, P. (1983) Word production and comprehension in Alzheimer's disease: the breakdown of semantic knowledge. *Brain and Language* **19**, 124–41.

Mateer, C. A. (1983) Localization of language and visuospatial functions by electrical stimulation. In A. Kertesz (ed.), *Localization in Neuropsychology*, pp. 153–83. New York: Academic Press.

Mayo Clinic, Section of Neurology and Section of Physiology. (1964) *Clinical Examinations in Neurology.* Philadelphia: Saunders.

McCleary, C. (1988) Semantic knowledge in aphasia. *Aphasiology* **2**, 343–45.

Murdoch, B., Chenery, H., Wilks, V. and Boyle, R. (1987) Language disorders in dementia of the Alzheimer type. *Brain and Language* **31**, 122–37.

Naeser, M. (1983) CT scan lesion size and lesion locus in cortical and subcortical aphasias. In A. Kertesz (ed.), *Localization in Neuropsychology*, pp. 63–119. New York: Academic Press.

Naeser, M., Hayward, R. W., Laughlin, S. and Zatz, L. M. (1981a) Quantitative CT scan studies in aphasia. Part I. Infarct size and CT numbers. *Brain and Language* **12**, 140–64.

Naeser, M., Hayward, R. W., Laughlin, S., Becker, J. M. T., Jernigan, T. and Zatz,

L. M. (1981b) Quantitative CT scan studies in aphasia. Part II. Comparison of the right and left hemispheres. *Brain and Language* **12**, 165–89.

Nicholas, M., Obler, L., Albert, M. and Helm-Estabrooks, N. (1985) Empty speech in Alzheimer's disease and fluent aphasia. *Journal of Speech and Hearing Research* **28**, 405–10.

Nielsen, J. (1946) *Agnosia, Apraxia, Aphasia.* New York: Hoeber.

Obler, L. and Albert, M. (1981) Language in the elderly aphasic and in the dementing patient. In M. Sarno (ed.), *Acquired Aphasia*, pp. 385–98. New York: Academic Press.

Obler, L., Albert, M., Estabrooks, N. and Nicholas, M. (1982). *Noninformative Speech in Alzheimer's Dementia and in Wernicke's Aphasia.* Paper presented at the meeting of the Academy of Aphasia, Lake Mohonk, NY.

Ojemann, G. A. (1979) Individual variability in cortical localization of language. *Journal of Neurosurgery* **50**, 164–9.

Ojemann, G. A., Fedio, P. and Van Vuren, J. M. (1968) Anomia from pulvinar and sub-cortical parietal stimulation. *Brain* **91**, 99–116.

Ojemann, G. A. and Mateer, C. A. (1979) Human language cortex: localization of memory, syntax and sequential motor-phoneme identification systems. *Science* **250**, 1401–3.

Ojemann, G. A. and Whitaker, H. A. (1978) Language localization and variability. *Brain and Language* **6**, 239–60.

Penfield, W. and Roberts, L. (1959) *Speech and Brain-Mechanisms.* Princeton, NJ: Princeton University Press.

Pick, A. (1931) *Aphasia.* Trans. and ed. J. W. Brown (1973). Springfield Illinois: Thomas.

Pitres, A. (1898) *l'Aphasie amnésiques et ses variétés cliniques.* Paris: Alean.

Porch, B. (1967) *Porch Index of Communicative Ability.* Palo Alto, CA: Consulting Psychologists Press.

Portnoy, R. (1979) Hyperkinetic dysarthria as an early indicator of impending tardive dyskinesia. *Journal of Speech and Hearing Disorders* **44**, 214–19.

Schuell, H. M. (1965) *Minnesota Test for Differential Diagnosis of Aphasia.* Minneapolis: University of Minnesota Press.

Schuell, H. M., Jenkins, J. J. and Jimenez-Pabon, E. (1964). *Aphasia in Adults: Diagnosis, Prognosis, and Treatment.* New York: Harper & Row.

Shewan, C. M. and Bandur, D. L. (1986) *Treatment of Aphasia: A Language-Oriented Approach.* San Diego: College-Hill.

Springer, S. P. and Deutsch, G. (1981) *Left Brain, Right Brain.* San Francisco: Freeman.

Stengel, E. (1964) Speech disorders and mental disorders. In A. DeReuck and M. O'Connor (eds), *Disorders of Language*, pp. 285–92. London: Churchill.

Weidner, W. E. and Jinks, A. F. G. (1983) The effects of single versus combined cue presentations on picture naming by aphasic adults. *Journal of Communication Disorders* **16**, 111–21.

Wepman, J. M., Bock, R. D., Jones, L. V. and Van Pelt, D. (1956) Psycholinguistic study of aphasia: a revision of the concept of anomia. *Journal of Speech and Hearing Disorders* **21**, 468–77.

Wernicke, C. (1874) *Der aphasische symptomenkomplex.* Breslau: Cohn & Weigert.

Wertz, R. (1978). Neuropathologies of speech and language: An introduction to patient management. In D. F. Johns (ed.), *Clinical Management of Neurogenic Communication Disorders*, pp. 1–101. Boston: Little, Brown.

Whitehouse, P., Caramazza, A. and Zurif, E. B. (1978) Naming in aphasia: interacting effects of form and function. *Brain and Language* **6**, 63–74.

Wilson, R., Kasniak, A., Bacon, L., Fox, J. and Kelly, M. (1982) Facial recognition memory in dementia. *Cortex* **18**, 329–36.

Wingfield, A. and Wayland, S. C. (1988) Object-naming in aphasia: word-initial phonology and response activation. *Aphasiology* **2**, 423–6.

Wynne, R. (1963) The influence of hospitalization on the verbal behaviour of chronic schizophrenics. *British Journal of Psychiatry* **109**, 380–9.

Chapter 4

Auditory Verbal Comprehension Impairment

Ed Schulte and Sara Dale Brandt

Introduction

How do people comprehend verbal messages? The concept of auditory comprehension ranges from a simple, literal decoding of the words of an utterance, to a deeper, complete understanding of what a speaker meant by what was said in a particular context (Clark 1978). In either case, auditory comprehension (AC) represents a very complex cognitive task, as evidenced by the difficulties of studying its disruption due to brain injury. While one of the most common characteristics of aphasia, auditory comprehension disorders can only be inferred from an aphasic individual's response to a stimulus (Reidel 1981).

Disorders of auditory comprehension associated with aphasia may be defined in several different ways: in cognitive terms, in behavioural terms, or in human terms as related to everyday skills. For purposes of illustration, a few prototypes of patients with impaired auditory comprehension associated with aphasia are described below.

1 An aphasic patient may repeat a word or phrase over and over without comprehending it, and/or make multiple errors when speaking and not comprehend them.
2 Aphasic patients may evidence great difficulty in comprehending a series of sounds and combining them into a word. They may request multiple repetitions (or repeat themselves) until grasping the sounds of word as a whole, ('sh—oes, sh—oes, . . . oh, you mean shoes!').
3 Aphasic patients may be able to respond to individual words, but fail when these same words are used in conversational contexts. Conversely, others may evidence accurate responses to words in context, but not in training tasks (e.g. 'What time is it?' vs. 'Point to your watch.').
4 Individuals with aphasia may recognize words, phrases, and sentences well, but be unable to keep up with the flow of words in a conversation, or to decode a message in which the word order is changed (e.g. 'Stop at the store after you pick up the kids.').

As illustrated in the examples, the disordered communication resulting from impaired auditory comprehension skills may be quite debilitating. Verbal misunderstandings are universally distressing, but for aphasics, they may pose a monumental barrier to normal functioning (Wulf 1979). The purpose of this chapter is to provide a general overview of auditory comprehension disorders in aphasia, including both functional and theoretical information.

History and theoretical issues

Aphasic disorders have almost certainly existed since people have been verbal, and were described in early medical literature by the Greeks and Romans. The modern study of aphasia dates from the time of Paul Broca and Carl Wernicke (1860–74). They provided a giant leap forward by linking left-hemisphere lesions with language disturbance including impaired auditory comprehension.

Wernicke's theories provided the basis for localizationist or multidimensional views of aphasia. This type of theory assumes that (1) abstract language processing mechanisms are localized in the brain, and (2) damage to different brain centres or pathways will result in different types of aphasia. The most popular contemporary classification system, derived from the Boston Diagnostic Aphasia Examination (BDAE, Goodglass and Kaplan 1972), extends this multidimensional view. The Boston system discriminates among types of aphasia based on syndrome patterns contrasting the type and relative degree of impairment observed on sets of linguistic tasks (e.g. auditory comprehension). Syndromes in which comprehension skills are 'relatively preserved' (e.g. anomic, Broca's, and conduction aphasias) are seen as different from those syndromes in which more significant impairment of auditory comprehension occurs (e.g. Wernicke's, sensory, and global aphasias). As shown in Table 4.1, the ability to repeat sounds, words, and sentences may also prove diagnostically significant, both in regard to the status of the auditory system and in differentiating among aphasic syndromes.

Table 4.1: Major aphasic syndromes: general effects on auditory comprehension and repetition

Fluent aphasias			Nonfluent aphasias		
Aphasic syndrome	AC of speech	Rep. skill	Aphasic syndrome	AC of speech	Rep. skill
Wernicke	poor	poor	Broca	good	good
Anomic	good	good	Global	poor	poor
Transcortical sensory	poor	good	Transcortical motor	good	good
Conduction	good	poor			

A contrasting set of theories are those featuring a holistic or unidimensional view of aphasia. Typified by Pierre Marie in the early 1900s, and more recently by Hildred Schuell (Schuell *et al.* 1964), this view holds that there is only one true aphasia. The different manifestations of symptoms result from differences in degree of impairment or from secondary motor or sensory impairments. Schuell felt that

> All aphasic patients show some impairment of vocabulary and of verbal retention span, with a proportionate amount of difficulty in formulating and responding to messages at some level of complexity (Schuell *et al.* 1964: p. 114).

Schuell did discriminate between 'auditory verbal agnosia' in which aphasic patients are unable to identify familiar objects named verbally, and deficits in 'reauditorization', the impaired ability to evoke or recall sound sequences used in language. However, a centralized dysfunction impacting on all language modalities remains the hallmark of the unidimensional view of aphasia.

The differences in theories has contributed to a wide range of classification systems used to describe aphasia in which disturbed auditory comprehension is a primary deficit. Table 4.2 provides a partial listing of these terms.

Table 4.2: Modern aphasia classification systems

Year	Author/authors	Categories related to AC deficit
1861	Broca	Verbal amnesia
1874, 1886	Wernicke	Sensory; subcortical sensory
1906, 1917	Marie	Temporal aphasia
1913, 1931	Pick	Impressive (temporal)
1926	Head	Syntactic
1934	Kleist	Word deafness
1935	Weisenburg, McBride	Receptive
1946	Nielson	Auditory verbal formulation agnosia
1948	Goldstein	Cortical sensory
1961	Wepman	Pragmatic jargon
1961	Brain	Pure word deafness
1962	Bay	Sensory
1963	Osgood	Decoding
1964	Luria	Sensory, acoustic-amnestic
1964	Jacobson	Similarity (selection)
1964	Schuell	I + II + III also auditory verbal agnosia, re-auditorization
1965	Howes, Geschwind	Type B (fluent)
1971	Benson, Geschwind	Wernicke's, pure word deafness
1972	Leischner	Sensory, mixed, sensory amnestic central
1972	Goodglass, Kaplan	Wernicke's
1977	Taxonomic	Wernicke's

Adapted from Kertesz (1979), p. 4.

Cognitive theory and AC disorders

Current theoretical models of AC impairments in aphasia are closely related to an information processing paradigm. Auditory comprehension is viewed as a process by which auditory verbal information is perceived, transformed into neural codes, analysed, compared with memory stores for meaning (application of knowledge and of rules for language use), and processed for storage and/or evocation of a response. A general model is presented in Figure 4.1.

Figure 4.1 An information processing model of cognitive processes related to language functions

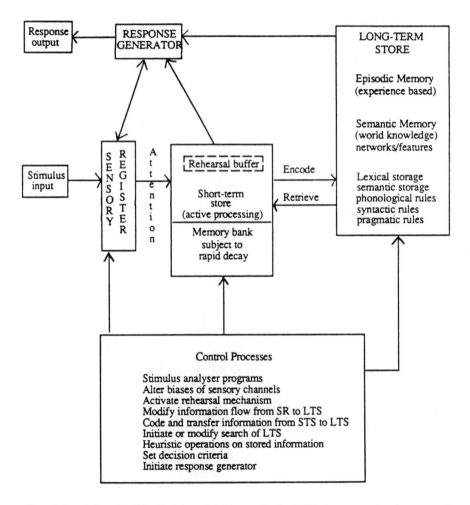

Note: Adapted from Shiffrin, R. M. and Atkinson, R. C. (1969) Storage retrieval processes in long-term memory, *Psychological Review* **76**, 179–93. Copyright 1969 by the American Psychological Association. Adapted by permission of the author.

Neurological considerations

Three major constructs are specifically related to understanding AC in aphasia: (1) issues of hemispheric asymmetry; (2) localization of function within the hemisphere; and (3) the relationship of cortical function to language function within the impaired system. First, both Broca and Wernicke noted the significant discrepancy in impairment of language skills among individuals with damage to the left brain hemisphere as compared to patients with right hemisphere damage. Recent studies suggest that the basis for this difference is a functional asymmetry in the way information is utilized by the two hemispheres: the left hemisphere of most individuals appears more proficient at manipulating sequential/analytic types of data; the right better at simultaneous/holistic tasks (Springer and Deutsch 1981; Code 1987). This asymmetry is related to theories of auditory comprehension disorders in aphasia because the linguistic content of verbal communication is largely sequential in nature. When received through the auditory modality, these signals consist of a rapid series of sound units which are perceived as phonemes/words/sentences, with associated production cues related to discourse (e.g. prosody). Thus, while incoming sensory information is largely available to both hemispheres, the linguistic superiority of the left hemisphere derives from fundamental differences in the way it processes, decodes, encodes, and arranges information.

The second construct relates to the organization of processing functions underlying language skills within the left hemisphere. Figure 4.2 shows a lateral view of the left hemisphere, including the major landmarks delineating the four lobes of the cortex and their major functions.

Figure 4.2 Major landmarks of the left hemisphere

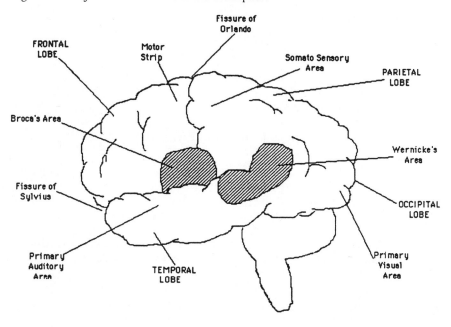

Analysis and initial processing of sensory information is organized in close proximity to sensory areas, with further cognitive integration of input in the area central to these input areas (i.e. Wernicke's area). Thus, in general, left hemisphere damage posterior to the Fissure of Rolando (central sulcus) may be expected to result in a more severe disruption of auditory comprehension than damage to frontal areas or to the opposite hemisphere, wherein more subtle disruptions of AC may be expected.

These two constructs (cortical asymmetry and localization of function) form the basis for the third construct: the relationship between cortical damage and communication impairments. Most aphasiologists agree on the behaviours associated with auditory comprehension impairments in aphasia. Terms such as auditory verbal agnosia are often used to describe an inability to recognize the sets of sound elements contained in single spoken words. Auditory retention span is nearly always reduced, as is recognition of the denotative and connotative meanings of words (a more extensive discussion of these variables will follow). However, much disagreement exists as to the functional basis for these deficits. A brief survey of three theoretical views may prove illustrative. They are: (1) disruption of the cognitive processes underlying language use; (2) non-language-specific performance deficits; and (3) disruption of the language code itself.

Many authorities such as Davis (1983) view aphasia as a breakdown at some stage of the cognitive system described earlier.

> Focal lesions can be thought of as producing a primary breakdown of a single component of the cognitive system which supports language function, and the primary breakdown leads to a variety of secondary disturbances. . . . Damage to Wernicke's area for example, might lead to a breakdown of auditory language processing which is considered to be the primary deficit. Direct observations of auditory comprehension deficiency reveal the primary symptoms of a Wernicke's aphasia. Other symptoms of this disorder are the secondary effects of the primary breakdown; secondary effects in Wernicke's aphasia include repetition failures, lack of awareness of jargon, reading deficits, and possibly, the jargon itself. Secondary symptoms appear because a single component of the cognitive basis for language function, however defined, interacts with all other components in the use of language. A primary disturbance, therefore, simply upsets the sometimes delicate balance among these intimately related subsystems (Davis, 1983: p. 93).

Other primary deficits that would relate specifically to auditory comprehension deficits in aphasia might include impairments of short-term memory, limiting the capacity for processing verbal stimuli; and impaired or disrupted search and retrieval processes for analysis of stimuli in relation to coded information in long-term memory.

A slightly different orientation to the problem is illustrated by McNeil (1983) who argues that 'nonlinguistic brain damage factors may account for much of the phenomenon of aphasia'. Reasons cited by McNeil include:

1 It is not likely that language in toto or subcomponents of language, or any

information-processing subcomponent will be found in a discrete area of any part of the brain.

2 Aphasic persons appear to have essentially preserved competence and that performance deficits account for the majority of their behaviours (as evidenced by transient aphasias; stimulability of aphasic language; the lack of qualitative differences between the aphasics and normals in special circumstances – such as when fatigued, hurried, or when dividing their attention); and finally, the fact that aphasic behaviours are highly variable across time, situations, and cognitive or linguistic task.

McNeil goes on to compile an extensive listing of the sensory, motor, higher cognitive, psychosocial and basic neurophysiological processes that are disturbed as a result of brain damage, which may be 'consequent to or independent from aphasia' (pp. 4–5). Prime candidates for much of the disruption of auditory comprehension skills seen as aphasia are:

1 a 'limited but variable capacity of attention of effort that can be allocated to any task or set of tasks at one time' (McNeil 1983: p. 14).
2 a disruption of bio-behavioural cycles related to internal neurological state.
3 interaction of the task and generalized brain damage factors (e.g. increased reaction/performance time, increased inertia in excitation and inhibition processes, etc.).

A third view supports a basic change in the structure of language itself. Lesser (1978) reviews several areas of research which support this hypothesis including:

1 Evidence related to an 'underlying impairment in semantic knowledge of word concepts, rather than to difficulty at a more peripheral stage' (Lesser 1978: p. 89).
2 Evidence of a 'central disruption of syntactic competence which extends to comprehension as well as speech' (ibid., p. 122).

Lesser goes on to conclude:

1 There is justification for theories of different levels of linguistic processing impairments in aphasia.
2 Linguistic investigations support the multiple nature of aphasia rather than its unitary quality.
3 Speech is not as autonomous from comprehension as had been thought. Anomia in speech is a sign of a central disorder at the semantic level which therefore affects comprehension as it does speech.

The major facet differentiating this view of auditory comprehension disorders from those covered previously is the focus on changes in linguistic abilities; the relationship of one behaviour (such as auditory comprehension) to different levels of central language dysfunction (semantic, syntactic, phonological).

In summarizing these views in regard to auditory comprehension, it is evident that much controversy remains as to the basis for the specific behavioural impairments seen. The hypotheses presented represent a broad continuum ranging from explanations which view auditory comprehension deficits as due to any number of non-language performance deficits characteristic of brain dysfunction (McNeil), to interruption at some stage in the sequence of cognitive processes underlying manipulation of language codes (Davis), to a fundamental change in the competence/organization of the language code itself (Lesser). Each of these views appears descriptive of auditory comprehension deficits in some patients, evidence of the wide variety of variables which must be considered in assessment and clinical management of this disorder.

Factors affecting auditory comprehension

Linguistic factors

A variety of factors can affect the aphasic patient's ability to correctly comprehend a spoken message. Some of these factors are linguistic aspects and others are factors such as contextual cues and timing variables. The relative effects of these variables are summarized in Table 4.3.

Length of the message   Almost all aphasic persons have some degree of deficit in short-term memory (Sarno 1981; Chapey 1986; Darley 1982). Therefore, the length of a sentence and the number of critical vocabulary elements within a sentence can affect the aphasic person's retention of material (Shewan and Canter 1971). Typically, aphasic persons retain short messages better than longer messages. As the message length increases, aphasic persons deteriorate in comprehension performance (Brookshire 1978; Chapey, 1986).

Syntactic complexity   Shewan and Canter (1971) reported that increases in syntactic complexity led to greater impairments in performance than increments in either length or vocabulary difficulty. This finding was the result of presenting sentences representing various levels of length, vocabulary difficulty, and syntactic complexity to 27 aphasic patients. Syntactic variations included both active and passive sentences with negative transformations. Shewan (1976) later found that despite some individual variation, the rank order of difficulty and type of error for aphasic patients was similar to normals. Some of the specific syntactic factors are discussed below.

(1) Voice and negatives   Normal subjects indicate the following order of difficulty to basic sentence types (easiest to most difficult):

    simple active affirmative sentence
        (the dog is chasing the boy)
    passive affirmative
        (the boy is being chased by the dog)
    active negative
        (the boy is not chasing the dog)

Table 4.3: Linguistic factors affecting auditory comprehension

Easier comprehension	*Moderate difficulty/neutral effect*
shorter sentences	prepositions
present tense verbs	colours
simple syntax (noun + verb +	numbers
object)	letters
active voice	articles (the, a)
affirmative	modality of input
directly worded	increased loudness
use of introductory phrases	
object names	
high frequency words	
meaningful words	*More difficult*
picturable words	negatives
emotional words	passive voice
realistic pictures	reversible nouns
redundancy	complex syntax
prominent location of target	transformations
decreased rate	body parts
pauses	connotative/emotional meanings
linguistic stress	semantically related choices
natural context	background noise
face to face presentation	
prosodic/affective cues	

Performance factors affecting auditory comprehension	
fatigue	scheduling
medication	illness
hearing loss	emotional state

negative passive
(the dog is not being chased by the boy)

Lasky *et al.* (1976) reported that fifteen aphasic patients followed the normal pattern and demonstrated better auditory comprehension of active affirmative sentences than of negative constructions. Further, these subjects better understood passive affirmative than active negative sentences and demonstrated difficulty with past and future tense. Pierce (1981) concluded that patients assume that a sentence is in present tense and that an underlying agent–action order is represented in any noun–verb–noun form.

Persons with aphasia have particular difficulty comprehending negation. The problem lies not so much with the negative marker but rather in the communicative intent (Wilcox *et al.* 1978). Aphasic patients had distinct difficulty comprehending sentences with negative intent ('Must you bite the pen?') but little difficulty with negative structures with affirmative intent ('Won't you sit down?'). Just *et al.* (1977) found that aphasic subjects processed affirmative statements more rapidly than negative statements. They also processed false negative statements faster than true negative statements.

(2) Expanded sentences Several studies (Goodglass *et al.* 1979; Brookshire and Nicholas 1983) investigated whether aphasic patients were better able to comprehend ideas which were expressed as a series of syntactically simple propositions or combined into one syntactically complex sentence. Three different types of linguistic constructions were used: embedding one simple proposition in another, using compound verb and noun phrases, and using prepositions of directionality or with–of agency. Subjects were better able to understand expanded utterances not containing transformations (the man was greeted by his wife and he was smoking a pipe) and had more difficulty with the sentences which were syntactically more complex (the man, smoking a pipe, was greeted by his wife.)

(3) Word order In some constructions, the subject and the object can easily be reversed (the boy is chasing the dog) whereas in others, they cannot (the boy is eating cake). Aphasic subjects tend to have more difficulty understanding reversible than nonreversible sentences (Caramazza *et al.* 1978; Lesser 1974). Subjects may also make use of a 'plausibility factor' (Deloche and Seron 1981) or knowledge of the real world to aid in interpretation of reversible sentences.

(4) Functors Several studies have pointed to problems in dealing with functors unique to Broca's aphasia. Goodenough *et al.* (1977) showed subjects three figures: a white circle, a black circle, and a black square. Subjects were given pointing instructions with either the appropriate or the inappropriate article (point to the black one). Broca's aphasic patients took no longer to respond to the incorrect direction than to the correct one, indicating no confusion from the linguistically incorrect article. Anomics took much longer to process the inappropriate directions. This is one of the first indications that Broca's aphasia involves a receptive problem with functors which corresponds to omission of these words in verbal expression.

(5) Prepositions The comprehension of locatives has usually been assessed by asking the listener to place an object in a spatial relationship to another object. A plausibility factor may aid in comprehension of this task. Patients with Broca's aphasia were more accurate when the preposition expressed a logical relationship between the object pairs (put the penny in the cup). Patients with Wernicke's aphasia could not make use of the semantic cues contained in the object pairs (Deloche and Seron 1981).

(6) Directness of wording Green and Boller (1974) varied the directness of wording of test items, contrasting directly worded items (point to the ceiling) with indirectly worded items (I would like you to point to the ceiling). Subjects gave more appropriate responses to the more directly worded items. They also performed better if the stimulus was preceded by an introductory sentence (Now here's something: point to the ceiling.)

(7) Prominence The positioning of the critical elements in a message may also affect comprehension. Darley (1976) suggests that placing the information-

carrying element in a prominent position such as at the end of the sentence may aid auditory comprehension.

Vocabulary The ability to understand the names of letters, numbers, colours and body parts should be examined. Wernicke's aphasics often fail badly with objects, yet do well with letters and numbers. The ability to point to a body part on oral request is often more severely impaired than object identification. Graphic input for single words is usually better than auditory comprehension, especially with body part names (Albert *et al.* 1981). Goodglass *et al.* (1968) found that comprehension of object names was the easiest, followed by action names, colour names, and number and letter names. This order of difficulty was different from the aphasics' production of the names on visual confrontation.

Schuell *et al.* (1961) compared the differences between semantic, phonetic/acoustic, and random errors to find that aphasics, regardless of the degree of comprehension impairment, made more semantic association errors than other types of errors.

Frequency of use Aphasic individuals are more likely to recognize words that have a high frequency of occurrence in their native language (Schuell *et al.* 1961). Further, aphasic subjects do better with short, meaningful, highly utilitarian words, as well as words that are personally familiar. Other vocabulary-related phenomena have been shown to affect comprehension. Brookshire and Nicholas (1982) found that aphasic subjects responded faster to written sentences containing highly picturable verbs than to verbs with low picturability.

Concreteness Using a reaction time task, Baker and Goodglass (1979) found a significant difference between Broca's and Wernicke's aphasics in comprehension of substantive words. The Wernicke's aphasics required more time to identify concrete object names than did Broca's aphasics whose response times approached that of normals. Meaning of words goes beyond the referential meaning (denotative) to emotional meanings (connotative). Anomic aphasics were more impaired in connotative/emotional judgements than Broca's or conduction aphasics (Gardner and Denes, 1973).

Redundancy Aphasic listeners typically profit from redundant information not essential for meaning in the message. Gardner *et al.* (1975) found that aphasic subjects comprehend redundant messages (the cat is furry) more easily than neutral sentences (the cat is nice). The use of repetitions and revisions is another means of providing message redundancy.

Timing factors

Rate Aphasic adults may respond better when spoken to at a slightly slower rate than normal. Weidner and Lasky (1976) and Lasky *et al.* (1976) concluded that aphasic subjects understand sentence material better at 110–20 words per minute than at 150 wpm.

Pauses Use of pauses within utterance boundaries and imposing a delay on subjects' response to stimuli can also affect comprehension. Studies by Liles and Brookshire (1975) and Lasky *et al.* (1976) found that pauses presented early in complex directives or which occurred between the major elements of sentences were generally helpful to aphasic patients. The effects of an imposed delay of response appear more difficult to interpret. Schulte (1986) identified an interaction between the length of imposed delay and the complexity of the task: individual subjects differed greatly in the effects of different periods of delay (0, 5, 10, and 20 seconds) and levels of complexity (directives containing 2, 3, 4, or 6 critical elements). Some aphasic patients were aided by imposing a delay which prevented premature responses, and allowed completion of processing while the performance of others deteriorated from inefficient retrieval, memory decay or deficit rehearsal mechanisms.

Attentional factors

Brookshire (1974) has described five types of auditory comprehension deficits, some of which are directly related to the patient's attention to the stimuli. These are summarized in Table 4.4.

Table 4.4: Auditory comprehension deficits (Brookshire, 1974)

'Slow Rise Time'	Listener misses beginning of message
'Noise Buildup'	Listener does better with initial messages; overloads with additional input.
'Information Capacity Deficit'	Cannot receive and process at same time; aided by use of pauses
'Retention Deficit'	Decreased performance as message increases in length
'Auditory Imperception'	Listener fades in and out

Context Aphasic patients frequently fail to comprehend items in a formal testing situation but demonstrate comprehension of a similar item in a natural context. Patients who are unable to 'point to the cigarette' on the PICA (Porch 1967) may reach into their shirt pocket when asked 'Do you have a cigarette?' Information contained in the speaker's facial expressions, tone of voice, or use of gestures as well as the setting appear to aid in comprehension. Assessment of the contribution of environmental context appears to be vital in counselling the family about the patient's understanding ability (Chapey 1986; Holland 1983).

Boller *et al.* (1979) studied the effect of emotional content with severe aphasics by presenting 30 sentences of high emotional content (e.g. 'Say "shit",' 'Do you wet the bed?') and 30 sentences judged to be neutral in emotionality. Results indicated that the items of high emotional content elicited more correct responses.

The emotional effect contained in speaker prosody may also contribute to the success of comprehension. Utterances in which prosodic cues mirror linguistic content may aid aphasics' comprehension (e.g. 'You look great!' spoken in a happy or positive manner). Conversely, use of contrasting prosodic or semantic cues may prove more difficult for aphasics to interpret (e.g. 'You look great!' spoken in a negative or sarcastic manner) (Schulte 1988).

Aphasic patients have demonstrated the ability to interpret correctly metaphorical language in context (Winner and Gardner 1977; Stachowiak *et al.* 1977). By choosing the correct picture, the patients could demonstrate comprehension of 'he lost his shirt' in the context of a poker game as 'he lost all his money'. To do so required integration of the statement into the context.

Performance factors

Fatigue Aphasic patients performed more poorly on the PICA (Porch 1967) following physical therapy (Marshall and King 1973) than when the testing followed a rest period. Likewise, fatigue within the therapy session may adversely affect performance.

Scheduling Other investigators (Tompkins *et al.* 1980; Marshall *et al.* 1980) found that 14 aphasic patients performed better on 11 subtests of the PICA in the morning than in the afternoon. Examination of the subtest scores indicated that the most difficult communicative tasks were the most affected.

Medication Medications that an aphasic patient may take for various problems such as seizures, high blood pressure, or pain may affect performance on all speech and language activities. Many medications prescribed for these problems may make the patient less attentive, more distractable and listless.

Illness Abrupt changes in a patient's performance may signal major physical events, such as another stroke. Any illness, however, can result in decreased attentiveness and therefore affect performance in comprehension tasks.

Hearing While the types of auditory comprehension deficits discussed here are not directly attributable to decreased hearing sensitivity, many aphasic patients may have coexisting hearing loss. Clinicians working with these patients will want to make use of techniques designed to maximize hearing acuity (Chapey 1986).

Emotional status Aphasic patients, like everyone else, are concerned with their families, marriages, money, friends, health, future, etc. Being preoccupied with similar concerns will surely affect comprehension abilities for tasks perceived by the patient as being less meaningful.

Presentation variables

Modality Various investigators have noted that one input modality may evoke better performance than another in individual patients. Combinations of two input channels may facilitate comprehension and performance in some patients.

Green and Boller (1974) found that listeners performed somewhat better with speakers who faced them and that live voice presentations were preferred over tape-recorded messages. Data are just beginning to be available on the effectiveness of computerized auditory comprehension training.

Two studies indicate that the modality used for stimulus presentation does not significantly affect comprehension performance. Gardner *et al.* (1975) studied the relative ability of aphasic patients to discover errors in sentences presented visually or auditorily. All of the patients did equally well under the two conditions. Goodglass *et al.* (1968) investigated the performance of 27 aphasic patients on naming of objects presented visually, tactilely, auditorily (from characteristic sounds), and through characteristic odours. No significant differences were found between naming performance in the various conditions, leading the investigators to conclude that the interruption between stimulus input and naming response is not specific to any one modality.

Stress Aphasic subjects are sensitive to linguistic stress. Aphasic persons could distinguish nouns and verbs (*con*vict vs. con*vict*) by stress alone (Blumstein and Goodglass 1972) and they responded more rapidly to words within sentences which were stressed (Swinney *et al.* 1980).

Choices The degree of semantic relatedness among stimulus items may affect comprehension. A patient may have little difficulty selecting a picture of an apple when the foils are a dog, a bed, and a flower but may exhibit increased difficulty when the foils are other kinds of fruit.

Power of stimulus Increasing the loudness of the presented stimuli does not improve the patient's comprehension abilities (McNeil 1977). Likewise, unilaterally increasing the loudness of one signal did not improve performance.

Background 'noise', either auditory signals or visual figure-ground confusions, appears to decrease comprehension performance. Interviews with aphasic patients have pointed out the distracting effect of background noise (Skelly 1975; Rolnick and Hoops 1969).

Assessment of auditory comprehension deficits

One of the initial challenges in the comprehensive assessment of aphasia is to determine the relative impairment of auditory comprehension. Because of the obvious confounding difficulties of relying on the patient's response, the assessment of auditory comprehension usually involves verbal input with a variety of nonverbal response modes. Identification of quantitative and qualitative differences in auditory comprehension is accomplished by changing the length and complexity of the verbal stimuli while maintaining the nonverbal requirements of the response as much as possible.

One of the first attempts to assess auditory comprehension was the famous 'three papers test' of Pierre Marie (as described by Weisenburg and McBride 1935). The patient was given three pieces of paper torn into different size pieces. The instructions were to 'throw the small one on the floor; put the middle sized piece in your pocket; and give the third one to me'. Current assessment methodology involves similar requests for the patient to point to pictures or objects, to manipulate objects in response to instructions, or to indicate yes or no in response to simple questions. Two problems with these response approaches have already been mentioned. First, the point-to response paradigm is an artificial one in that people rarely are required to point to objects or pictures in real activities. Secondly, aphasic patients can often manipulate real objects in natural contexts, such as reaching for their glasses when asked if they wear glasses, but not be able to 'point to your glasses' when requested to do so.

A summary of tests frequently used to assess auditory comprehension in aphasia is found in Table 4.5.

Accuracy of the patient's response

Evaluation of auditory comprehension involves assessment of the accuracy of the patients' responses, but information beyond the rightness or wrongness is of potential benefit in treatment planning. Chapey (1986) describes several behavioural features that are worthy of note during the assessment of auditory comprehension.

Some aphasic patients need increased time (latency) to process statements of increasing syntactic complexity. These delays seem to serve a useful function and may facilitate comprehension.

Patients often need or request additional information which the clinician can supply in the form of a repetition, a revision, or an assistive cue. Caution is extended that the clinician not confuse the need for additional processing time with the need for information and supply information when none has been requested or required.

Clinicians should be aware of patient responses which are erroneous but phonemically or semantically related to the target. Related responses can often indicate progress from totally erroneous responses and may be shaped towards even more accurate responses.

The amount of self-correction offered by the patient is of interest. Two kinds of self-correction behaviour are noted in auditory comprehension tasks. One is the revision of a frank error. Another is a request for repetition or additional information to avoid making an error.

On auditory comprehension tasks, a patient will often repeat an incoming stimulus or portions of it. This can be detrimental if the patient repeats the stimulus incorrectly, but can be a useful technique if monitored appropriately.

Treatment for auditory comprehension deficits

The communicative paradigm contains, at the very least, a sender of messages (speaker), the message transmitted within a context, and a receiver (listener). Rehabilitation may focus on any one of these parts of the communicative interaction. In the case of impaired auditory comprehension (listener), it may be advisable and facilitory to manipulate other aspects of the communicative paradigm. Various aspects of the message which can be adjusted to maximize auditory comprehension were discussed earlier and summarized in Table 4.3. Treatment, then, might first focus on further adjustments by the speaker prior to or in addition to direct training for the listener.

Table 4.5: Assessment of auditory comprehension

Test	Author	Areas Assessed	Comments
Token	De Renzi Vignolo 1962	Brief commands with 20 tokens of 5 colours, 2 shapes, 2 sizes	8+ versions of this test; commands increase in number of elements or syntactic complexity; few confounding factors (IQ, education, SES)
ACTS	Shewan 1979	Vocabulary, sentence length, syntax varied in systematic manner	Subject selects 1 of 4 line drawings to match auditory sentence; foils vary by 1 critical item
ALPS	Keenan Brassell 1975	1 of 4 scales is 'listening'. 10 items increase in difficulty.	First item is response to being called by name; last is 5 step command
BEST	Fitch-West Sands 1987	Select objects, point to pictures on command	Tasks begin with most complex, scoring notes amount of cueing needed
BDAE	Goodglass Kaplan 1983	Objects, letters, verbs, colours, numbers, shapes, body parts, R/L discrimination	Follow commands from simple commands to short paragraphs
WAB	Kertesz 1979	Yes/no questions follow directions	Similar to BDAE, uses real objects
MTDDA	Schuell 1965	Identify pictures, letters, yes/no questions, follow commands, serial item identification, follow commands digit span	Semantically and phonetically similar foils
PICA	Porch 1967	Point to objects by name/function	Author notes test picks up 'slow rise time' and 'noise buildup' by error pattern

Key:
ACTS – Auditory Comprehension Test for Sentences
ALPS – Aphasia Language Performance Scales
BEST – Bedside Evaluation and Screening Test
BDAE – Boston Diagnostic Aphasia Examination
WAB – Western Aphasia Battery
MTDDA – Minnesota Test for Differential Diagnosis of Aphasia
PICA – Porch Index of Communicative Ability

Adjustments by the speaker

The child language literature has recently noted ways in which mothers and other caregivers accommodate to the developing communicative abilities of children. Typical 'Motherese' accommodations include simpler syntax, slower rate, higher pitch, fewer grammatical errors, and fewer false starts. There have been numerous attempts to equate the linguistic deficits of aphasic patients to stages of linguistic development in children (Caramazza *et al.* 1978). In both cases, normal adults attempt to communicate with linguistically impaired or underdeveloped listeners.

Several studies have documented modifications by speakers when talking to impaired adult listeners. When the speech of normal college students was distorted so that normal listeners understood only 50 per cent of the directions they were given, the speakers made three adjustments: they lengthened their descriptions, they used a more redundant vocabulary, and they decreased their speaking rate (Longhurst and Siegel 1973).

When various health care workers were asked to talk to aphasic listeners, they reduced the length of their utterances and increased redundance of the vocabulary in comparison with normal listeners (Gravel and LaPointe 1982; 1983). Linebaugh *et al.* (1983; 1984) conducted two studies regarding communication with aphasic family members in which they asked normal adults to describe pictures to normal listeners and to an aphasic family member. They found that speakers used significantly more words, a redundant vocabulary, and took more time to describe the pictures to aphasics than to normal listeners.

Brandt (1987) asked spouses of aphasic patients and spouses of normal elderly persons to describe a series of action pictures to aphasic listeners and to normal listeners. The speakers all made adjustments for the auditory comprehension deficits of the aphasic listeners. They simplified the speech to the aphasic listeners by using fewer different words, decreasing the length of utterances, using fewer complex sentence types, and using more simple present, past, and future tense verbs. Speakers also talked more to the aphasic listeners; they used more utterances to describe each picture and the descriptions were longer. A summary of speaker accommodations to auditory comprehension deficits can be seen in Table 4.6.

Table 4.6: Adjustments by speakers to maximize auditory comprehension

Lengthened descriptions	Increased redundancy
Decreased length of utterance	Use of pauses
Decreased speaking rate	Reduced complexity

Direct training for auditory comprehension deficits

Direct therapy for auditory comprehension deficits should begin with auditory input in which the goal is to increase the patient's ability to recognize, discriminate, retain, sequence, and recall language units of increasing length and complexity (Darley 1982). The exact point to begin must be determined by each individual patient's comprehension abilities, identified previously through assessment. Therapy should begin at a point where the patient can achieve some success but is not totally accurate on the task provided. Specific activities can be varied to keep the task interesting and progressive in difficulty.

If comprehension deficits are so severe that the patient is unable to process linguistic information, Shewan (1976) suggests beginning with auditory perception tasks in which the patient first indicates the awareness of nonspeech auditory stimuli, such as raising a hand when music is played. This task might be followed by a task discriminating speech from nonspeech stimuli by having the patient point to a picture of a person when a voice is heard and a picture of a musical instrument when music is heard. Further discrimination of environmental sounds such as a telephone ringing, a horn honking, etc. might be an additional step.

Visual Action Therapy (VAT) (Helm-Estabrooks *et al.* 1982) is another method of early training designed to develop basic comprehension skills. In this training program, the approach is mainly nonverbal and consists of a series of increasingly difficult matching tasks. Patients progress from matching two like objects to more abstract matches (unlike but similar objects, objects to pictures, different size pictures, etc.) in order to prepare the patient for the linguistic task of matching an auditory signal (the word 'cup') to the object for which the linguistic unit stands.

Ultimately, the goal is, of course, to have the patient comprehend increasingly difficult speech signals. Darley (1982) lists the following hierarchy of auditory tasks:

Recognition of spoken words
    select objects or pictures
Process a series of two and three word phrases
    'spoon and book'
Execute one step commands
    'point to the book'
Execute one-step, three unit commands.
    'put the book in the box'
Execute two-step commands:
    'point to the spoon, give me the book'
Execute complex commands
    'after pointing to the torn book, give me the good book'
Answering yes/no question
    'Is the window broken?'
Answering questions about oral sentences and paragraphs

Kearns and Hubbard (1977) presented aphasic patients with a battery of 13 auditory comprehension tasks. From this list they identified a four-step hierarchy which was most useful in planning treatment of auditory comprehension deficits. The hierarchy is as follows:

Point to one common object by function

Point in sequence to two common objects by name
Carry out in sequence two verb instructions
Follow three sequential verb instructions

Treatment considerations

Selection of appropriate tasks is crucial to the therapeutic process (Chapey 1986). Patients generally perform better if the task is meaningful to them. For example, identifying members of their family from photo albums or identifying items of food on the mealtime tray may be more acceptable and more useful than identifying geometric shapes or random pictures. Patients will also generally respond more enthusiastically if the therapist explains the purpose behind the activity. Families often complain that the therapist asks the patient to do 'silly' tasks. Making family and patient aware of the purpose and reason for the activity may increase everyone's compliance.

In a similar manner, the materials used in auditory comprehension training should be appropriate for adults and of interest to the individual patient. Using functional materials and activities (telephone books, ads in newspapers, trade or professional materials appropriate for a specific patient) will increase interest and generalization of the tasks.

More and more therapeutic activities are being developed for the computer. As the capabilities of computers increase, auditory comprehension activities will be more readily available.

Conclusions

Auditory comprehension disorders in aphasia represent a microcosm of the complex issues involved in aphasia itself. While some general patterns of dysfunction are identifiable, individual differences between patients and variability within patients must be anticipated in both therapeutic and research contexts. Research using an information processing approach is promising, but has also demonstrated the enormous complexities involved in inferring internal cognitive processes. Various theoretical points of view provide different orientations to auditory comprehension disorders with implications for many types of neurogenic communication disorders. However, these differences in theory raise many questions. Do the discrepancies in AC skills among aphasic individuals reflect differences in degree of impairment (quantitative) or in type of impairment (qualitative)? Can we effectively discriminate between impairments which may have a linguistic basis versus those which may be common to other types of cognitive deficits following brain damage? If fundamentally distinct deficits do exist, are divergent methods of rehabilitation indicated or will common intervention techniques succeed in spite of the different mechanisms involved? Such questions will form the basis of research for years to come as we strive to learn more about the facets of the complex disorder known as aphasia.

References

Albert, M. L., Goodglass, H., Helm, N. A., Rubens, A. B. and Alexander, M. P. (1981) *Clinical Aspects of Dysphasia*. New York: Springer-Verlag.

Baker, E. and Goodglass, H. (1979) Time for auditory processing of object names by aphasics. *Brain and Language* **8**, 355–66.

Brandt, S. D. (1987) 'Aphasic-ese': A description of how spouses talk to their aphasic mates. Unpublished doctoral dissertation, University of Kansas.

Blumstein, S. F. and Goodglass, H. (1972) The perception of stress as a semantic cue in aphasia. *Journal of Speech and Hearing Research* **15**, 800–6.

Boller, F. (1978) Comprehension disorders in aphasia. *Brain and Language* **5**, 149–65.

Boller, F., Cole, M., Vrtunski, B., Patterson, M. and Kim, Y. (1979) Paralinguistic aspects of auditory comprehension in aphasia. *Brain and Language* **7**, 164–74.

Brookshire, R. H. (1974) Differences in responding to auditory verbal materials among aphasic patients. *Acta Symbolica* **5**, 1–18.

Brookshire, R. H. (1978) Auditory comprehension and aphasia. In D. F. Johns (ed.), *Clinical Management of Neurogenic Communication Disorders*. Boston: Little, Brown and Co.

Brookshire, R. H. and Nicholas, L. E. (1982) Comprehension of directly and indirectly pictured verbs by aphasic and nonaphasic listeners. In R. H. Brookshire (ed.), *Clinical Aphasiology Conference Proceedings*. Minneapolis, MN.: BRK Publishers.

Caramazza, A., Zurif, E. B. and Gardner, H. (1978) Sentence memory in aphasia. *Neuropsychologia* **16**, 661–9.

Chapey, R. (ed.) (1986) *Language Intervention Strategies in Adult Aphasia*, 2nd edn. Baltimore, MD.: Williams & Wilkins.

Clark, H. H. (1978) Inferring what is meant. In W. J. M. Levilt and G. B. Flores d'Arcais (eds), *Studies in the Perception of Language*. New York, NY: Wiley Press.

Code, C. (1987) *Language, Aphasia, and the Right Hemisphere*. West Sussex, England: John Wiley & Sons.

Darley, F. L. (1976) Maximizing input to the aphasic patient. In R. H. Brookshire (ed.), *Clinical Aphasiology Conference Proceedings*. Minneapolis, MN.: BRK Publishers.

Darley, F. L. (1982) *Aphasia*. Philadelphia, PA.: W. B. Sanders Co.

Davis, G. A. (1983) *A Survey of Adult Aphasia*. Englewood Cliffs, NJ.: Prentice-Hall, Inc.

Deloche, G. and Seron, X. (1981) Sentence understanding and knowledge of the world. *Brain and Language* **14**, 57–69.

De Renzi, E. and Vignolo, L. A. (1962) The token test: a sensitive test to detect receptive disturbances in aphasics. *Brain* **85**, 665–78.

Fitch-West, J. and Sands, E. S. (1987) *Bedside Evaluation and Screening Test of Aphasia*. Aspen Publishers: Fredrick Maryland.

Gardner, H., Albert, M. L. and Weintraub, S. (1975) Comprehending a word: the influence of speed and redundancy on auditory comprehension in aphasics. *Cortex* **11**, 155–62.

Gardner, H. and Denes, G. (1973) Connotative judgments by aphasic patients in a pictorial adaptation of the semantic differential. *Cortex* **9**, 183–96.

Goodenough, C., Zuirf, E. B., Weintraub, S. and Von Stockert, T. (1977) Aphasics: attention to grammatical morphemes. *Language and Speech* **20**, 11–19.

Goodglass, H., Barton, M. J. and Kaplan, E. F. (1968) Sensory modality and object-naming in aphasics. *Journal of Speech and Hearing Research* **11**, 488–96.

Goodglass, H., Blumstein, S. E., Gleason, J. B., Hyde, M. R. and Statlender, S. (1979) The effect of syntactic encoding on sentence comprehension in aphasia. *Brain and Language* **7**, 201–9.

Goodglass, H. and Kaplan, E. (1972) *The Assessment of Aphasia and Related Disorders* (1st edn.). Philadelphia: Lea & Feiberger.

Goodglass, H. and Kaplan, E. (1983) *The Assessment of Aphasia and Related Disorders* (revised). Philadelphia, PA: Lea & Feiberger.

Goodglass, H., Klein, B., Carey, P. W. and Jones, K. J. (1966) Specific semantic word categories. *Cortex* **2**, 74–89.

Gravel, J. S. and LaPointe, L. L. (1982) Rate of speech of health care providers during interactions with aphasic and nonaphasic individuals. In R. H. Brookshire (ed.), *Clinical Aphasiology Conference Proceedings*, pp. 208–11. Minneapolis, MN: BRK Publishers.

Gravel, J. S. and LaPointe, L. L. (1983) Length and redundancy in health care providers' speech during interactions with aphasics and nonaphasic individuals. In R. H. Brookshire (ed.), *Clinical Aphasiology Conference Proceedings*, pp. 211–17. Minneapolis, MN: BRK Publishers.

Green, E. and Boller, F. (1974) Features of auditory comprehension in severely impaired aphasics. *Cortex* **10**, 133–45.

Helm-Estabrooks, N., Fitzpatrick, P. M. and Barresi, B. (1982) Visual action therapy for global aphasics. *Journal of Speech and Hearing Disorders* **47**, 385–9.

Holland, A. L. (1983) Remarks on observing aphasic people. In R. H. Brookshire (ed.), *Clinical Aphasiology Conference Proceedings*. Minneapolis, MN: BRK Publishers.

Just, M. A., Davis, G. A. and Carpenter, P. A. (1977) A comparison of aphasic and normal adults in a sentence verification task. *Cortex* **13**, 402–23.

Kearns, K. and Hubbard, D. J. (1977) A comparison of auditory comprehension tasks in aphasia. In R. H. Brookshire (ed.) *Clinical Aphasiology Conference Proceedings*. Minneapolis: BRK Publishers.

Keenan, J. S. and Brassell, E. G. (1975) *Aphasia Language Performance Scales*. Murphreesboro, TN: Pinnacle Press.

Kertesz, A. (1978) *Western Aphasia Battery*. New York: Grune and Stratton.

Lasky, E. Z., Weidner, W. E. and Johnson, J. P. (1976) Influence of linguistic complexity, rate of presentation, and interphase pause time in auditory-verbal comprehension of adult aphasic patients. *Brain and Language* **3**, 386–95.

Lesser, R. (1974) Verbal comprehension in aphasic: an English version of three Italian tests. *Cortex* **10**, 247–63.

Lesser, R. (1978) *Linguistic Investigations of Aphasia*. New York, NY: Elsevier North-Holland.

Liles, B. Z. and Brookshire, R. H. (1975) The effects of pause time on auditory comprehension of aphasic subjects. *Journal of Communication Disorders* **8**, 221–35.

Linebaugh, C. W., Pryor, A. P. and Margulies, C. P. (1983) A comparison of picture descriptions by family members of aphasic patients to aphasic and nonaphasic listeners. In R. H. Brookshire (ed.), *Clinical Aphasiology Conference Proceedings*, pp. 218–26. Minneapolis, MN: BRK Publishers.

Linebaugh, C. W., Margulies, C. P. and Mackisack-Morin, E. L. (1984) The effectiveness of comprehension-enhancing strategies employed by spouses of aphasic patients. In R. H. Brookshire (ed.), *Clinical Aphasiology Conference Proceedings*, pp. 188–97. Minneapolis, MN: BRK Publishers.

Longhurst, T. M. and Siegel, G. M. (1973) Effects of communication failure on speaker and listener behavior. *Journal of Speech and Hearing Research* **16**, 128–40.

McNeil, M. R. (1977) *Effects of Diotic and Selective Binaural Intensity Variations on Auditory Processing in Aphasia*. Unpublished doctoral dissertation, University of Denver.

McNeil, M. R. (1983) Aphasia: neurological considerations. *Topics in Language Disorders* **3**(4), 1–19.

Marshall, R. C. and King, P. S. (1973) Effects of fatigue produced by isokinetic exercise in the communicative ability of aphasic adults. *Journal of Speech and Hearing Research* **16**, 227–30.

Marshall, R. C., Tompkins, C. A. and Phillips, D. S. (1980) Treatment scheduling: effects on communicative ability of aphasic subjects. *Journal of Communication Disorders* **13**, 105–14.

Pierce, R. S. (1981) Facilitating the comprehension of tense related sentences in aphasia. *Journal of Speech and Hearing Research* **46**, 364–8.

Porch, B. E. (1967) *Porch Index of Communicative Ability*, Vol. I: *Theory and Development*. Palo Alto, CA: Consulting Psychologists Press.

Rolnick, M. and Hoops, H. R. (1969) Aphasia as seen by the aphasic. *Journal of Speech and Hearing Disorders* **34**, 48–53.

Reidel, K. (1981) Auditory comprehension in aphasia. In M. T. Sarno (ed.), *Acquired Aphasia*. New York: Academic Press.

Sarno, M. T. (ed.) (1981) *Acquired Aphasia*. New York: Academic Press.

Schuell, H. M. (1972) *Minnesota Test for Differential Diagnosis of Aphasia*. Minneapolis, MN: University of Minnesota Press.

Schuell, H. M., Jenkins, J. J. and Jimenez-Pabon, E. (1964) *Aphasia in Adults*. New York, NY: Harper and Row.

Schuell, H. M., Jenkins, J. J. and Landis, L. (1961) Relationship between auditory comprehension and word frequency in aphasia. *Journal of Speech and Hearing Research* **4**, 30–6.

Schulte, E. J. (1986) Effects of imposed delay of response and item complexity on auditory comprehension by aphasics. *Brain and Language* **29**, 358–71.

Schulte, E. J. (1988) *Comprehension of Speaker Intent by Aphasic, Right-Brain Injured, and Normal Adult Males*. Unpublished doctoral dissertation, University of Kansas.

Shewan, C. M. (1976) Error patterns in auditory comprehension of adult aphasics. *Cortex* **12**, 325–36.

Shewan, C. M. (1979) *Auditory Comprehension Test for Sentences*. Chicago, Ill.: Biolinguistics Clinical Institutes.

Shewan, C. M. and Canter, G. J. (1971) Effects of vocabulary, syntax, and sentence length in auditory comprehension in aphasic patients. *Cortex* **7**, 209–26.

Skelly, M. (1975) Aphasic patients talk back. *American Journal of Nursing* **75**, 1140–2.

Springer, S. P. and Deutsch, G. (1981) *Left Brain Right Brain*. San Francisco: W. H. Freeman and Company.

Stachowiak, F. J., Huber, W., Poeck, K. and Kerschensteiner, M. (1977) Text comprehension in aphasia. *Brain and Language* **4**, 177–95.

Swinney, D. A., Zurif, E. G. and Cutler, A. (1980) Effects of sentential stress and word class upon comprehension in Broca's aphasia. *Brain and Language* **10**, 132–44.

Tompkins, C. A., Marshall, R. C. and Phillips, D. S. (1980) Aphasic patients in a rehabilitation program: Scheduling speech and language services. *Archives of Physical Medicine and Rehabilitation* **61**, 252–4.

Weidner, W. E. and Lasky, E. Z. (1976) The interaction of rate and complexity of stimulus in the performance of adult aphasic subjects. *Brain and Language* **3**, 34–40.

Weisenburg, T. H. and McBride, K. E. (1935) *Aphasia*. New York, NY: Commonwealth Fund.

Wilcox, M. J., Davis, G. A. and Leonard, L. L. (1978). Aphasics comprehension of contextuality conveyed meaning. *Brain and Language* **6**, 362–77.

Winner, E. and Gardner, H. (1977). Comprehension of metaphor in brain damaged patients. *Brain* **100**, 717–29.

Wulf, H. H. (1979) *Aphasia, My World Alone*. Detroit, MI: Wayne State University Press.

Chapter 5

Agrammatism and Paragrammatism

Marjorie Perlman Lorch

Introduction

The neurologist Arnold Pick was one of the early clinical aphasiologists to focus on disorders of sentence construction. He emphasized the appearance of agrammatism in the course of recovery, stating that the grammatical disturbance may be initially masked by other difficulties but will become more evident as recovery progresses, and in milder cases may be observed from early on. Pick's definition of agrammatism includes what we now refer to as paragrammatism. Unlike more recent approaches he considered disturbances in sentence production alone and did not examine the related issues in sentence comprehension. Pick stated 'Agrammatism is that form of pathologically changed speaking, in which the processes operating in the grammatical and syntactic construction of language are disturbed in multiple ways . . .' (p. 203, trans. in de Bleser 1987).

History of the notions of agrammatism and paragrammatism

The interest in agrammatism as a disorder of sentence production dates from the earliest work in the scientific study of the aphasias. The first description of agrammatism is attributed to a case report by Deleuze (1819), in which it was noted that 'The patient in question used exclusively the infinitive of verbs and never used any pronoun' (p. 1, trans. in Goodglass and Menn 1985). Steinthal (1871) referred to agrammatism as the incapacity to build sentences; an impairment with respect to the 'methods (laws, rules) and means (small words, inflections) to interconnect images into a sentence' (p. 485, trans. in Kolk *et al.* 1985).

It is notable that many of the early reports of agrammatism were from cases of German speaking aphasics. Indeed, Low (1931) pointed out the significant lack of descriptions of agrammatism in English. This was due, in part, to sociological factors which accounted for the greater sophistication of the German school of aphasiology at the turn of the century (Howard 1985).

But there is another reason why there were so many well documented cases in German and French, and, until recently (within the last 25 years), very few in English. This is due to the fact that both German and French are highly inflected languages, i.e. they have a multitude of grammatical word endings. Thus, the presence of agrammatism, as a deficit affecting these bound grammatical inflections, would be particularly striking in such languages. Indeed, Alajouanine (1968) noted that 'the richer a language is in distinctions of these types of grammatical differentiation in inflection, the more glaring agrammatism will appear' (p. 4, trans. cited from Goodglass and Menn, 1985).

The early descriptions of the agrammatic deficit in German and French are fairly comparable, in that they both note the loss of inflections marking person, number, and gender agreement and the predominance of the infinitive form of verbs. In contrast to French, German and other highly inflected languages, English has few grammatical endings (bound grammatical inflections). Instead there is a general reliance on the use of word order and auxiliary verbs to signal syntactic distinctions. Although the grammatical forms in English show these differences, descriptions of agrammatism in English have been influenced by the clinical reports of patients who were speakers of the more heavily inflected languages (e.g. Goldstein 1948; Luria 1970). However, owing to the general lack of inflections in English these descriptions placed less emphasis on the impairment in bound morphology, and more emphasis on the omission of functors (auxiliaries, prepositions, pronouns) and word order. (See Crystal 1988 for a discussion of the interaction between language factors and morphological versus syntactic level descriptions.)

The distinction between agrammatism and paragrammatism was first drawn by Kleist in 1934, prior to which all grammatical disturbances were referred to as agrammatisms. What is the basis for this distinction? In clinical aphasiology this dichotomy is based on both anatomical and linguistic grounds.

Clinical descriptions

Traditionally, agrammatism is considered to be a symptom which is typically found as a part of the larger syndrome of Broca's aphasia. This aphasic syndrome which includes agrammatism as part of its symptom complex is also referred to as motor aphasia (Goldstein 1948); syntactic aphasia (Wepman and Jones 1964); efferent motor aphasia (Luria 1970); and is included in the more general categories of expressive aphasia (Weisenburg and McBride, 1935) and non-fluent aphasia (Goodglass et al. 1964; Howes 1967). Clinical descriptions given under these various terminological distinctions are quite similar. The agrammatic aspect is characterized by a difficulty with function words and inflections with relative sparing of substantive words. Prepositions, articles and pronouns, as well as grammatical inflections, are omitted or substituted. Speech production is typically made up of short declarative sentences composed primarily of nouns, verbs and adjectives. This agrammatic form of production is also referred to as *telegraphic speech*.

Some examples of agrammatic speech productions (taken from Schwartz

1987: p. 169) elicited by picture description (a girl presenting flowers to her teacher) are as follows:

'The young . . . the girl . . . the little girl is . . . the flower'
'The girl is . . . going to flowers'
'The girl is flower the woman'
'The girl is . . . is roses. The girl is rosin''
'Girl is handing flowers to teacher.'

These transcriptions (as well as the paragrammatic ones which follow below) do not include information on the intonation, stress, and articulation of the speech (see Crystal 1988 for discussion of this problem).

In contrast, paragrammatism is associated with the syndrome of Wernicke's aphasia. The aphasic syndrome which includes paragrammaism as one of its symptoms is also referred to as sensory aphasia (Goldstein 1948); syntactic aphasia (Head 1926); acoustic aphasia (Luria 1970); pragmatic aphasia (Wepman and Jones 1964); and as part of the more general categories of receptive aphasia (Weisenburg and McBride 1935); and fluent aphasia (Goodglass and Kaplan 1972). The paragrammatic disorder is typically described as the inappropriate juxtaposition of words and inflections. It may include the presence of semantic paraphasia and neologisms. The speech of paragrammatics is notable for its facile articulation, and may tend towards logorrheia. Despite the structural richness and variety of the sentences, the word strings are empty of semantic content.

Examples of paragrammatic speech production elicited by picture description ('The cookie theft.') (from Buckingham 1981: pp. 54–9) follow:

These were [ɛksprɛ́šəz], [əgræšənz] *and with the type of mechanic is standing like this . . . and then the . . . I don't know what she* [gɔ́in] *other than* [?]. *And this is* [dɛ́li] *this one is the one and this one and this one and . . . I don't know.*

I mean, she is a beautiful girl. And this is the same with her. And now its coming there and [?]. *Now what about here or anything like that . . . what any.*

This is a boy, this is a boy. I forget the boy and a boy. This one ever which ever one is right and a boy. Then this one is right here, right here. And . . . nice right in here.

Well, this is a little girl boy. And that's a little girl, he's a [trə tráksər] *candy. And, my lights are, oh* [kǽθəl dúnət], [kǽnə dónət]. *And he was up on the* [ráksər], *but it's a wonder he wasn't* [ɔ́fə] *fell* [ɔ́fə] *there.*

It must be emphasized that these two classifications are empirically derived rather than theoretically motivated. Agrammatism is typically associated with anterior lesions centred around the left premotor cortex and nonfluent, motor aphasia. Paragrammatism is associated with posterior lesions centred around the auditory association area of the left temporal lobe and/or parietal lobe, and a fluent, sensory aphasia.

The specific site of lesion responsible for the disorder of agrammatism is a topic of debate. It is generally attributed to the dominant (left) prefrontal gyrus – the third frontal convolution, but whether it involves this structure alone or involves the parietal operculum and insula in addition (Mohr 1976) and whether the adjacent periventricular white matter is crucially implicated (Naeser *et al.* 1982) remains unsettled.

Both of these disorders refer to the sentence level of language behaviour. They are generally seen in conjunction with difficulties at the single word level, involving both lexical semantics and phonology. These aspects are dealt with separately in Chapter 6 on paraphasia by Buckingham and Chapter 2 on fluency by Poeck. The majority of discussion in this chapter will be taken up with agrammatism which has been a primary focus of research in sentence production in modern neurolinguistics. Paragrammatism will be dealt with secondarily. For a variety of reasons, the research concerning these patients has typically focused on semantic and phonological processes affecting word production rather than the syntactic processes involved in sentence level production.

Linguistic and psycholinguistic research

Initial scientific reports in English described agrammatics as having: (a) shortened phrase length (Goodglass *et al.* 1964); (b) a limited inventory of the types of words produced (Wepman and Jones 1964; Goodglass and Hyde 1969); and (c) reduced speaking rate (Howes and Geschwind 1962; Howes 1967). As a clinical diagnostic category, agrammatism has primarily been used to refer to a simplification of sentence form chiefly reflected in an over-reliance on content words (Geschwind 1970; Goodglass and Kaplan 1972).

While this clinical picture has been well documented for years, the symptoms considered to be central to the disorder, and the models used to describe them, have changed considerably. It is questionable whether a unitary explanation of agrammatism has yet been devised (Berndt and Caramazza 1980). A multitude of arguments have been offered to explain the quality of this disorder. Currently, there is little consensus of opinion on the nature of the disturbance (see Kean 1985 for eight different viewpoints.)

A plurality of views have been put forth to account for the distribution of spared and impaired grammatical forms in agrammatic speech. Appeals have been made to such general cognitive factors as 'effort' (Spreen 1973; Lenneberg 1967), redundancy (Goodglass and Hunt 1958; de Villiers 1974; 1978), saliency (Goodglass *et al.* 1967), and meaningfulness (Goodglass and Menn 1985).

Arguments based upon more linguistic notions have also been advanced – phonological stress and clitics (Kean 1977; 1979), contiguity (Jakobson 1971), semantic complexity (de Villiers 1974 based on Brown 1973) and discourse-location notions (Lapointe 1985). Different formal linguistic models have been employed over the years – phrase structure grammar (Myerson and Goodglass 1972), transformational grammar (Marshall 1977), stratificational grammar (Schnitzer 1982), and government and binding (Grodzinsky 1984a). Various levels of psycholinguistic processing have also been implicated – thematic (Saffran *et al.* 1980b), morpho-lexemic (Schnitzer 1982), syntactic (Berndt and Caramazza 1980), morpho-syntactic (Grodzinsky 1984a) and phonological (Kean 1977).

While both clinical and experimental evidence in English indicates that agrammatic aphasics have difficulties producing functor words (free grammatical morphemes) and inflectional morphology (bound grammatical morphemes), not all of these grammatical formatives appear to be equally affected. There seems to be some order to the frequency of occurrence of these grammatical entities in the spontaneous speech of agrammatics. For example, the overly frequent use of the verb with the '-ing' inflection in agrammatic speech has been noted by Goodglass (1968).

Various studies have explored the order of difficulty that agrammatics have in producing noun and verb inflections. Jakobson (1956) was the first linguist to address the issue. He characterized the agrammatics' behaviour as being due to a 'contiguity disorder'. This deficit was characterized as a syntagmatic impairment considered to reflect a dissolution of grammatical rules resulting in the loss of government and concord. Jakobson's notion of contiguity accurately predicts a higher degree of difficulty with verb inflection in comparison to noun inflections. It also successfully captures the ordering of difficulty of the production of certain grammatical morphemes (plural 's' is more frequent than possessive 's' which is more frequent than third singular present tense 's') based on the size of the constituent structures over which the government reaches (Jakobson 1964). It is not clear how well Jakobson's model can be extended to predict the varying degrees of susceptibility in other grammatical forms. This model would seem to erroneously predict the equal vulnerability of all verb inflections, as they all mark government in the larger unit of the clause (de Villiers 1974).

General psycholinguistic factors have been used to account for some aspects of the agrammatics' pattern of grammatical formative omissions. In a series of studies, Goodglass and co-workers demonstrated the effects of such factors as redundancy, stress saliency and frequency (Gleason *et al.* 1975; Goodglass and Hunt 1958; Goodglass and Berko 1960; Goodglass *et al.* 1967). Grammatical affixes were analysed as being affected relative to the syllable structure of the target word. In a sentence completion task, aphasics were shown to be more likely to omit the non-syllabic form of the possessive morpheme than the syllabic form (e.g. 'dog's' was harder than 'horse's'). But the impairment was not thought to be characterizable exclusively in phonological terms (cf. Kean 1977); syntactic function was also recognized to play a role. Goodglass and Berko (1960) verified Jakobson's (1956) theoretical prediction that the /Iz/ morpheme was more likely to be produced as a plural than as a marker for the third-person singular present tense, and the third singular was more likely to be produced than the possessive (genitive) marker.

De Villiers (1974) carried out a study of the occurrence of fourteen morphological inflections in spontaneous samples of agrammatic speech. This study examined the heterogenous group of bound inflections serving various grammatical functions. In attempting to explain the distribution pattern of her findings, many different theoretical models were examined and rejected. Initially, Brown's (1973) hierarchy of semantic complexity was considered to be one of the more promising alternatives, since it was developed to capture the order of acquisition of inflectional morphology. However, when it was applied to the aphasic speech data, only half of the cases could be accounted for. De Villiers concluded that some notion of redundancy (Goodglass and

Hunt 1958) must be appealed to. She argued that this notion does predict the loss of the third person singular 's' on the grounds that number agreement is unnecessary, being determined by the subject.

This explanation falls short in several instances. For example, it fails to account for the preservation of plural 's' in Broca's aphasics' speech in the context of relatively frequent use of number words modifying the plural nouns. The idea of redundancy cannot account for the loss of tense markings; these are not in general recoverable because the agrammatics rarely use adverbs of time. A more serious shortcoming results from the difficulty of specifying the notion of redundancy. De Villiers (1978) points out that the concept of redundancy must be related to factors defined by the surrounding context. Due to the nature of the reduced grammatical form of agrammatic speech some indeterminacy does exist.

Early theories of agrammatism also relied on a notion similar to that of redundancy. In light of the motoric aspects of the disorder which commonly co-occur in agrammatics – the dysarthia, dysprosody and effortful quality of speech – the strain of speaking was once thought to account for the agrammatic quality. The principle of 'minimum effort' was invoked to explain the patients' over-reliance on content words as a conscious attempt to maximize the amount of information with the fewest words (Isserlin 1922; and Pick, discussed in Spreen 1973). In a more elaborate version, Lenneberg (1975) also attributed the source of omission of 'redundant' elements and need for economy of effort to the muscle coordination difficulties of articulation. The difficulty with these accounts is that they lack any principle which would determine what elements of the message are essential and need to be retained and which elements are unnecessary and may be omitted. Recently, Badecker and Caramazza (1985) reopened this debate, making the claim that the words which will be omitted in agrammatic speech can accurately be predicted by frequency and abstractness variables. Kolk *et al.* (1985) and Heeschen (1985) have pursued a related line of reasoning based on the idea that agrammatic speech represents a form of adaptation strategy based on the normal process of ellipsis. (See Butterworth 1985 for a parallel argument that the paragrammatic impairment is secondary to a failure of control.)

While the evidence from clinical and experimental studies suggests that there may be some underlying regularity to the pattern of production in agrammatism, there has been a general lack of success in determining a coherent view. This is reflected in the plurality of theoretical approaches and experimental paradigms under current exploration. One response to this state of affairs has been to question the integrity of the syndrome (Badecker and Caramazza 1985; Goodglass and Menn 1985; Kolk and Van Grunsven 1985). Another result has been a trend towards studies focused on isolated aspects of the agrammatics' deficits.

Agrammatics have traditionally been considered to have an impairment in closed class items (function words and inflections), and it has been generally assumed that open class items (content words) were not a problem (Kolk 1978). Research has examined properties of prepositions (Beyn *et al.* 1979; Frederici 1982), and complements (Grodzinsky 1984b). These studies were carried out to examine specifically closed class function words. Recently, however, there have been arguments raised which call for closer scrutiny of the behaviour of main verbs in agrammatism with regard to both lexical and inflectional issues (Saffran *et al.* 1980a; Miceli *et al.* 1984; Grodzinsky 1984a; Wales and Kinsella 1981; McCarthy and Warrington 1985).

It has been noted that agrammatics produce fewer verbs than nouns in spontaneous speech (Myerson and Goodglass 1972; Hand *et al.* 1979; Martin *et al.* 1976). Wales and Kinsella (1981) found that verbs were less often produced than nouns, prepositions or particles in a highly constrained sentence completion task. Additionally, in a task comparing naming of pictured objects and actions agrammatics were found to be impaired on verb targets relative to noun targets (Miceli *et al.* 1984). Other experimental paradigms have been employed by Jones (1984) and Lesser (1984) to document agrammatic (comprehension) deficits in verb semantics.

In clinical descriptions of the spontaneous speech of English-speaking agrammatics, it has been noted that main verbs are typically produced in one of two forms: (a) the uninflected form (e.g. 'walk'), and (b) the verb + ing (e.g. 'walking') (Goodglass 1968; Goodglass and Geschwind 1976; Jakobson 1964; Luria 1970). The former productions might be considered alternatively as infinitives, bare stems, or 'default forms', while the latter might be considered as participles (adjectival), or as gerundive (nominalized) forms (Lorch 1986). De Villiers (1974) documented that the '-ing' form was used twice as often as any other verb form. The difficulty with the syntactic representation of these forms is due to the fact that they serve multiple grammatical functions.

In normal speech these verbs are used in different sentence structures which distinguishes their grammatical role. In the reduced sentence structures produced by agrammatics, there is some confusion as to how these forms should be characterized (Myerson and Goodglass 1972). This is due to the limited structure apparent in the agrammatics' productions. Agrammatic utterances generally contain few adverbs or complements which could be used to disambiguate the syntactic function of these forms.

Goodglass and Geschwind (1976) suggested that these prevalent '-ing' forms represent nominalizations (i.e. a naming form). Agrammatics have been found to produce derived nominalizations instead of active verbs in elicitation tasks. Whitaker (1972) employed a task which required the generation of sentences with the inclusion of a target noun or verb. He found that certain aphasics who had difficulty producing verb forms frequently supplied derived nominalizations (e.g. decide→decision, engage→engagement, p. 67). Similar findings are reported by Saffran *et al.* (1980b). They also suggest that such '-ing' forms are being used 'to name' the action normally expressed by the verb as a predicate. The implication of all of these arguments is that agrammatics have a deficit in predication (cf. Luria 1970). That is, in using the '-ing' form as a nominal, agrammatics are referring to the action without expressing the grammatical relations between sentence constituents.

The case reported by Saffran *et al.* (1980a) is regarded as counter-evidence to the notion of the nominalization of verbs and implied deficit in predication. This patient's picture descriptions include examples of 'verbified nouns' e.g. 'she is bookening it' (reading), 'the girl is polaroid the flowers' (photograph-ing), 'the baby bottle-ing' (drinking a bottle). These observations are interpreted by these authors as a difficulty affecting the form in which predicates are expressed rather than a loss of predication *per se*.

To summarize, agrammatics' speech is typically comprised of substantive words with few functors or inflections in reduced sentence structures. The loss of control of grammatical morphemes in agrammatism is typically manifest as omission (at least in English-speaking patients). By contrast, studies of neologism and paraphasia in paragrammatic aphasics indicates the opposite pattern: major lexical categories are particularly vulnerable to phonological distortion, while syntactic categories are relatively spared (Butterworth 1979; Lecours and Rouillon 1976; Schwartz 1987). Of course, the grammatical inflections may not be syntactically appropriate to the sentence frame which gives the paragrammatic quality, i.e., substitution errors (Caplan *et al.* 1972; Buckingham and Kertesz 1976).

Additional research issues

Spontaneous versus elicited speech   Generally, the clinical characterization of aphasic speech as agrammatic or paragrammatic is based upon the assessment of spontaneous speech (Goodglass and Kaplan 1972; Albert *et al.* 1981). Heeschen (1985; and Goldstein 1948) warns against drawing conclusions regarding a patient's deficit on the basis of spontaneous speech. The characterization of agrammatic (and paragrammatic) speech will differ depending on how the speech is elicited. The entire grammatical repertoire of the agrammatic is unlikely to be obtained in a narrative sample (Myerson and Goodglass 1972). This may lead to an inaccurate impression of the patients' level of impairment.

Saffran (1982) states that evidence of agrammatism is more pronounced in less structured settings; the spontaneous speech elicited in open-ended interviews will reveal the highest degree of impairment. On the contrary Heeschen (1985) found that the quality of agrammatic speech was altered in nature by the manner in which it was elicited. In spontaneous speech, (German) agrammatics were found to produce speech which contained 39 per cent omission of case markings. When required to produce sentences in a constrained elicitation task, the agrammatics omitted case markings only 20 per cent of the time. However, they now produced 23 per cent erroneous case markings, i.e. substitution errors, which had not been present in their spontaneous speech. The paragrammatic patients in this study, by contrast, did not produce different patterns of speech in the two contexts. The point that both errors of omission and substitution can occur in the same patient has long been recognized (Isserlin, in Droller *et al.* 1985; Weisenburg and McBride 1935).

Comprehension   The issue of syntactic comprehension in these patients must be raised if only briefly. The classical German writings on agrammatism described agrammatism as a disorder specific to speech production. Salomon (1914) was the first to raise the question of grammatical comprehension in these patients. Based on findings of impaired grammatical comprehension performance (e.g. Zurif and Caramazza 1976; Bradley *et al.* 1980), modern aphasiologists considered agrammatism to be the result of a central syntactic disorder (Kean 1985; Berndt and Caramazza 1980; Saffran *et al.* 1980a; Zurif 1980). Subsequently, there were reports of agrammatic patients in whom dissociations between receptive and expressive modalities were demonstrated (Miceli *et al.* 1983; Kolk *et al.* 1985; Nespoulous *et al.* 1988). It also seems that poor comprehension is not necessarily always found in conjunction with paragrammatic production (Butterworth 1985).

The issue of syntactic comprehension deficits (which may or may not occur in conjunction with sentence production deficits) have become the focus of a great deal of research activity in the past five years. Much of this work focuses on meta-syntactic tasks such as grammaticality judgement (e.g. Linebarger *et al.* 1983; Schwartz *et al.* 1987). Demonstrations of the ability to perform grammaticality judgements in agrammatics is taken as evidence for intact syntactic knowledge; thus the impairment is inferred to be the result of a processing deficit (cf. Martin and Blossom-Stach 1986).

Treatment

There have been a number of treatment procedures which have been suggested for helping agrammatic patients. Crystal *et al.* (1976) propose that syntactic structures should be introduced into rehabilitation programmes in order of their acquisition in children. This approach is motivated by the assumption that the aphasic is suffering from the loss of syntactic knowledge and therefore must be treated with a reteaching programme.

The use of programmed instruction procedures to retrain specific declarative sentence structures have been carried out by Holland and Levy (1971) and by Naeser (1975) with agrammatic patients. While the former study showed some improvement but no generalization, the latter study showed carryover to untrained sentences and some facilitation of untrained syntactic skills. Weigl-Crump (1976) used repetition to retrain specific sentence structures in expressive aphasics. These subjects improved on the trained sentences and on untrained sentences as well. For a survey of training studies see Howard and Hatfield (1987).

Approaches to treatment of syntactic disorders also exist which are based on the view that the agrammatics have an impaired access to syntactic knowledge. Studies carried out at the Boston Veterans Hospital using a story completion paradigm suggested that patients did have intact syntactic knowledge although their ability to employ it was variable (Goodglass *et al.* 1972; Gleason *et al.* 1975). The syntax stimulation procedure developed by Helm uses the story completion strategy in conjunction with visual stimuli to facilitate production of specific target sentence structures of increasing syntactic complexity (Albert *et al.* 1981). A case study of treatment using this technique documented generalized improved performance on a standard syntax test (Helm-Esta-brooks *et al.* 1981).

Visual stimuli are also used in the functional grammar approach advocated by Hatfield and Shewell (1983). Emphasis is placed on the expression of the meaningful elements of the picture and their relationship. This production of clause structure precedes work on the more difficult aspect of phrase structure, with function words being introduced last. This approach is suggested for patients with severe agrammatism, patients with more residual syntactic skills are treated with conversational practice working on 'surface structures'.

Recently, two treatment programmes have been developed which focus on the agrammatic impairment in theme assignment. The thematic role maps the semantic role on to a syntactic role. Both Byng and Coltheart (1986) and Jones (1986) demonstrated specific treatment effects in agrammatic aphasics ability to understand thematic roles. These studies reflect the increasing cognitive and neuropsychological underpinnings of current efforts to capture the essence of the agra matic deficit.

References

Alajouanine, Th. (1968) *L'Aphasie et le langage pathologique*. Paris: J-B Bailliere et Fils.

Albert, M., Goodglass, H., Helm, N., Rubens, A. and Alexander, M. (1981) *Clinical Aspects of Dysphasia*. Vienna: Springer-Verlag.

Badecker, W. and Caramazza, A. (1985) On considerations of method and theory governing the use of clinical categories in neurolinguistics and cognitive neuropsychology: the case against agrammatism. *Cognition* **20**, 97–125.

Berndt, R. and Caramazza, A. (1980) A redefinition of the syndrome of Broca's aphasia: implications for a neuropsychological model of language. *Applied Psycholinguistics* **1**, 225–78.

Beyn, E., Vinzel, T. and Hatfield, F. (1979) Aspects of agrammatism in aphasia. *Language and Speech* **22**, 327–46.

Bleser, R. de (1987) From agrammatism to paragrammatism: German aphasiological traditions and grammatical disturbances. *Cognitive Neuropsychology* **4**, 187–256.

Bradley, D., Garrett, M. and Zurif, E. (1980) Syntactic deficits in Broca's aphasia. In D. Caplan (ed.), *Biological Studies of Mental Processes*. Cambridge: MIT Press.

Brown, R. (1973) *A First Language*. Cambridge: Harvard University Press.

Buckingham, H. (1981) Where do neologisms come from? In J. Brown (ed.), *Jargonaphasia*. New York: Academic Press.

Buckingham, H. and Kertesz, A. (1976) *Neologistic Jargon Aphasia*. Amsterdam: Swets and Zeitingler.

Butterworth, B. (1979) Hesitation and the production of verbal paraphasias and neologisms in jargon aphasia. *Brain and Language* **8**, 133–61.

Butterworth, B. (1985) Jargon aphasia: processes and strategies. In S. Newman and R. Epstein (eds), *Current Perspectives in Dysphasia*. Edinburgh: Churchill Livingstone.

Byng, S. and Coltheart, M. (1986) Aphasia therapy research: methodological requirements and illustrative results. In E. Hjelmquist and L. Nilsson (eds), *Communication and Handicap*. Amsterdam: Elsevier.

Caplan, D., Kellar, L. and Locke, S. (1972) Inflection of neologisms in aphasia. *Brain* **95**, 169–72.

Crystal, D. (1988) Linguistic levels in aphasia. In F. Rose, R. Whurr and M. Wyke (eds), *Aphasia*. London: Whurr Publications.

Crystal, D., Fletcher, P. and Garman, M. (1976) *The Grammatical Analysis of Language Disability*. New York: Elsevier.

Droller, H., Howard, D. and Campbell, R. (1985) On agrammatism. *Cognitive Neuropsychology* **2**, 303–45.

Frederici, A. (1982) Syntactic and semantic process in aphasic deficits: the availability of prepositions. *Brain and Language* **15**, 249–58.

Geschwind, N. (1970) The organisation of language in the brain. *Science* **170**, 940–4.

Gleason, J., Goodglass, H., Green, E., Ackerman, N. and Hyde, M. (1975) The retrieval of syntax in Broca's aphasia. *Brain and Language* **2**, 451–71.

Goldstein, K. (1948) *Language and Language Disturbances*. New York: Grune and Stratton.

Goodglass, H. (1968) Studies on the grammar of aphasics. In S. Rosenberg and J. Kopin (eds), *Developments in Applied Psycholinguistics Research*. New York: Macmillan.

Goodglass, H. and Berko, J. (1960) Agrammatism and inflectional morphology in English. *Journal of Speech and Hearing Research* **3**, 257–67.

Goodglass, H., Fodor, I. and Schulhoff, C. (1967) Prosodic factors in grammar – evidence from aphasia. *Journal of Speech and Hearing Research* **10**, 5–20.

Goodglass, H. and Geschwind, N. (1976) Language disorders (aphasia). In E. C. Carterette and M. P. Friedman (eds), *Handbook of Perception*, Vol. VII. New York: Academic Press.

Goodglass, H., Gleason, J., Bernholtz, N. and Hyde, M. (1972) Some linguistic structures in the speech of a Broca's aphasic. *Cortex* **8**, 191–212.

Goodglass, H. and Hunt, J. (1958) Grammatical complexity and aphasic speech. *Word* **14**, 197–207.

Goodglass, H. and Hyde, M. (1969) How aphasics begin their utterances. Unpublished Progress Report, USPHS Grant NS 07615, Boston.

Goodglass, H. and Kaplan, E. (1972) *The Assessment of Aphasia and Related Disorders*. Philadelphia: Lea and Febiger.

Goodglass, H. and Menn, L. (1985) Is agrammatism a unitary phenomenon? In M-L. Kean (ed.), *Agrammatism*. New York: Academic Press.

Goodglass, H., Quadfasel, F. A. and Timberlake, W. H. (1964) Phrase length and the type and severity of aphasia. *Cortex* **1**, 133–58.

Grodzinsky, Y. (1984a) The syntactic characterization of agrammatism. *Cognition* **16**, 99–120.

Grodzinsky, Y. (1984b) *Differential Sensitivity to Vocabulary Type in Agrammatic Aphasia*. Manuscript. Brandeis University, Waltham.

Hand, C., Tonkovich, J. and Aitchison, J. (1979) Strategies of a chronic Broca's aphasic. *Linguistics* **17**, 729–59.

Hatfield, F. and Shewell, C. (1983) Some applications of linguistics to aphasia therapy. In C. Code and D. Muller (eds), *Aphasia Therapy*. London: Edward Arnold.

Head, H. (1926) *Aphasia and kindred disorders of speech*. New York: Macmillan.

Heeschen, C. (1985) Agrammatism versus paragrammatism: a fictitious opposition. In M-L. Kean (ed.), *Agrammatism*. New York: Academic Press.

Helm-Estabrooks, N., Fitzpatrick, P. and Barresi, B. (1981) Response of an agrammatic patient to a syntax stimulation program for aphasia. *Journal of Speech and Hearing Disorders* **46**, 422–7.

Holland, A. and Levy, C. (1971) Syntactic generalization in aphasics as a function of relearning an active sentence. *Acta Symbolica* **2**, 34–41.

Howard, D. (1985) Agrammatism. In S. K. Newman and R. Epstein (eds), *Current Perspectives in Dysphasia*. Edinburgh: Churchill Livingstone.

Howard, D. and Hatfield, F. (1987) *Aphasia Therapy: Historical and Contemporary Issues*. London: Lawrence Erlbaum Associates.

Howes, D. (1967) Hypotheses concerning the functions of the language mechanism. In S. Salzinger and K. Salzinger (eds), *Research in Verbal Behaviour and Some Neurophysiological Implications*. New York: Academic Press.

Howes, D. and Geschwind, N. (1962) Statistical properties of aphasic speech. Unpublished Progress Report, USPHS Grant M-1802. Boston Veterans Administration Hospital, Boston.

Isserlin, M. (1922) Ueber Agrammatismus. *Zeitschrift für die gesamte Neurologie und Psychiatrie* **75**, 332–410.

Jakobson, R. (1956) Two aspects of language and two types of aphasic disturbances. In R. Jakobson and M. Halle (eds), *Fundamentals of Language*. The Hague: Mouton.

Jakobson, R. (1964) Towards a linguistic typology of aphasic impairments. In A. de Reuck and M. O'Connor (eds), *Disorders of Language*. London: Churchill.

Jakobson, R. (1971) *Studies on Child Language and Aphasia*. The Hague: Mouton.

Jones, E. (1984) Word order processing in aphasia: effect of verb semantics. *Advances in Neurology* **42**, 159–81.

Jones, E. (1986) Building the foundations for sentence production in a non-fluent aphasic. *British Journal of Disorders of Communication* **21**, 63–82.

Kean, M-L. (1977) The linguistic interpretation of aphasic syndromes: agrammatism in Broca's aphasia, an example. *Cognition* **5**, 9–46.

Kean, M-L. (1979) Agrammatism, a phonological deficit? *Cognition* **7**, 69–83.

Kean, M-L. (1985) *Agrammatism*. New York: Academic Press.

Kleist, K. (1934) *Gehirnpathologie*. Leipzig: Barth.

Kolk, H. (1978) The linguistic interpretation of Broca's aphasia: a reply to Marie-Louise Kean. *Cognition* **6**, 353–61.

Kolk, H. and Van Grunsven, M. (1985) Agrammatism as a variable phenomenon. *Cognitive Neuropsychology* **2**, 347–84.

Kolk, H., Van Grunsven, M. and Keyser, A. (1985) On parallelism between production and comprehension in agrammatism. In M-L. Kean (ed.), *Agrammatism*. New York: Academic Press.

Lapointe, S. (1985) A theory of verb form use in the speech of agrammatic aphasics. *Brain and Language* **24**, 100–55.

Lecours, A. and Rouillon, F. (1976) Neurolinguistic analysis of jargonaphasia and jargonagraphia. In H. Whitaker and H. Whitaker (eds), *Studies in Neurolinguistics*, Vol. II. New York: Academic Press.

Lenneberg, E. (1967) *Biological Foundations of Language*. New York: John Wiley.

Lenneberg, E. (1975) In search of a dynamic theory of aphasia. In E. Lenneberg and E. Lenneberg (eds), *Foundations of Language Development: A Multidisciplinary Approach*, Vol. 2. New York: Academic Press.

Lesser, R. (1984) Sentence comprehension and production in aphasia: an application of lexical grammar. *Advances in Neurology* **42**, 193–201.

Linebarger, M., Schwartz, M. and Saffran, E. (1983) Sensitivity to grammatical structure in so-called agrammatic aphasics. *Cognition* **13**, 361–92.

Lorch, M. (1986) *A Cross-linguistic Study of Verb Inflections in Agrammatism*. Doctoral Dissertation. Boston University, Boston.

Low, A. (1931) A case of agrammatism in the English language. *Archives of Neurology and Psychiatry* **25**, 556–97.

Luria, A. (1970) *Traumatic Aphasia*. New York: Basic Books.

McCarthy, R. and Warrington, E. (1985) Category specificity in an agrammatic patient: the relative impairment of verb retrieval and comprehension. *Neuropsychologia* **23**, 709–27.

Marin, O., Saffran, E. and Schwartz, M. (1976) Dissociations of language in aphasia: implications for normal language function. *Annals of the New York Academy of Sciences* **280**, 868–84.

Marshall, J. (1977) Disorders in the expression of language. In J. Morton and J. Marshall (eds), *Psycholinguistics: developmental and pathological*. Ithaca: Cornell University Press.

Martin, R. and Blossom-Stach, C. (1986) Evidence of syntactic deficits in a fluent aphasic. *Brain and Language* **28**, 196–234.

Menn, L. and Obler, L. (In press) *Agrammatic Aphasia: Cross-linguistic Narrative Sourcebook*. Amsterdam: John Benjamins.

Miceli, G., Mazzuchi, A., Menn, L. and Goodglass, H. (1983) Contrasting cases of Italian agrammatic aphasia without comprehension disorder. *Brain and Language* **19**, 65–97.

Miceli, G., Silveri, M., Villa, G. and Caramazza, A. (1984) On the basis for the agrammatics' difficulty producing main verbs. *Cortex* **20**, 207–20.

Mohr, J. (1976) Broca's area and Broca's aphasia. In H. Whitaker and H. A. Whitaker (eds), *Studies in Neurolinguistics*, Vol. I. New York: Academic Press.

Myerson, R. and Goodglass, H. (1972) Transformational grammars of three aphasic patients. *Language and Speech* **15**, 40–50.

Naeser, M. (1975) A structured approach to teaching aphasics basic sentence types. *British Journal of Disorders of Communication* **10**, 70–6.

Naeser, M., Alexander, M., Helm-Estabrooks, N., Levine, H., Laughlin, S. and Geschwind, N. (1982) Aphasia with predominantly subcortical lesion sites: description of three capsular/putaminal aphasia syndromes. *Archives of Neurology* **39**, 2–14.

Nespoulous, J-L., Dorain, M., Perron, P., Ska, B., Bub, D., Caplan, D., Mehler, J. and Lecours, A. (1988) Agrammatism in sentence production without comprehension deficits: reduced availability of syntactic structures and/or of grammatical morphemes? A case study. *Brain and Language* **33**, 273–95.

Saffran, E. (1982) Neuropsychological approaches to the study of language. *British Journal of Psychology* **73**, 317–37.

Saffran, E., Schwartz, M. and Marin, O. (1980a) The word order problem in agrammatism: production. *Brain and Language* **10**, 3–280.

Saffran, E., Schwartz, M. and Marin, O. (1980b) Evidence from aphasia: isolating the components of production. In B. Butterworth (ed.), *Language Production, Vol. I: Speech and Talk*. New York: Academic Press.

Salomon, E. (1914) Motorische Aphasie mit Agrammatismus und sensorisch-agrammatischen Stoerungen. *Monatsschrift fuer Psychiatrie und Neurologie* **35**, 181–275.

Schnitzer, M. (1982) The translation hierarchy of language. In M. Arbib, D. Caplan and J. Marshall (eds), *Neural Models of Language Processes*. New York: Academic Press.

Schwartz, M. (1987) Patterns of speech production deficit within and across aphasia syndromes: application of a psycholinguistic model. In M. Coltheart, G. Sartori, and R. Job (eds), *The Cognitive Neuropsychology of Language*. London: Lawrence Erlbaum Associates.

Schwartz, M., Linebarger, M., Saffran, E. and Pate, D. (1987) Syntactic transparency and syntactic interpretation in aphasia. *Language and Cognitive Processes* **2**, 85–113.

Spreen, O. (1973) Psycholinguistics and aphasia: the contribution of Arnold Pick. In H. Goodglass and S. Blumstein (eds), *Psycholinguistics and Aphasia*. Baltimore: John Hopkins University Press.

Villiers, J. de (1974) Quantitative aspects of agrammatism in aphasia. *Cortex* **10**, 36–54.

Villiers, J. de (1978) Fourteen grammatical morphemes in acquisition and aphasia. In A. Caramazza and E. Zurif (eds), *Language Acquisition and Language Breakdown*. Baltimore: John Hopkins University Press.

Wales, R. and Kinsella, G. (1981) Syntactic effects in sentence completion by Broca's aphasics. *Brain and Language* **13**, 301–7.

Weisenburg, T. and McBride, K. (1935) *Aphasia*. New York: The Commonwealth Funds.

Wepman, J. and Jones, L. (1964) Five aphasias: a commentary on aphasia as a regressive linguistic phenomenon. *Research Publications of the Association for Research in Nervous and Mental Disease* **42**, 190–203.

Whitaker, H. (1972) Unsolicited nominalizations by aphasics. *Linguistics* **78**, 62–71.

Wiegl-Crump, C. (1976) Agrammatism and aphasia. In Y. Lebrun and R. Hoops (eds), *Recovery in Aphasics*. Amsterdam: Swets and Zeitinger.

Zurif, E. (1980) Language mechanisms: A neuropsychological perspective. *American Scientist* **68**, 305–11.

Zurif, E. and Caramazza, A. (1976) Psycholinguistic structures in aphasia: studies in syntax and semantics. In H. Whitaker and H. Whitaker (eds), *Studies in Neurolinguistics*, Vol. I. New York: Academic Press.

Chapter 6

Phonological Paraphasia

Hugh W. Buckingham, Jr

Introduction

Karl Wernicke (1874) in his groundbreaking monograph on sensory aphasia observed and analysed what he referred to as 'word transpositions' and 'word confusions' (Eggert 1977). By word transpositions, Wernicke meant segmental alterations within some word, and by word confusions he meant full-word substitutions, where the error bore a similarity relation to the target – either phonological or semantic. A. Kussmaul (1877) coined the term 'paraphasia' and applied it to the distinction drawn earlier by Wernicke. Kussmaul called word transpositions 'literal paraphasias', and word confusions, 'verbal paraphasias'. The term 'literal' simply reflected the existing confusion between sounds and letters. We now know that phonemes are involved – not graphemes. The form 'para-' relates to the Greek word meaning 'akin to, associating with, and closely related' and involves substitution. The form 'phasia' comes from the Greek word for speech in the broad sense of the word. Accordingly, Kussmaul's term paraphasia indicated that some linguistic form substituted for another, but where the two forms bore some resemblance to each other.

In this chapter, I will provide a brief outline of the basic processes and constraints on phonemic errors. Then, I will chart some of the important early studies of these errors, ranging from Wernicke (1874) to Blumstein (1973). Next, I will sketch some contemporary psycholinguistic models of production within which one can locate the precise locations of computational derailments that lead to phonological paraphasias. Subsequently, I will discuss some of the more recent model-oriented studies that examine phonological paraphasia, and finally I will comment on some future directions for these kinds of investigations.

Basic processes of phonemic paraphasia

In the first place, I will use the modifiers 'phonemic' and 'phonological' interchangeably. I will not include discussion at the level of archiphonemes or morphophonemes, nor will I treat the many types of phonetic problems seen in apraxia and dysarthria.

Substitution

The first type of phonological error is the substitution, where the substituting phoneme does not emanate from the immediate context of the error expression. This point is of utmost importance, since there are many substitution errors where the intruding unit is already present in the phonetic context. The absence of a contextual source means that the phonemic substitution is strictly paradigmatic (vertical) in nature. The no-source phonemic substitution further assumes that there is some sort of *selection* problem among simultaneously available phonemes that are quite similar in their featural makeups and that have equal or very similar frequency counts for the language as a whole.

Transposition

Transpositions are of three types: anticipatory (regressive), perseverative (progressive), and metathesis (full exchange). Anticipatory errors involve a right-to-left movement of some segmental unit – usually a phoneme or a cluster. The initial consonants of syllables down line in an utterance are usually those which are anticipated. Anticipations may be substitutive or additive. That is, the anticipated /n/ in the word *nondon* for *London*, substitutes for the target /l/. On the other hand, the anticipated /p/ in the error *papple* for *apple*, is additive, since there was no consonant in the initial position for the target word. Anticipations may or may not remain in their original positions. When they do, of course, a 'doublet' is created.

Perseverations are also typical of transposition errors; they move left-to-right. As with anticipations, perseverative errors may be substitutive or additive, and the perseverate may or may not remain in its original position.

Exchanges represent the last type of transposition error, and although they occur relatively frequently in slips-of-the-tongue, they occur only rarely in aphasia. These would be the classical 'spoonerisms' (Potter 1980, and other citations in Fromkin 1980).

Additions

Additive phonemic errors (like phoneme substitutions in the strict sense) may or may not come from the immediate phonetic context. That is, one sort of addition paraphasia will be a no-source addition. We just saw that many of the transposition errors may *add* the moved segment into a previously unfilled slot in some word.

Deletion

Omission of segments is also seen in phonemic paraphasia. It is often the consonant cluster that is the site of a deletion error. In a sense, it is a simplification. The word *sleep* may become *seep*, for instance, or *black* may become *back*. It is usually the second member of an initial consonant cluster that is deleted (see also Stemberger and Treiman (1986) for the same observation in slips-of-the-tongue). Intervocalic consonants are rarely, if ever, deleted.

Segment perseveration blending into other words

Aphasics will often perseverate on segments, clusters or full syllable types (see Buckingham 1985). These perseverates can then blend in various ways with ensuing lexical items forming coalesced forms. A patient studied in Buckingham *et al.* (1979) with neologistic jargon and perseveration (the two are rarely dissociated) at one point was perseverating on initial /kr-/ and /fr-/ clusters, thus forming words such as *kremon* (for *lemon*) and *krubanana* (for *banana*). These are not, however, to be confused with the blending of two words that present themselves to the selection mechanism simultaneously.

Constraints on paraphasic processes

Many phonemic paraphasias are constrained by high-level, overriding properties of the phonological system. Some properties are universal and others are language specific. It has been observed that segmental slips-of-the-tongue obey these same conditions (Buckingham 1980).

Parallel syllable structure

The first condition is that of cross-syllable slot matching. Fromkin (1971) and many others have observed this constraint in segmental slips-of-the-tongue, and Buckingham and Kertesz (1976) correlated these observations with the structure of perseverative transpositions in neologistic jargon. Most characterizations of the constituent structure of the syllable initially divide the syllable into an onset and a core (or rime). The onset position is made up of zero or more consonants, and it stands apart from the rest of the syllable. The core consists of the peak of the syllable, which is the vocalic portion that serves as the site of stress placement, and the coda, which consists of zero or more consonants that close the syllable. Onset and core consonants that are unambiguously members of some syllable, and only that syllable, are referred to as 'tautosyllabic'. Internal consonants in certain specific environments may belong to the syllable to the right or to the left; they are referred to as 'ambisyllabic'. Generally, in English a (C)VCV word with tonic accent on the first syllable will have an ambisyllabic internal consonant. The word *apple*, for instance, will have an ambisyllabic internal /p/, whereas the word *appeal*, will not. The words *funny* and *pony* both have ambisyllabic /n/. To be ambisyllabic, there have to be other words where the consonant in question may be a tautosyllabic onset or coda.

The parallel syllable structure constraint simply says that transposed items may switch from syllable to syllable, but they tend to end up in the same syllable position. That is, onsets go to onset positions, peaks go to peak positions, and codas move to coda positions. It would therefore be expected that ambisyllabic consonants might be free to move to either position, which turns out to be the case (Buckingham 1980; Stemberger 1982). Blumstein (1978) discusses this constraint in detail. It should be noted, however, that when there is a transposition within the confines of one syllable this constraint is broken, since quite often a coda moves to the onset position. The error *fafter* is a good example of this, where an unmarked, initial CV has been produced for the word *after*, the coda /f/ being anticipated to an onset position.

Phonotactics

The language-specific phonotactic patterns serve as a very important conditioning factor for phonemic paraphasias. For instance, when consonants transpose to other syllables that already have consonants in either the onset or the coda, they will only move if the resulting cluster is permitted by the sequencing rules of the language. This applies as well to transpositions within neologisms. On one occasion, a jargon aphasic produced the neologism *fawbreiber*, only to produce *frawbeiber* in the following sequence. Note that *fr* and *br* are permissible onset consonants clusters in the English language. In addition, the CV syllable type is very common, and therefore unmarked. Accordingly, it has been observed that with CCV targets, the second C (and not the first, for reasons other than phonotactics, as we will see) will be deleted, resulting in an unmarked CV form. If the target word is a CVC, the tendency is for the final C to be omitted, thus again resulting in the unmarked CV. For similar reasons, vowel-initial words with internal consonants will often be the site of anticipatory transpositions, moving the internal C to the unfilled onset position, again creating the unmarked CV.

Sonority

Another very important syllabic structure condition, one which interrelates with phonotactics but is essentially different, is the so-called 'sonority' principle. Blumstein (1978), Beland *et al.* (1985), Beland and Nespoulous (1985), and Buckingham (1987a; 1987b) have, for slightly different purposes, made reference to this principle. Syllables seem to be universally constructed from least sonorous to most sonorous and back to least sonorous again. Sonority is defined in terms of maximum perceptual/acoustic salience correlated with a maximally open vocal tract, so that in general syllables start with a consonant produced with less vocal tract opening and move to the vocalic part where the tract is maximally open, and then to the coda where the vocal tract again approaches the closed gesture. In terms of ascending sonority, the hierarchy goes: obstruent, nasal, liquid, glide and vowel. From the peak of the syllable to the end of the coda, sonority would descend in mirror image fashion. The human phonological system likes things to go this way. It also likes sequences of sounds that are maximally separated on this hierarchy, so that the CV syllable /ba/ is preferred over /na/, which is preferred to /la/ and /ra/, both of which are preferred to the CV's /ya/ and /wa/. Sequences of two sounds that share the same place in this hierarchy are highly marked, although they obviously do occur in languages. This relates to the fact that consonant clusters usually consist of consonants that are not next to each other on the hierarchy (Harris 1983). Languages tend to have more /pl-/ clusters than /ps-/ clusters. Note that clusters like *sp* in the word *sport* violate this principle; the two segments are obstruents.

Conditioned by this principle, any error that would otherwise leave two segments of the same sonority value together is likely to be subsequently altered to avoid the situation. Therefore, if a consonant is transposed from an intervocalic position, it is very likely that a doublet will be created by ensuring that the moved item *remains* in its original position between the two vowels. Inspection of doublet creating errors in the aphasia literature (e.g. Lecours and Lhermitte 1969) reveals that in most cases they involve intervocalic consonants that are misordered but remain in their original slots. For further details, see Buckingham (1987b: pp. 395–8).

Moreover, it is important to distinguish sonority from phonotactics, although as I mentioned above, the two do interrelate. For instance, it has been observed (Blumstein 1973, 1978; Stemberger and Treiman 1986) that when clusters reduce through consonant deletion/omission, it is most often the second of the consonant group that deletes. Why? Phonotactic constraints will not help here. For example, if the /l/ of the word *black* were omitted, the result would be *back*. If the /b/ were deleted, the result would be *lack*. Phonotactic constraints do not differentiate between /l/ and /b/ onset consonants. So, why is it that more often the /l/ deletes in these cases? Sonority is a better explanation, because *that* principle clearly would favour *back* to *lack* due to the fact that /b/ and the vowel are further apart than /l/ and the vowel on the sonority hierarchy. On the other hand, phonotactics would do just as well as sonority in explaining certain addition paraphasias. For instance, if an /l/ were added to the word *base* to form *blase*, it would be in its correct sonority position, but on that account so would an /n/, but an /n/ would never be added after the /b/ of *base*, because the phonotactics of English rule out clusters of /bn-/.

Range of transposition

Another important conditioning factor for phonemic transposition paraphasias is the range within which segments can move around. Until we have outlined in a bit more detail the actual psychological models for language production, our discussion will be somewhat restricted. Suffice it to say here that the ranges that are involved for segmental placement and ordering can span either an isolated word (such as on single-word tasks), or they can span up to a phrase or a clause in sentence production. That is, we see phonological seg-ments transposed at times within syllables, within words, within phrases, and even across phrases (but still within clauses). What we rarely, if ever, see are segments transposing across sentence (clause) boundaries. So, in general, anticipations, perseverations, and exchanges of segments are confined to phrases or at most the single clause.

Finally, of the transposition errors, anticipations appear to be the most numerous, and onset segments are the ones most likely to be transposed – even more so if the segment is not only a syllable onset but a word-initial, syllable onset as well (see Shattuck-Hufnagel 1987). At least for slips-of-the-tongue, there is evidence that consonants that are onsets in tonically accented word-initial syllables are subject to some sort of separate processing (as opposed to the rest of the syllable) that in some way renders them particularly vulnerable to confusion or disruption. A clear example of this for conduction aphasia is discussed in Buckingham (1987b: p. 392), where the patient was attempting to read the printed word *telephone*. The /t/ is not only in syllable onset position, but it is in word-initial position and in the tonically accented syllable of the word. In this first set of attempts to repeat, the patient made approximately 25 attempts at the polysyllabic word. Not once did he get the initial /t/. The forms ranged from *pelephone* to *felepone* to *lelephone* to *felephone*. Most attempts came out *felephone* or *lelephone*. His tonic accent, however, was on the first syllable in practically every instance. Interestingly enough, he made the same type of error on a repetition task for the word *telephone*, producing in order: *felephone*, *felepone*, and *felephone*.

Earlier works

I will now briefly outline the continuity and change in the observation and analysis of phonemic paraphasia. In my treatment of the work of the nine-teenth-century German school, I am greatly indebted to Eggert (1977).

Wernicke (1874) observed the different types of intralexical transpositions of segments we have outlined and hypothesized that they arose from a disturb-ance of acoustic images and of proprioceptive (kinaesthetic) 'muscle sense'. Wernicke utilized the notion of muscle sense (akin to the concept developed over a hundred years earlier by David Hartley (1746) – see Buckingham (1984) for an historical outline of the notion of 'muscle sense' – and combined it with his own ideas of acoustic imagery to develop a precursor to the modern concept of a speech programmer. The system that drove speech production consisted of sensory information coded in terms of the acoustic and motor-kinaesthetic elements of words. Taken together, but excluding semantics, these formed the 'word-concept'. This system selected and ordered speech units. With acoustic information disrupted, the motor system would run on unchecked or unmonitored, and paraphasias would arise accordingly.

Kussmaul (1877) observed and wrote about the same sorts of phonemic paraphasias, but instead of emphasizing the role of damaged sensory impres-sions that inhibit the operation of some sort of speech programmer, Kussmaul theorized that paraphasic disorders stemmed from diminished, or disturbed, attention mechanisms. Impaired attention, for Kussmaul, incorrectly lead to the arousal (or revivification) of associated sounds and words that resembled the targets – either a similar sound or a word that was similar based on sound or meaning. As Eggert (1977: p. 51) writes:

> Further exploration of the problem of paraphasia in the post-Wernickean period tended to take two directions. One school pursued Kussmaul's idea relating this disorder to impaired attention. Adherents of the second school expanded Wernicke's notion of 'word-concept' leading to development of the idea of a speech programmer.

Hugo Liepmann (Eggert 1977: p. 51) concurred with Wernicke's notion of a mechanism that manipulated speech sounds, but he developed slightly different theories in terms of planning processes. Initially, Liepmann had constructed models for various sorts of complex limb movements and their disorders – the apraxias. In relating this work to speech, Liepmann assumed that an 'acoustic plan' was basic to normal articulatory production. Speech output was viewed as a complex set of movements by the articulators, which Liepmann viewed simply as special types of limbs. He assumed that these plans consisted of the appropriate serial ordering of the acoustic components of words and that they worked in tandem with the motor elements of word production. Accordingly, Liepmann conceived that damage to the acoustic images might lead to the internal disintegration of words, 'characterized by the repetition or contamination of preceding sounds and syllables or the anticipation of sounds to be produced' (Eggert 1977: p. 51). Liepmann made the analogy of phonemic paraphasias to ideational and ideokinetic limb apraxias and related these types of paraphasias to posterior cerebral systems. Buckingham (1983) draws this analogy in his distinction between 'apraxia of speech' and 'apraxia of language', whereby he linked phonemic paraphasia phenomena to ideational apraxia. As it turns out, it may be more precise to say that phonemic level paraphasia reflects the linguistic counterpart of general ideokinetic (or ideomotor) limb apraxias. In a very modern description, Liepman described paraphasia in terms of (Eggert 1977: p. 51), 'syllable perseveration, premature production of syllables, word slips with changes in sound and meaning, mixtures of appropriate word-segments and those mutilated in sound and meaning, word-perseverations and combinations of word components evoked by chance sensory stimuli or associations'. The recent work of Kimura (1982) and Roy (1982) alludes to Liepmann's contribution to the study of general movement systems as it relates to higher-level articulatory movement planning and execution.

Kleist contributed as well to the early study of paraphasia (Eggert 1977). He, as Wernicke, Kussmaul, and Liepmann before him, contributed to the conceptualization of speech programmers. Kleist coalesced the notions of the 'word-concept' and the 'word-plan' into an overall system that determined the organization or arrangement of speech sounds into temporal and rhythmic patterns. Kleist conceived of a special serializing or sequencing mechanism as part of the function of the temporal lobe – a mechanism that imparted order to tonal images and acoustic engrams (i.e. to sensory elements). He claimed that there was a similar ordering mechanism in Broca's area for the proper sequencing of motor elements. For normal speech production as a whole, Kleist argued that there had to be a tight interaction among the motor and acoustic ordering devices. Thus, Eggert (1977: p. 52) writes, 'Kleist viewed paraphasia as an impairment of the temporal acoustic serializing mechanism and its influence on that of the motor speech system'. Again, Kleist's appreciation for the need of some sort of serial ordering mechanism for phonological production is a clear precursor of modern notions of the seriation of speech.

Arnold Pick (1931) provides detailed commentary on phonemic paraphasia. He proposes a transmission mechanism for the selection and ordering of speech sounds and further establishes attention mechanisms for the proper functioning of the mechanism. Properly functioning attentional processes allow for the normal operation of excitation and inhibition of units in Pick's view. Pick (1931: p. 57) writes, 'Disinhibition is also a causal factor in word distortion, a purely descriptive term for *literal paraphasia.*' For Pick, damage to the left temporal lobe in the language areas 'loosens up' the segmental coherence of words. The coherence is then not firm enough to disinhibit phonemes evoked by association or to disinhibit a misordering among similar phonemes in analogous syllabic slots. The result is the substitution and transposition of sound units. Pick also notices the parallels with segmental slips-of-the-tongue. Not only do slips have the same error taxonomy as phonemic paraphasias, but they, too, seem to be the result of abnormal excitatory/inhibitory processes during speech production. Drawing analogies between phonemic paraphasia and slips-of-the-tongue, Pick (1931: p. 57) writes,

> According to our knowledge of normal slips of the tongue, the separate forms of disorder [phonemic paraphasia] may be explained as anteception, metaception, postception, and paraception.

At this point in the quote, Pick refers to the classic study of slips by Meringer and Mayer (1895). The term anteception refers to a right-to-left transposition, while metaception refers to an exchange of sounds (spoonerism). Postception is a term for left-to-right movement, and paraception was used to refer to a substitution. Pick continues (p. 57),

> To these may be added contamination [blending] and perseveration. The not infrequent mixture of verbal and literal paraphasia presumably corresponds to the simultaneous occurrence of disinhibition in both the stages in question.

Here, for the first time that I can find in the literature, is the suggestion that phonemic paraphasic distortions can be applied to the output of a verbal paraphasia. Pick mentions that this two-stage error is involved in jargon aphasic production, and that the bizarre neologisms seen in jargon aphasia may stem from phonological alteration of a word that is already in error. Buckingham and Kertesz (1976) evaluated this account of jargon in the current thinking of A. Luria (1970), Lecours and Lhermitte (1972) and J. Brown (1972; 1988), as it relates to theories of neologistic production (see Chapter 7 on jargon and neologisms in this book).

More recent studies

In any discussion of paraphasia in aphasia, Roman Jakobson's (Jakobson and Halle 1956; Jakobson 1964; 1980) contribution must be credited. I have previously alluded to the notion of similarity, which plays an important role in aphasic paraphasias. Rounding out the picture of similarity is the other side of that coin – selection. That is, as Jakobson pointed out (obviously bringing in the classical terms handed down from the structuralist movement), where there is an error based upon a similarity metric, the problem is one of *selecting* the wrong item. Selection interlocks with similarity, and the process is referred to as 'paradigmatic'. In contradistinction to similarity, there is 'contiguity', which does not relate to selection, but rather to combination. As similarity correlates with selection, contiguity correlates with combination. The combination process is not paradigmatic, but rather 'syntagmatic'; it is linear. Jakobson's principal weakness was his rigid limitation of paradigmatic processes to posterior areas (and therefore to sensory aphasia) and syntagmatic processes to frontal areas (motor aphasia). We now know that many derailments of sensory aphasics involve precisely syntagmatic processes of serial ordering.

The next landmark work on paraphasia is to be found in Lecours and Lhermitte (1969). This study was the first major, in-depth investigation of phonological errors in fluent aphasia using the notion of distinctive features to measure the complexity of the errors. The analysis was cast in a structural framework, characteristic of the linguistics of the modern French linguist, André Martinet (1964). Lecours and Lhermitte showed very clearly that there are all sorts of linear errors, left-to-right and right-to-left. At times doublets were created or pairs in the target were even destroyed. They noted many substitutive errors as well, and typically observed that many of them differed by one distinctive feature only. By devising a taxonomy of error types including addition, deletion, transposition and substitution, they developed a sophisticated metric in terms of transformation.

The final milestone study of paraphasia is Blumstein (1973). To begin with, many of the points I will raise concerning this study have been broached by Lecours and Caplan (1975). Blumstein studied the spontaneous speech output of 17 aphasics: 6 Broca's, 5 Conductions and 6 Wernicke's. She looked at the following types of paraphasia: substitution (purely paradigmatic with no source in the phonetic context, presumably), simplification (deletion), environmental (linear transposition), and addition (a presumably no source addition of some segment that was not in the immediate phonetic context). After all counts were in, she found that the proportional frequency of error types was about the same in the three groups. Every group had more substitution errors, followed by simplification errors, environmental and addition errors, respectively.

The great majority of substitution errors differed from their targets by one distinctive feature, and the errors went from a more marked phoneme to a less marked phoneme. Out of a total of 1,346 substitution errors, 571 (42.4 per cent) occurred at the beginning of words, before a vowel. The fewest occurred in word-final position (57, or 4.2 per cent). Most of the substitutions involved single consonants. Clusters tended to act as protective environments for the consonants, as far as substitutions were concerned. Blumstein concentrated on consonantal substitutions to practically the complete exclusion of vowels. Vowels do tend to be more stable in phonemic paraphasia than consonants, but they may be altered nevertheless.

The first issue one can raise with her analysis of substitution is that, not unlike her mentor (who was Jakobson), Blumstein drew too sharp a distinction between the paradigmatic and the syntagmatic, and thus appeared to fail to distinguish those substitutions that had no contextual sources from those that did have contextual sources. Lecours and Caplan (1975) levelled this criticism quite sharply. Had she made this distinction, she would have been obliged to mix syntagmatic and paradigmatic processes. Jakobson's rather hard-line division between these types of computations perhaps prevented Blumstein from appreciating the problem.

Another criticism is that some of the phonemic substitution errors (and especially the phonemic errors of the Broca's group) could have been phonetic in their origin (Lecours and Caplan 1975: p. 243). Buckingham (1979; 1986) and Buckingham and Yule (1987) provide more discussion of the pracical and theoretical problem of a speaker's phonetic aberration giving rise to the perception of a phonemic level substitution on the part of the hearer. The problem is one of 'phonemic false evaluation', and recognition of this confounding speaker–hearer mismatch goes back to the latter part of the nineteenth century and appears again in the classic Prague School phonological study of N. Trubetzkoy (1939/1969).

Simplification (deletion) phonemic errors were more often found in clussters of consonants or with the final consonant in a CVC word. Both types of simplification follow general principles of syllable structure. When a consonant is deleted in an onset cluster, for instance, it is the second of the two which is deleted. Since the principle of sonority predicts that the second consonant of an onset cluster will be more sonorous than the first, the deletion of the second will set up a more preferred CV type, because the initial consonant which remains will contrast more sharply in sonority from the vowel. As mentioned previously, phonotactic constraints do not explain this.

Environmental errors, according to Blumstein, are either anticipations (regressive), perseverations (progressive), or metatheses, and they occur within and across morphemes (most often involving contentive morphemes), usually within the confines of the phrase. Anticipations are the most numerous, and these transpositions are more typical of the Broca's and the Conductions, according to Blumstein. The sequences resulting from these transpositions nevertheless conform to the phonotactics of the language. As I have pointed out above, transposed segments either end up substituting for some other phoneme or are added to some unfilled slot. Again, the doubling of the moved segment only occurs if it also remains in its original position.

Addition errors occur in the smallest numbers for all aphasic groups. Presumably, here, Blumstein is ruling out all of the additions that stem from environmental misorderings, but again, her strict division between the paradigmatic and the syntagmatic prevent her from emphasizing that there are no-source additions as well as source additions (again, see Lecours and Caplan's (1975) criticism). In her analysis of additive errors, she found that they quite often create consonant clusters from singletons, thus producing something *more* complex (more marked) than the target. On the other hand, additions were often produced within target words with initial vowels, thereby creating the unmarked CV. Blumstein also observed that there were many approximants that were added to oral stop, onset singletons to form typical clusters. Predictably, the approximants were added to the right of the target singletons, but this would be conditioned by phonotactic constraints as well as by the principle of sonority. Initial /bl-/ clusters follow the ordering in terms of increasing sonority, but it is also the fact that initial /lb-/ clusters are ruled out by phonotactics. The tight interaction between sonority and phonotactics is evident here. On the other hand, no /n/ would ever be added to the right of an oral stop in English, although the sequence oral stop + nasal follows the sonority ordering scale perfectly. Therefore, phonotactics constrain many of the addition errors, or lack thereof.

In any consideration of phonological errors in aphasia Blumstein's (1973) findings must be scrutinized and her contribution credited. Much has taken place since that study, and certainly Blumstein would now concur with many of the criticisms that have been levelled against it. There can be no doubt, though, that her investigations stimulated much subsequent fruitful work.

Contemporary production models

The 1970s marked a period of unpredecented growth in the modern study of slips-of-the-tongue (e.g. Fromkin 1971, 1973, 1980; Garrett 1975; Shattuck-Hufnagel 1979; Fay and Cutler 1977; Cutler and Fay (eds) 1978), and pursuant to this, those studies were brought to bear on aphasia research (Buckingham and Kertesz 1976; Buckingham 1980; Garrett 1982, 1984; Kohn 1984, 1985; Schwartz 1987), much the same way that the work on slips by Meringer and Mayer (1895) had been brought to bear on aphasia by nineteenth- and early twentieth-century investigators such as Freud and Pick. In my opinion, the most applicable model to emanate from psycholinguistics for the study of aphasia is that of Merrill Garrett (e.g. Garrett 1984, 1988). In order to provide mechanisms that more carefully manipulate phonological segments, I have inserted certain components from other models developed by Shattuck-Hufnagel (1979) and Butterworth (1979) into the overall framework of Garrett, thereby enriching the computational power of that model. A view of his model and my augmentations to it are seen in Figure 6.1.

The model is composed of levels of representative knowledge and sets of computations that interrelate them. At the Functional Level of representation the basic relational aspects of propositions are developed. Here, words are appreciated and accessed on the basis of their meanings; representative forms of words are not accessed. However, the meaning access establishes some sort of 'linking address' with the form, so that in the normal situation the form selected in the second access computation will match the prior accessed meaning. The second lexical look up is a computation of word selection based upon the underlying phonological form of the word. Form-based selection is one of the computations that map from the Functional Level to the Positional Level in Garrett's model. The other Positional Level computations are: the determination of clausal matrices (one clause at a time) that specify positions for functors and contentives, as well as the overall intonational envelope for

Figure 6.1 Merrill Garrett's model for language production

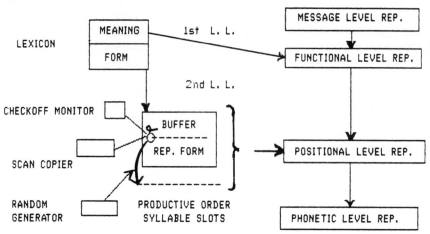

An augmented schematic diagram of Merrill Garrett's model for language production. The first lexical lookup (1st L.L.) is based solely on meaning/function and forms part of the computations that lead to the Functional Level. The rest of the processes in this diagram belong to the operations that map from the Functional Level to the Positional Level. The second lexical lookup (2nd L.L.), based upon the representative form, feeds units into the buffer and eventually they are placed into the Positional Level matrices. The scan-copier and checkoff monitor manipulate symbols in the buffer, ultimately copying representative forms on to productive order syllable slots. If the second lexical lookup fails, segmental items may be inserted into the buffer by the random generator. The mechanisms proposed by Shattuck-Hufnagel and Butterworth are thus readily seen to fit into Garrett's model as part of the computational system that maps the Functional Level of representation on to the Positional Level of representation (from Buckingham 1987b: p. 382)

the sentence. The contentives, having been accessed in terms of their shapes are then placed into their respective slots in the matrix. The slots come coded with grammatical category information. By entirely separate computations, the functors, both free and bound, are placed into their respective positions. At the Positional Level, the actual utterance order is more directly reflected than it is at the Functional Level. The functors are manipulated as segmentally unanalysable whole units as they are placed into their respective positions at the Positional Level, but the segments of the content words are imparted a second ordering for utterance level purposes as those content words are being positioned into their respective matrix slots. Again, the window sizes of the buffer and of the matrix have to match and be appreciated simultaneously, because many scanning errors occur over the range specified by the Positional Level matrices. This is where Shattuck-Hufnagel's operations come in, being added as they are to the set of Positional Level computations.

Within their respective window sizes (usually a phrase length, but possibly as much as a clause), content words are accessed from the lexicon on the basis of their shapes and placed into the buffer. Two processes are operating in tandem here. The full words are going into their respective matrix slots, but at the same time the sequential ordering mechanism is imparting productive order to their segments. The mechanism that computes this is the scan copier, and it is viewed as doing just that – copying segments in their representative order on to productive order syllable templates. The scanner copies syllable by syllable, working on onsets simultaneously, and then peaks and codas simultaneously. As each segment is copied on to productive template slots, that segment is cleared from the buffer by a device referred to as the checkoff monitor. It checks off segments once they are copied so that they will not continue to be copied reiteratively. There are apparently times when nothing gets into the buffer, but things still get uttered. Word retrieval deficits usually involve the second lexical lookup and not the first. That is, there is hard evidence that quite often a patient will know the meaning of some form but not be able to access the form of that word. If the patient is fluent, lacks sufficient self-monitoring, has comprehension deficits, and some sort of pragmatic need to continue conversing, he may fill in the slot of the missing word with a neologism.

In some cases, that neologism may not come from perseverated units but rather from some capacity to produce syllabic sequences based upon the knowledge all speakers have about possible words in their language. Butterworth (1979) labelled the mechanism that could do this a random phoneme generator. When Butterworth counted the phonemes in his corpus of bizarre neologisms – neologisms that were preceded by pauses of 250 msec or more, indicating lexical search – their numbers did not match expected phoneme frequency counts of English. In this sense, they are random. One must be careful not to claim that the neologisms so produced are comprised of phonemic units randomly juxtaposed. Syllable pattern conditions operate to ensure that random strings do not obtain, so that even the most bizarre of neologisms are 'possible' words in the language. That is, they are pronounceable and, accordingly, follow phonotactic dictates. If the generator is considered to produce syllable-sized chunks, then the phonotactics could be built into the syllables themselves and no unpermitted sequences would ever show up. (See Ch. 7 below on jargon aphasia for a fuller treatment.)

The string of elements at the Positional Level would be close to underlying phonemic units, to which regular allomorphic and allophonic computations would apply. All phoneme and morpheme transpositions would have to occur first, so that their allophones and allomorphs would be properly realized by the regular phonological processes. Errors at the Positional Level are always accommodated. Since this is the case, there is at least a kind of logical ordering to the processes involved, rendering any *strict* parallel processing view suspicious. In any event, phonological paraphasias as I have been describing them in this chapter seem to be characterizable as derailments of certain computations at the Positional Level (Garrett 1988: p. 83). More specifically, they seem to result from computational abnormalities of the scan copier and the checkoff monitor. It is also assumed that the scan copier and checkoff monitor operate on segments in the buffer, and therefore there must be something in the buffer for phonemic paraphasias to occur in the first place. The material either (1) gets into the buffer from the lexicon, in which case its representative shape can be accessed; (2) it gets there from some other competing source that slips into the planning elements; (3) it gets there from the random generator; or (4) items previously there do not get erased. Obviously the wrong word form may be placed into the buffer in case the linking address attaches erroneously to a word that is similar to the target, but that is not phonemic paraphasia, unless of course, the scan copier and/or the monitor derail subsequently on the lexical error itself, which, of course, is just a modern, model-oriented version of Pick (1931: p. 57).

Although, as I said above, these components, except the random generator, have been established to account for data from slips-of-the-tongue, their derailments seem to be quite close to computational disruptions that would lead to the production of phonological paraphasias. In a real sense, we now have the modern counterparts of the speech programmers and planners of Kussmaul, Kleist and Liepmann. But, note a very important consideration: our phonological error generating mechanisms only have access to elements in the buffer. Extraneous segments are difficult to come by. This is the reason we worry so much about the supposed non-source phonemic error. Does it exist? If so, where does the segment come from? This problem is most acute when dealing with the so-called pure paradigmatic phoneme substitution, because for that to actually happen, two similar planning phonemes must be simultaneously available to the scan copier that would select and copy the wrong one. Where would the similar, but non-target, phoneme come from? This represents no frivolous question and suggests that there may be no such thing as the no-source phonemic substitution (i.e., the purely paradigmatic substitution). Shattuck-Hufnagel (1979: p. 317) suggests several possible locations for the source; Buckingham and Yule (1987) suggest yet another and related it to the phenomenon of 'phonemic false evaluation'.

It is now easy to see that all sorts of transpositional errors can be described through breakdowns in these ordering computations (again, see Garrett (1988: p. 83)). The scanner can anticipate some onset consonant and copy it too early, either adding it to an onset position for a new consonant singleton or forming a cluster with some target phoneme, providing, of course, that the resulting cluster is permitted in the language. The anticipated element may substitute for a target item as well, and in both cases it may or may not be checked off by the monitor. The same works for perseveration transpositions. Whether the checkoff monitor works or not after the transposition seems to depend upon the resulting sequence of the items surrounding the transposed phoneme. If that sequence is unmarked, such as a vowel and a consonant, then it is more likely that the checkoff monitor will erase the moved item from its original slot. On the other hand, if the remaining sequence would result in two vowels falling together, then it is very unlikely that the monitor would check off the moved consonant. It would remain, and a doublet would thereby be created.

Later model oriented studies

We can now consider some more recent studies of phonemic paraphasia with reference to the overall model just sketched. By doing so, we can more precisely pinpoint the levels and computations that are involved. To begin with, as mentioned earlier, Buckingham (1980), following a well-established line of reasoning, showed the usefulness of incorporating psycholinguistic models constructed on data from slips-of-the-tongue to characterize aphasic errors and to make clear various well-known distinctions. In Buckingham

(1983) the attempt was made to distinguish, through psycholinguistic mechanisms, apraxia of speech (i.e. those phonetic aberrations made by Broca's aphasics – often referred to as phonetic disintegration or anarthria by the French School) and phonemic paraphasia. There, it was argued that *if* the so-called apraxias of speech truly comprised phonemic level errors, then it is as much an 'apraxia of language' as an 'apraxia of speech', since phonemes are abstract units which underly actual speech sounds. At the level of phonemic planning, and in accordance with the general schema of apraxias handed down by Liepmann, the apraxia of language is more like an ideational or ideomotor (ideokinetic) disorder than a limb-kinetic one, and therefore the 'apraxia' that would be involved in phonological paraphasic disruptions would be more correctly referred to as an apraxia *of language* and not of speech. That is, aphasic breakdowns with mechanisms such as the scan copier and checkoff monitor are higher order planning disruptions and the analogy to apraxia, if one is to be made (and there is no reason not to make it), is to a higher level apraxia, closer to what Liepmann had in mind with his ideational apraxias or ideomotor apraxias, since those are the more fluent apraxic disorders. (See Roy (1982) for a detailed treatment of the higher level apraxias.)

Other recent studies of paraphasia have attempted to provide answers to questions like: which types of aphasics make which kinds of paraphasic errors? or, which response elicitation techniques condition this or that paraphasic response, and in which types of patients? Kohn (1984, 1985, 1988) has devoted a good deal of effort to distinguishing segmental error typology in Wernicke's, Conduction, and Broca's aphasics. First off, she argues that if one is to unambiguously tap phonological knowledge in aphasics, then it is best to work only with confrontation naming of visual stimuli – as opposed to oral reading or repetition. No elements of the phonological patterns of words are provided in naming tasks, whereas in oral reading and repetition, many aspects of the underlying phonology come with the stimuli provided the patient. She claims that different responses are conditioned by different elicitation procedures, but Caplan *et al.* (1986) find that this is not the case. In any event, Kohn's investigations led her to conclude that Wernicke's aphasics have problems in accessing the representative lexical shapes of words, whereas Conduction aphasics have difficulty in readying and sequencing phonemic segments in the construction of phonological strings for productive ordering. Broca's aphasics have problems with phonetic implementation. In terms of our model, she locates the Wernicke's problem at the accessing stage, the Conduction's problem at the stage of scanning for order, and the Broca's problem at the stage of 'regular' phonological processing below the Positional Level.

Many of Kohn's findings are based on in-depth analyses of phonological approximations to targets that are provided by patients as they make repeated attempts to provide the required behaviours. This is referred to, in French, as 'conduit d'approche', and in fact, as Kohn points out, much additional data had been provided by earlier studies of these kinds of approximations (e.g. Joanette *et al.* 1980a and Joanette *et al.* 1980b). Kohn notes that Conductions seem to get closer to the target in their approximations, but that Wernicke's patients do not. In fact, the Wernicke's patients will often provide a different number of syllables than those of the target, and they will variously produce different CV patterns from the target. There is often very little match in terms of the number of phonemes in the target and the number of phonemes in the responses. As they go on, they will often get *further* from the target – or at least no closer. In addition, Kohn shows that the Wernicke's are poorer at utilizing phonemic cuing, and they reveal little if any 'tip-of-the-tongue' information for the sought after target. To this I would only add that the Wernicke's often recover to an anomia, which implies that they had had anomia all along. Theirs is, accordingly, a problem with accessing underlying forms.

Conduction aphasics demonstrate through greater agreement in their errors with the overall underlying shapes of words that theirs is not one of word access, but rather one of constructing phonemic strings, which can be characterized in terms of scan copying, etc. Kohn attempts to demonstrate that the actual lexical phonological forms are coded in terms of morphophonemes, and that these are only later translated into phoneme-like units to be manipulated at the level of string construction. Kohn concludes that Wernicke's aphasics have a phonological (whereby she means underlying morphophonemic lexical representations and access to them) deficit, conduction aphasics have a phonemic (on the assumption that phonemes are a step less abstract than morphophonemes but not abstract enough to be considered phonetic) deficit, and finally, that the Broca's have a phonetic deficit. Kohn (1985) gives an in-depth treatment to many of these questions and should be consulted for further details.

The usefulness of more detailed psycholinguistic models is made clear when one compares studies such as Kohn's with work such as Canter *et al.* (1985). The latter authors contrast apraxia of speech with phonemic paraphasia, but seem to find little that essentially differentiates the conductions and the Wernicke's in their fluent phonemic disorders. In this study, the ten paraphasics consisted of 5 conductions and 5 Wernicke's; there were 10 Broca's patients with apraxia of speech. The speech samples were elicited through spontaneous speech and repetition. They found a non-significant trend in the paraphasic group towards substitutions of more than one feature, and while the paraphasics made more sequencing errors, the Broca's with apraxia of speech made more transitionalization errors (smooth transitions between contiguous segments). Fine differences between Kohn's Wernicke's and conductions were not noted in the Canter *et al.* study.

Several studies have not concentrated as much on the nature of the paraphasic processes themselves as on the specific stimulus parameters that bring about, or encourage, paraphasic responding. We have reasoned, following Kohn, that naming (as opposed to oral reading and repetition) may very well elicit more paraphasic responses, since the stimulus provides no phonological information. Words vs. non-words have also been noted differentially to evoke paraphasic responses on oral reading and repetition tasks (Friedrich *et al.* 1984; Caramazza *et al.* 1986). It has often been observed that patients can repeat real words but perform miserably on non-words. This has led many to believe that there is a 'lexical route' to reading and something like a 'phonological route' to repeating. In the normal case, we would repeat a word through the information we have on that form as a stored item in our lexicon, and not through some non-lexical acoustic/phonological/motor system. On the other hand, normal subjects have little if any difficulty in repeating non-sense words, which are nevertheless 'possible' words in the language. Related to this is the definite fall off that is observed in the ability to repeat very low frequency words, so that low-frequency words will stimulate more phonemic paraphasia. In addition, it has been shown that conduction aphasics, for example, demonstrate far greater numbers of phonemic transpositions on multisyllabic words. In all these cases, the quality of the paraphasias is not involved, rather the quantity of them is enhanced.

Another detailed study of error type, comparing Broca's aphasics with conduction aphasics is found in Nespoulous *et al.* (1987). They compare these two groups on repetition and reading. First, they note that the Broca's errors are more stable and predictable; conduction aphasics were more variable. Conduction aphasics did worse on repetition, while the Broca's had the most difficulty with oral reading. At a finer level of comparison, however, these authors showed that on repetition, the conductions had a significantly greater proportion of transposition errors than the Broca's subjects. No significant differences were found between the groups regarding additions, omissions, or substitutions. On oral reading, there were no significant differences in additions, transpositions or substitutions for both groups, but on this kind of task the Broca's aphasics produced significantly more omissions than did the conductions.

Caplan (1986) have studied single-word production in a conduction aphasic on naming, repetition, and reading aloud. Unlike Kohn, these authors find no real differences in the paraphasic performance on these different tasks. They find that their conduction patient has no problem with access and verbal short-term memory for words when there is no verbal output required (i.e. on pointing and recognition tasks). Underlying word representations are intact therefore. And in fact, Caplan *et al.* claim that there are underlying phonological (in name only, apparently) representations that are modality-neutral with respect to the characterization of the segmental/suprasegmental aspects of the sounds of language. They even claim that there is no reason to think of them as auditory or articulatory representations, *per se*. Perhaps, they should not be called 'phonological' then. In any event, what needs to be done is to map these deep lexical forms on to 'superficial' phonological representations, which play more directly into the verbal output system. It is here, that the conduction disruption is assumed to take place, and it is these superficial lexical segments that are submitted to the ordering computations in verbal outputing – computations that breakdown in conduction aphasia.

The problem that Caplan *et al.* (1986) see here is that the phenomena involve single word construction, and not something that necessarily takes place in phrasal matrix positioning computations. I see no real reason however why we cannot consider that in certain circumstances the window size of the buffer is reduced to the situation at hand, and if we only need to produce one word, the buffer receives only one word. I see no real problem in using the scan copier, buffer, etc., in all this. We simply claim that in these circumstances the matrix at the Positional Level is narrowed down to the word, and that after the segments of the superficial representation are copied on to the syllabic templates, they are positioned into the matrix. I can not see the logic of suggesting a distinct production model, just to handle single word production for the laboratory tasks of naming, reading and repetition. Why not use the machinery of the normal cognitive system as used in typical settings and adjust that machinery in certain ways to be able to handle unreal language settings, such as responding in unnatural ways to the stimuli set forth by some examiner?

The last set of studies to be mentioned are Buckingham (1985, 1986, 1987a,b; and Buckingham and Yule 1987). In Buckingham (1985) the perseverative phonological paraphasias of fluent neologistic jargonaphasia is analysed in terms of Garrett's model, with Shattuck-Hufnagel's and Butterworth's mechanisms placed at the Positional Level. Buckingham (1986) presents more details regarding the characterization of phonemic paraphasias through the levels and computations in Garrett's model, while Buckingham (1987b) addresses more theoretical problems in the interpretation of the very bizarre-looking neologisms (called 'abstruse' in Lecours (1982); again, see Ch. 7 below on jargon for more details) in jargonaphasia. In this paper, there is further discussion of the principle of sonority and how it plays a role in determining the operation of the scan copier and the checkoff monitor in creating doublets in transposition errors. Finally, Buckingham and Yule (1987) present a detailed discussion of the problem of phonemic false evaluation, a problem that, if gone unappreciated, can lead to many incorrect analyses and interpretations in aphasia as well as in other domains of language analysis. If the hypothesis of phonemic false evaluation holds in the realm of phonemic substitutions that are of the so-called no source type, then we will have further reason to believe that there is simply no such thing as the pure, paradigmatic (no source) phonemic substitution, and, as mentioned above, this in turn would accord well with Shattuck-Hufnagel's (1979) theories.

Future directions

In order to avoid further misunderstanding and misrepresentation, investigators will have to take increasing care to avoid slips-of-the-ear and unwitting perceptual categorizations that lead to false interpretations of the intentional encoding of aphasic speakers. This will require increased attention and care in unassisted transcription of tape-recorded speech samples – especially in the 'fluent' aphasias, because in sensory aphasia, any subtle motoric aberrations that might affect the acoustic properties of speech sounds may go undetected because of the overall appearance of an unemcumbered articulatory flow in that population.

As we gain more knowledge of language through work in linguistics and psycholinguistics, future research will pay increased attention to underlying and deep-seated phonological principles that are at work in conditioning error typology. Accordingly, we will be able to go beyond mere observation and cataloguing to provide principled *explanations* of why certain errors occur. More work regarding CV phonology and principles such as the sonority hierarchy will continue to offer real explanations for phonological paraphasias.

Psycholinguistic models will continue to be pushed to their limits in the characterization of aphasic breakdown, and researchers will seek to discover precisely where those models work and where they do not. It is expected that new mechanisms will be suggested and placed into the total set of computations in models such as Garrett's. We have seen how devices such as the scan copier or the random generator have been placed into the set of mental computations at the Positional Level. More work will certainly be done with respect to additional operations at the level of the lexicon, which feeds into the Functional and the Positional levels. In a similar vein, slips-of-the-tongue will continue to be the focus of future research, and it is to be expected that from these studies we will gain further insight into the processes of aphasic derailments.

Increased inquiry will likely focus on more precise delineations of which aphasics produce more or less of which kinds of phonological paraphasias and why they do so. Localization of brain damage may help us understand some of the variable phenomena here, but future research will also have to consider the stimulus settings and elicitation procedures and techniques before one can say for sure just why some patients produce this or that type of phonological error, or why they produce more of one type of error on one task and more of another type of error on another task.

Finally, it is to be expected that out of much of the laboratory research will come new ideas for therapeutic intervention with aphasics. For instance, we have seen that a very salient aspect of phonological paraphasia is the abnormal amount of post-activation of phonological material. Perseveration (Buckingham *et al.* 1979; Buckingham 1985; Sandson and Albert 1984, 1987; Albert and Sandson 1986) is extremely widespread in most all of the aphasias and seems to result from damage to several different zones of the nervous system (thalamus, supplemental motor region, the frontal lobes, and the parietal lobes). It is also of several types: contiguous/close order reiteration vs. perseveration of units spread across larger stretches of material. Helm-Estabrooks *et al.* (1987) have reported on some new techniques they have devised to inhibit perseveration, which, if successful, will have a cascading effect in the overall rehabilitation of the aphasia in general. Additional new ideas for diagnosis and treatment in aphasia therapy have been reported in Lesser (1985) and Albert and Helm-Estabrooks (1988a, b). In the best of all possible worlds, sophisticated theory and research will ultimately point the way towards enlightened techniques for rehabilitative intervention. This is what we hope for the future.

References

Albert, M. L. and Helm-Estabrooks, N. (1988a) Diagnosis and treatment of aphasia. Part I. *Journal of the American Medical Association* **259**, 1043–7.

Albert, M. L. and Helm-Estabrooks, N. (1988b) Diagnosis and treatment of aphasia. Part II. *Journal of the American Medical Association* **259**, 1205–10.

Albert, M. L. and Sandson, J. (1986) Perseveration in aphasia. *Cortex* **22**, 103–15.

Beland, R. and Nespoulous, J.-L. (1985) *Recent Phonological Models of Aphasic Disorders*. Paper presented at The Academy of Aphasia, Pittsburgh, PA.

Beland, R., Caplan, D. and Nespoulous, J.-L. (1985) *Lexical Phonology and Performance Errors in a Conduction Aphasia Case*. Paper presented at the BABBLE Conference, Niagara Falls, Ontario.

Blumstein, S. E. (1973) *A Phonological Investigation of Aphasic Speech*. The Hague: Mouton.

Blumstein, S. E. (1978) Segment structure and the syllable in aphasia. In A. Bell and J. B. Hooper (eds), *Syllables and Segments*. Amsterdam: North-Holland.

Brown, J. W. (1972) *Aphasia, Apraxia and Agnosia*. Springfield, IL: C. C. Thomas.

Brown, J. W. (1988) *The Life of the Mind*. Hillsdale, NJ: Lawrence Erlbaum.

Buckingham, H. W. (1979) Explanation in apraxia with consequences for the concept of apraxia of speech. *Brain and Language* **8**, 202–26.

Buckingham, H. W. (1980) On correlating aphasic errors with slips-of-the-tongue. *Applied Psycholinguistics* **1**, 199–220.

Buckingham, H. W. (1983) Apraxia of language vs. apraxia of speech. In R. A. Magill (ed.), *Memory and Control of Action*. Amsterdam: North-Holland.

Buckingham, H. W. (1984) Early development of association theory in psychology as a forerunner to connection theory. *Brain and Cognition* **3**, 19–34.

Buckingham, H. W. (1985) Perseveration in aphasia. In S. Newman and R. Epstein (eds), *Current Perspectives in Dysphasia*. Edinburgh: Churchill Livingstone.

Buckingham, H. W. (1986) The scan-copier mechanism and the positional level of language production: Evidence from phonemic paraphasia. *Cognitive Science* **10**, 195–217.

Buckingham, H. W. (1987a) *The Principle of Sonority, Doublet Creation and the Checkoff Monitor*. Paper presented at the BABBLE Conference, Niagara Falls, Ontario.

Buckingham, H. W. (1987b) Phonemic paraphasias and psycholinguistic production models for neologistic jargon. *Aphasiology* **1**, 381–400.

Buckingham, H. W. and Kertesz, A. (1976) *Neologistic Jargon Aphasia*. Amsterdam: Swets & Zeitlinger.

Buckingham, H. W., Whitaker, H. and Whitaker, H. A. (1979) On linguistic perseveration. In H. Whitaker and H. A. Whitaker (eds), *Studies in Neurolinguistics*, Vol. 4. New York: Academic Press.

Buckingham, H. W. and Yule, G. (1987) Phonemic false evaluation: theoretical and clinical aspects. *Clinical Linguistics and Phonetics* **1**, 113–25.

Butterworth, B. (1979) Hesitation and the production of verbal paraphasias and neologisms in jargon aphasia. *Brain and Language* **8**, 133–61.

Canter, G., Trost, J. and Burns, M. (1985) Contrasting speech patterns in apraxia of speech and phonemic paraphasia. *Brain and Language* **24**, 204–22.

Caplan, D., Vanier, M. and Baker, C. (1986) A case study of reproduction conduction aphasia I: Word production. *Cognitive Neuropsychology* **3**, 99–128.

Caramazza, A., Miceli, G. and Villa, G. (1986) The role of the (output) phonological buffer in reading, writing, and repetition. *Cognitive Neuropsychology* **3**, 37–76.

Cutler, A. and Fay, D. (eds) (1978) Introduction. *Versprechen und Verlesen*. Amsterdam: J. Benjamins.

Eggert, G. (ed.) (1977) *Wernicke's Works on Aphasia: A Sourcebook and Review*. The Hague: Mouton.

Fay, D. and Cutler, A. (1977) Malapropisms and the structure of the mental lexicon. *Linguistic Inquiry* **8**, 505–20.

Friedrich, F. J., Glenn, C. and Marin, O. S. M. (1984) Interruption of phonological coding in conduction aphasia. *Brain and Language* **22**, 266–91.

Fromkin, V. A. (1971) The non-anomalous nature of anomalous utterances. *Language* **47**, 27–52.

Fromkin, V. A. (ed.) (1973) *Speech Errors as Linguistic Evidence*. The Hague: Mouton.

Fromkin, V. A. (ed.) (1980) *Errors in Linguistic Performance: Slips of the Tongue, Ear, Pen, and Hand*. New York: Academic Press.

Garrett, M. F. (1975) The analysis of sentence production. In B. Gorden (ed.), *The*

Psychology of Learning and Motivation: Advances in Research and Theory. New York: Academic Press.

Garrett, M. F. (1976) Syntactic processes in sentence production. In R. J. Wales and E. Walker (eds), *New Approaches to Language Mechanisms.* Amsterdam: North-Holland.

Garrett, M. F. (1982) Production of speech: Observations from normal and pathological language use. In A. W. Ellis (ed.), *Normality and Pathology in Cognitive Functions.* London: Academic Press.

Garrett, M. F. (1984) The organization of processing structure for language production: Applications to aphasic speech. In D. Caplan, A. R. Lecours and A. Smith (eds), *Biological Perspectives of Language.* Cambridge, Mass.: The MIT Press.

Garrett, M. F. (1988) Processes in language production. In F. Newmeyer (ed.), *Linguistics: The Cambridge Survey, III. Language: Psychological and Biological Aspects.* Cambridge: Cambridge University Press.

Harris, J. W. (1983) *Syllable Structure and Stress in Spanish: A Non-linear Analysis.* Cambridge, Mass.: The MIT Press.

Hartley, D. (1746) *Various Conjectures on the Perception, Motion, and Generation of Ideas.* Trans. from Latin by R. E. A. Palmer. Notes and introduction by M. Kallich. Reprinted by The Augustan Reprint Society. William Andrews Clark Memorial Library. Univ. of Calif., Los Angeles, 1959.

Helm-Estabrooks, N., Emery, P. and Albert, M. L. (1987) Treatment of aphasic perseveration (TAP) program: A new approach to aphasia therapy. *Archives of Neurology* **44**, 1253–5.

Jakobson, R. (1964) Towards a linguistic typology of aphasic impairments. In A. De Reuck and M. O'Connor (eds), *Disorders of Language.* London: Churchill.

Jakobson, R. (1980) *The Framework of Language.* Ann Arbor, MI: Michigan Studies in the Humanities.

Jakobson, R. and Halle, M. (1956) *Fundamentals of Language.* The Hague: Mouton.

Joanette, Y., Keller, E. and Lecours, A. R. (1980a) Sequences of phonemic approximations in aphasia. *Brain and Language* **11**, 30–44.

Joanette, Y., Keller, E., Viau, A. and Lecours, A. R. (1980b) Une approache dynamique a l'étude des séquences d'approximations phonémiques dans l'aphasie. *Grammatica* **7**, 217–37.

Kimura, D. (1982) Left-hemisphere control of oral and brachial movements and their relation to communication. *Philosophical Transactions of the Royal Society of London* **B298**, 135–49.

Kohn, S. (1984) The nature of the phonological disorder in conduction aphasia. *Brain and Language* **23**, 97–115.

Kohn, S. (1985) Phonological breakdown in aphasia. Unpublished doctoral dissertation. Boston: Tufts University.

Kohn, S. (1988) Phonological production deficits in aphasia. In H. Whitaker (ed.), *Phonological Processes and Brain Mechanisms.* New York: Springer-Verlag.

Kussmaul, A. (1877) *Die storungen der Sprache.* (Disturbances of Speech). Leipzig: Vogel. (Cited in Brown (1972) as: Kussmaul. 1877. Disturbances of Speech. *Cyclop. Pract. Med.* **14**, 581–875.)

Lecours, A. R. (1982) On neologisms. In J. Mehler, E. C. T. Walker and M. Garrett (eds), *Perspectives on Mental Representation: Experimental and Theoretical Studies of Cognitive Processes and Capacities.* Hillsdale, NJ: Lawrence Erlbaum.

Lecours, A. R. and Caplan, D. (1975) A review of 'A phonological investigation of aphasic speech' by S. E. Blumstein (1973). *Brain and Language* **2**, 237–54.

Lecours, A. R. and Lhermitte, F. (1969) Phonemic paraphasias: Linguistic structures and tentative hypotheses. *Cortex* **5**, 193–228.

Lecours, A. R. and Lhermitte, F. (1972) Recherches sur le langage des aphasiques: 4.

Analyse d'un corpus de néologismes; notion de paraphasie monémique. *Encephale* **61**, 295–315.

Lesser, R. (1985) Aphasia therapy in the early 1980's. In S. Newman and R. Epstein (eds), *Current Perspectives in Dysphasia*. Edinburgh: Churchill Livingstone.

Luria, A. R. (1970) *Traumatic Aphasia*. The Hague: Mouton.

Martinet, André (1964) *Elements of General Linguistics*. Chicago: University of Chicago Press.

Meringer, R. and Mayer, C. (1895) *Versprechen und verlesen, eine psychologisch-linguistische studie*. Stuttgart: Goschense Verlagsbuchhandlung.

Nespoulous, J.-L., Joanette, Y., Ska, B., Caplan, D. and Lecours, A. R. (1987) Production deficits in Broca's and conduction aphasia: repetition vs. reading. In E. Keller and M. Gopnik (eds), *Motor and Sensory Processes of Language*. Hillsdale, NJ: Lawrence Erlbaum.

Pick, A. (1931) *Aphasia*. Trans. by J. W. Brown. C. C. Thomas, 1973.

Potter, J. M. (1980) What was the matter with Dr. Spooner? In V. A. Fromkin (ed.), *Errors in Linguistic Performance: Slips of the Tongue, Ear, Pen, and Hand*. New York: Academic Press.

Roy, E. A. (1982) Action and performance. In A. W. Ellis (ed.), *Normality and Pathology in Cognitive Functions*. London: Academic Press.

Sandson, J. and Albert, M. L. (1984) Varieties of perseveration. *Neuropsychologia* **22**, 715–32.

Sandson, J. and Albert, M. L. (1987) Perseveration in behavioral neurology. *Neurology* **37**, 1736–41.

Schwartz, M. (1987) Patterns of speech production deficit within and across aphasia syndromes: Application of a psycholinguistic model. In M. Coltheart, G. Sartori and R. Job (eds), *The Cognitive Neuropsychology of Language*. London: Lawrence Erlbaum.

Shattuck-Hufnagel, S. (1979) Speech errors as evidence for a serial ordering mechanism in speech production. In W. E. Cooper and E. C. T. Walker (eds), *Sentence Processing: Psycholinguistic Studies Presented to Merill Garrett*. Hillsdale, NJ: Lawrence Erlbaum.

Shattuck-Hufnagel, S. (1987) The role of word-onset consonants in speech production planning: New evidence from speech error patterns. In E. Keller and M. Gopnik (eds), *Motor and Sensory Processes of Language*. Hillsdale, NJ: Lawrence Erlbaum.

Stemberger, J. P. (1982) The nature of segments in the lexicon: Evidence from speech errors. *Lingua* **56**, 235–59.

Stemberger, J. P. and Treiman, R. (1986) The internal structure of word-initial consonant clusters. *Journal of Memory and Language* **25**, 163–80.

Trubetzkoy, N. S. (1939/1969) *Principles of Phonology*. Trans. by C. A. M. Baltaxe. Berkeley and Los Angeles, CA: Univ. of California Press.

Wernicke, K. (1874) *Der aphasische Symptomencomplex; Eine psychologische studie auf anatomischer Basis*. Breslau: Cohn & Weigert.

Chapter 7

Jargonaphasia

Sarah S. Christman and Hugh W. Buckingham

Introduction

The language behaviour identified as neologistic jargonaphasia is an intriguing phenomenon that has inspired study since it was first defined by Bastian (1869) as 'a series of speech sounds without meaning' (Brown 1981). Although much is now known about the linguistic characteristics of that behaviour, the mechanisms underlying neologism genesis still engender controversy and resist unambiguous definition. This chapter will address current issues in neologistic jargonaphasia through an analysis of the frequently documented linguistic characteristics found in that syndrome. Discussion of the possible mechanisms underlying production of neologisms will be accomplished through exploration of two competing models in cognitive psychology: the hierarchical model of sentence production developed by Merrill Garrett (1975; 1976; 1980; 1982; 1984) and the interactive activation model of sentence production developed by McClelland and Rumelhart (1981) and Stemberger (1982; 1984; 1985).

Clinical and linguistic characteristics

Neologistic jargonaphasia is typically found in an adult with an acquired brain lesion in the posterior temporal lobe of the dominant language hemisphere (Schwartz 1987) and it may be associated with Wernicke's aphasia, conduction aphasia and transcortical sensory aphasia (Lecours and Rouillon 1976). The speech pattern of jargonaphasia is typically characterized as fluent, easily articulated and free of arthric qualities (Benson and Geschwind 1971; Buckingham 1982a; Buckingham and Kertesz 1976; Buckingham and Yule 1987; Wernicke 1874). However, recent research suggests that subtle motor difficulties may underly speech production in posterior aphasics (Blumstein *et al.* 1980; Buckingham and Yule 1987; MacNeilage *et al.* 1981; Tuller 1984) as evidence points to a greater motoric role for dominant posterior cortex (Ojemann 1983; Galaburda 1982, 1984; Amaducci *et al.* 1981; Glick and

Shapiro 1984). If so, the classical dichotomy that Broca's patients have phonetic control problems and Wernicke's patients have phoneme selection problems may be inadequate (Tuller 1984). A growing suspicion is that similar
linguistic phenomena may characterize all types of aphasias (Blumstein 1973;
MacNeilage 1982).

If motor difficulties are associated with posterior aphasia, then a listener
could inadvertently misidentify phonemes that a patient has selected. For
example, lesions in Wernicke's area typically yield a phonemic aphasia where
phonologic rather than phonetic programming is disturbed. Thus, a patient
may incorrectly select a phonemic category but subsequently correctly produce the phone for that phoneme (Buckingham 1982b). In this case, the
patient has selected the incorrect phoneme, and the listener would perceive it
as such. However, if subtle motor difficulties alter a patient's cue productions
of a correctly selected phoneme enough to cause categorical shifts in listener
perception, then listeners may falsely evaluate the patient's phonemic selections. Of course, an incorrect phoneme could be selected and also subsequently
phonetically altered, creating a phonological and a phonetic error. Therefore,
although it is difficult to find striking articulatory disruptions in posterior
aphasics, it is necessary to consider the possibility that speech production in
those patients may not be entirely error free. Although Buckingham and Yule
(1987) did not suggest that phonemic false evaluation played any confounding
role in the interpretation of neologisms, we do not want to rule it out —
especially if some neologisms can be said to arise from phonemic substitutions.

Speech production in the jargonaphasic has often been described as
logorrheic, with an irresistible press for speech and inability to self-monitor
(Buckingham and Kertesz 1976). In fact, the receptive aphasia of Wernicke's
patients often leaves them with comprehension deficits that render them
unable to link sound and meaning (Buckingham and Kertesz 1976; Naeser
1974; Lesser 1978) though they may not perform any worse than other aphasics on tests of phoneme perception (Naeser 1974). These patients may have
difficulty accessing the phonological representations of intended words even
when they are able to retrieve most of their meaning (Buckingham 1982b);
their aphasia is often masked by the production of neologisms; novel word
creations that sound bizarre and that have been described variously as nonsense
or gibberish. Quite often, the underlying word source is unidentifiable (Buckingham 1979; Schwartz 1987). Syntactic linguistic processes tend to remain
intact though some sentences are not necessarily well formed (Schwartz 1987).
Patients may correctly use anaphora and distinguish between identity of sense
and identity of reference (Buckingham 1979). They may correctly construct
complex grammatical structures involving sentential coordination and subor-
dination (Buckingham and Kertesz 1976) and correctly use syntactic morphology (Schwartz 1987) even as they violate selection restriction (Buckingham and Kertesz 1976) and affix selection rules (Caplan *et al.* 1972).
Examples of neologisms are presented in Table 7.1 (Buckingham 1981: p. 41).

By far the most puzzling characteristic of jargonaphasia is the neologism
and it is this to which we now turn our attention. Neologisms can be divided
into subtypes with implications for different accounts of their production
(Schwartz 1987: pp. 172–3). One subtype is synonymous with phonemic
paraphasia, such that any word-like form produced that is not in the lexicon

Table 7.1 Examples of neologisms

---

1. I [spo´li] but the labor of the speaker down here in New York.
2. You know, it's quite a [dɪ´səp`ai] the way I talked with him.
3. What is that [fæ´nəti] that [fɪts]?
4. I'd write the [mɛd] a [lɛdi] at the paper to the [æ´tətʃəbi] at the [tɛi´səmæ´dɪk].
5. The leg [vi´ltəd] from here down.
6. He [vɔ´ntd] the [də´rsɪz].
7. But they did have to [væn] my toes.
8. I never always forget the name of the [pei´ðə] when I call it.
9. This is the [krei´bəkræ´ks] where the [fɔ́dzəz] get out after the [tʃuw].
10. I used to be on [di´zɪ̆ks] on a [zi´dɪ̆k] on a [vi´zɪ̆ks].
11. I guess the [bu´lwi] the [wæ´lɪ̆k] and the [bi´li] is exactly, and then, of course, the [gi´fku].
12. No, it is not just a [dɔ´itʃ], it's not a [bɔ´it] or a [bi´vɪ̆k].

---

of the speaker's language may be termed a neologism (Butterworth 1979; Lecours 1982). A second subtype includes neologisms that contain recognizable pieces of real words from the speaker's language, as in the monemic (i.e. morphemic) paraphasias of Lecours and Rouillon (1976) and Lecours (1982). The third subtype is the 'abstruse' neologism (Lecours 1982), a term that refers to a form with no identifiable source in the speaker's native language. Buckingham and Kertesz (1976: p. 13) and Buckingham (1981: p. 40) have defined abstruse neologisms as 'phonological forms produced by the patient for which it is impossible to recover with any reasonable degree of certainty some single item or items in the vocabulary of the subject's language as it presumably existed prior to the onset of the disease'. These distinctions will be explored in more detail later when we explore the mechanisms underlying neologistic production.

In general, neologisms sound nonsensical but they are nevertheless actually highly rule-governed in form with respect to a speaker's language. An English speaker will produce novel words constructed only from phonemes in the inventory of his language and they will be constructed so as to obey the phonotactic constraints of English, which include rules about acceptable phoneme sequences and rules for stress assignment (Buckingham and Kertesz 1976; see also Ch. 6 above on phonological paraphasia). Neologisms also have a particular distribution, occurring in sentence locations marked for major lexical items and primarily replacing nouns and attributive adjectives (Lecours and Rouillon 1976). For example, Lecours (1982) analysed 447 abstruse neologisms in the connected speech of a Wernicke's aphasic and reported the following distributions: (i.e. neologisms occurring in the place of. . .) Nouns: 284 (63.5 per cent), Verbs 74 (16.6 per cent), Names 32 (7.2 per cent), Adjectives 27 (6.0 per cent), Unclassifiable 25 (5.6 per cent), Lexical Adverbs 5 (1.1 per cent). Some categories received no counts: articles, pronouns, prepositions, conjunctions, and relative pronouns. Although it is not always possible to determine which grammatical categories neologisms represent, especially if excessive productions are present, jargonaphasics typically have phrasal constructions sufficiently well defined to allow assignment (cf. Perecman and Brown 1981; Schwartz 1987). Butterworth (1979) reported that his patient K.F. exhibited classifiable neologisms for different grammatical categories as follows: Nouns (61 per cent), Verbs (20 per cent) and Adjectives (14 per cent). Similarly, Buckingham and Kertesz (1976) identified the following proportions of classifiable neologisms in their patient's (B.F.) speech: Nouns (73.6 per cent) and Verbs (23.6 per cent).

Apparently, major lexical content is more vulnerable to neologistic alteration than is the functor system, which explains why syntactic morphology is largely intact. Support for this argument is founded not only upon the distribution phenomena described above but also upon the operation of affixation processes, as when appropriate syntactic inflections are attached to neologistic root forms (e.g. Buckingham and Kertesz 1976; Butterworth 1979; Caplan *et al.* 1972; Lecours and Rouillon 1976). Even if the inflections are not correct, they are subject to application of morphophonemic 'accommodation' rules (Schwartz 1987). Because syntactic functor morphemes appear to be dissociated from neologisms, it is possible that they are accessed from a different location in the lexicon (cf. Bradley 1978) or are accessed in a different manner (i.e. as whole units rather than as conglomerations of separable segments) from content words (Schwartz 1987).

Miller and Ellis (1987) have presented an alternative explanation for this apparent content/functor word distinction by proposing that neologistic distribution trends may be accounted for by word frequency effects. They state that neologisms appear to occur less frequently for functors because they are more frequently used in the English language and are thus more easily activated for lexical retrieval than are the less frequently occurring content words. Therefore, they dismiss the often cited content/functor neologism distribution as an artifact of word frequency phenomena.

Although various possibilities have been suggested, the precise nature of 'the neologism-creating mechanism' is unclear and merits further discussion. One explanation for neologisms is that they result from severe phonemic distortions of the underlying phonological forms of target words. This view is seen in Brown (1977), Ellis (1985), Kertesz and Benson (1970), Lecours (1982) and Luria (1970), who generally describe abstruse neologisms as those resulting from phonemic distortions of words. Lecours (1982) defines the abstruse neologism as 'any word-like entity that cannot be positively identified as a phonemic paraphasia (or related entity), nor as a morphemic deviation'. This would imply that the patient is able to retrieve an intended word and access its phonemic array before subsequent distortion by excessive phonemic paraphasias (Buckingham 1982b, 1987; Lecours 1982). The degree of distortion would determine whether the neologism was recognizably target-related (few phonemic errors) or abstruse (excessive phonemic errors) and would thus account for all three subtypes of neologism (Buckingham 1987). If, in fact, all neologisms are created by one mechanism and differentiated by degree of distortion, then excessive phoneme errors might not be necessary for creation of the abstruse subtype. For example, if an aphasic attempts to produce an infrequently occurring word in his language and then distorts it via just one or two phonemic errors it may nevertheless render the word opaque to the hearer and thus appear abstruse (Ellis *et al.* 1983; Ellis 1985; Miller and Ellis 1987) *to him.*

One difficulty with a theory of quantitative distinction among neologisms is that, historically, phonemic paraphasias and neologisms have been treated as separate entities. Evidence for a qualitative difference among neologism subtypes is found in a Butterworth (1979) report that described a patient who often hesitated 250 msec or longer immediately before production of an abstruse neologism. Butterworth did not note these hesitations before production of either phonemic paraphasias or verbal paraphasias in his patients.

Additional support for qualitative distinctions among neologisms is found in phoneme frequency counts (Butterworth 1979). It appears that the distribution of phoneme frequencies for neologisms does not correspond to the phoneme frequency patterns found in normal English production. However, frequency counts for phonemic and verbal paraphasias do correspond to those of normal English. Butterworth concluded that some form of random segment or syllable generator could account for the random distribution of phonemic segments comprising abstruse neologisms (Buckingham 1987). Note that the randomness only pertains to the fact that the neologistic segments do not follow normal frequency distributions; they do abide by phonotactic constraints. So, the randomness is not helter skelter in any sense.

An important assumption underlying the concept of phonemic paraphasia as an explanation for neologistic production is the implied accessibility of the underlying phonological form prior to distortion (Buckingham 1979). Some word blends and hybrids are neologistic in final form even though the sources of their composition are recoverable. In these cases, however, lexical forms have been accessed and no word retrieval problem is evident. On the other hand, there is evidence that suggests that patients may not always be able to retrieve the appropriate phoneme arrays associated with a word they nevertheless understand (Butterworth *et al.* 1981; Buckingham 1979), and in many cases neologistic sources are not recoverable. Accordingly, some researchers have postulated an anomic component to jargonaphasia, such that a patient may not have in mind the word he desires at the time of neologism production (Buckingham and Kertesz 1974, 1976; Buckingham 1977, 1979, 1981, 1982b; Lecours and Lhermitte 1972; Pick 1931). For example, the hesitations noted in jargonaphasics prior to neologisms may indicate lexical access difficulties since pausing represents lexical search and mental processing activity (Butterworth 1979; see also Goldman-Eisler 1968). When periods following hesitation are filled by neologisms, they mask retrieval difficulty by acting as gap fillers and indicate unsuccessful access of lexical forms (Buckingham 1979, 1987; Buckingham and Kertesz 1974; Lecours and Rouillon 1976; Weinstein and Puig-Antich 1974). If phonological form retrieval (rather than phonological form distortion) is what is involved in the patient's word-finding difficulty, then explanation via phonemic paraphasia cannot account for subsequent neologism productions (Buckingham 1979, 1982b). The random segment or syllable generator mentioned above has potential as a second explanation of neologism production in this case.

The notion of a random root morpheme generator was first proposed by Butterworth (1979) to explain the production of neologisms when no underlying phonological form was available. The device worked by randomly selecting phonemes and ordering them into phonotactically acceptable sequences for subsequent placement into a buffer. The generator operated whenever form-based lexical retrieval was blocked and thus would function in conjunction with an underlying anomia. For example, if a patient were unable to retrieve the phonological form of a word, he might search unsuccessfully until some critical period passed after which the device would begin to randomly construct a word for production in place of the intended lexical item (usually a content word). Thus, the device could account for the genesis of a no-source abstruse neologism without recourse to explanation via phonemic paraphasia (Buckingham 1987). Buckingham (1981, 1982b, 1987) has suggested conceptualization of the device as a random syllable generator such that the minimal syllabic units manipulated by the device are already coded with appropriate language-specific phonotactic constraints. This characterization of the generator would eliminate the need to invoke subsequent phonotactic filtering mechanisms to ensure that the neologisms are pronounceable.

There is evidence to suggest that the random generator is a component of normal human cognition prior to brain damage rather than a 'de novo' device created post-morbidly, despite concerns expressed by Ellis (1985) to this effect. Normal speakers know the phonemic inventory of their language and the phonotactic rules that constrain its use (Buckingham 1987). In fact, phonotactics may be considered to be a 'hard-wired' aspect of the language system and thus relatively resistant to loss from brain damage when compared with other components of cognition (Sussman 1984). Although they typically access real lexical forms from a fully specified dictionary (Butterworth 1983), speakers are nevertheless able to use this system to create permissible new words and to judge the acceptability of newly encountered words even when they are not yet part of the language (Aronoff 1976; Butterworth 1983; Halle 1973, Vennemann, 1974). This knowledge of word formation rules is the likely database for operation of the random generator. Therefore, just as normal speakers are capable of creating permissible nonsensical strings at will (Garrett 1982), aphasic patients who are unable to retrieve phonological forms for intended words might draw upon their intact knowledge of word formation rules and create novel items in place of targets. However, these patients may not recognize their productions as non-words due to impaired comprehension and self-monitoring skills. Thus a normally little-used but nevertheless inherent component of cognition could be released into accelerated activity under circumstances of lexical access difficulties subsequent to brain damage (Buckingham 1987).

It is important to note that the random generator manipulates phonological material at a level dissociated from meaning, i.e. it handles general phonological information that is separate from the specific sets of phonemes associated with words in the lexicon. This concept is supported by the work of Clements and Keyser (1983), Sussman (1984), Van Lancker *et al.* (1983), and Perecman and Brown (1981).

A third proposed mechanism for jargon production considers the neologism to be the result of a two-stage error, which goes back to the work of Pick (1931). With explanation via phonemic paraphasia, it is assumed that the target word has been correctly selected with respect to meaning and phonological form with subsequent distortion of that form by varying quantities of phonemic paraphasias. However, it is possible that a patient could incorrectly select a word with respect to meaning and then modify that form through phonemic distortion (Brown 1972; Buckingham and Kertesz 1976; Lecours and Lhermitte 1972; Luria 1970; Pick 1931). Consequently, it is possible to have a combination of failure at lexical selection and at phonological implementation. Subsequent phonemic alteration of phonological forms associated with verbal paraphasias will easily render the target word unrecognizable because the error word would not fit the context in the first place (Buckingham 1981). A commonly noted behaviour among aphasics is that they may have more difficulty retrieving some word meanings than others. Phonological, emotive, contextual and perceptual factors can account for ease of word access, as can word frequency and grammatical influences (Lesser 1978). Word frequency may interact with word access in such a way as to account for some occurrences of two-stage errors as described below.

High frequency words may be more easily retrieved and more frequently produced than low frequency words in anomia (Buckingham 1982a). Rochford and Williams (1962, 1965) conducted a series of naming studies with results suggesting that high frequency of usage was the primary factor responsible for easy word access. Howes (1964) demonstrated that the word frequency distribution in aphasic speech actually resembles that used by normals although it often appears that aphasics use words of higher frequency in their language. Howes noted that this approximation of the normal curve is affected, however, by the severity of the aphasia and the quantity of brain damage. Beyn and Vlasenko (1974), in a verb-naming study, reported that patients with all degrees of Wernicke's aphasia often made dynamic word misnamings, reflecting the difficulty they had naming verb actions. Instead of intended targets, these patients sometimes produced novel words that also contained phonemic paraphasias (two-stage errors). One might predict that if high-frequency words facilitate retrieval, then fluent aphasics may produce more two-stage errors when attempting to access low-frequency words. As mentioned above, Miller and Ellis (1987) explain neologistic production on content words as resulting from the fact that content words are less frequent in occurrence than are function words.

Recovery patterns in aphasia often illuminate the processes at work in the production of neologisms (Alajouanine 1956; Buckingham 1981, 1987; Kertesz and Benson 1970; Peuser and Temp 1981). In early stages of jargon resolution, hesitations and pauses commonly precede the neologisms that mask word-finding blocks (Butterworth 1979). Neologisms and jargon are present when patients engage in discourse and when they answer questions (Weinstein and Puig-Antich 1974). As recovery progresses, they often show a significant reduction in neologisms with increased numbers of indefinite pronouns, definitions, circumlocutions, hesitations and confabulations (Buckingham and Kertesz 1976; Green 1969; Kertesz and Benson, 1970; Lecours and Joanette, 1980). They also produce stereotypic responses, clichés, malapropisms and puns instead of neologisms to fill gaps when word-finding difficulties exist (Weinstein and Puig-Antich 1974). After comprehension and self-monitoring skills improve patients still appear to have the severe word-finding difficulties resembling those of severe anomia (Buckingham 1981, 1987).

This type of recovery pattern lends support to the characterization of the neologism (via the random generator) as a function of word-retrieval difficulty rather than distortion by phonemic paraphasia. If the latter were the case, then patients would become more accurate in target production rather than more anomic. It is likely that anomia was always present but was masked by the gap-filling function of neologisms. As neologisms subside, the anomia becomes more evident (Buckingham 1987), but it has been present all along.

An alternative recovery pattern could be characterized by reduction in abstruse neologistic production with a corresponding increase in target-related neologisms (i.e. phonemic paraphasia). If recovery progressed to production of simple paraphasias and finally to elimination of all paraphasias, then the argument for phonemic distortion of phonological representations (by a mechanism such as scan-copier malfunction, to be discussed later) would be supported. No underlying anomia would be suggested. This second pattern of recovery, however, has not been clearly and unambiguously documented (Buckingham 1987).

In this section we have presented the common linguistic behaviours observed in jargonaphasia, with particular emphasis on possible origins of target-related and abstruse neologisms. Discussion has centred around questions concerning the availability of semantic and/or phonological representations for the different types of neologisms and, we have presented a mechanism capable of explaining neologistic production in the absence of phonological representations. However, this discussion has not drawn upon any particular model of sentence production. In the following sections, two diverse models will be described with reference as to how each may account for neologisms. The first is the hierarchical model developed by Merrill Garrett (1975, 1976, 1980, 1982, 1984, also sketched in Ch. 6 above on phonological paraphasia), and the second is the interactive activation model developed by McClelland and Rumelhart (1981), Stemberger (1982, 1984, 1985) and others.

The Garrett model

Arnold Pick (1931), Karl Lashley (1951), Freida Goldman-Eisler (1968) and Victoria Fromkin (1971) have, in various ways, contributed to the thinking involved in the construction of models of sentence production. Merrill Garrett, as well, has described sentence production more precisely as a collection of independent computational processes that correspond to one or more levels of linguistic representation. Analyses of slips of the tongue in normal speakers have provided the data base for Garrett's model. From these errors, inferences about the nature of underlying mental operations were made, but formal interpretations for some aspects of the model (such as the nature of the linguistic representations) have not yet been made (Garrett, 1980).

In general Garrett's model (1975, 1976, 1980, 1982, 1984) (Fig. 7.1) consists of 5 sets of computational processes that map levels of linguistic representations to each other in an hierarchical manner as follows:

Figure 7.1 A schematic diagram of the various representation levels and sets of computations that map one level onto another in the model constructed by Merrill
Garrett (see Chapter 6 in this book on phonological paraphasias for a more
detailed schematic of the computations that map the functional level onto
the positional level.)

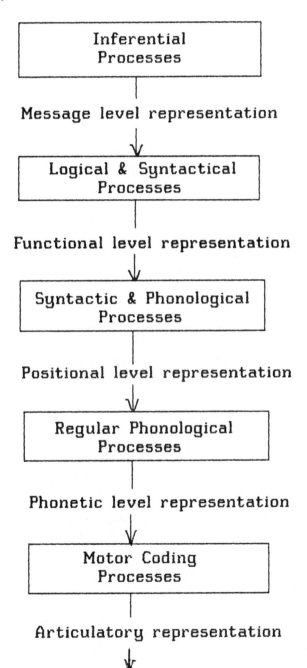

Inferential processes

These computations map conceptual structures to the Message level of representation. These are the high-level linguistic processes responsible for such activities as coding semantic states, determining the nature of speech acts and interpreting given/new information. They work in real time to help determine the very abstract form of sentence level constructions (Garrett 1982).

Logical/syntactic processes

These computations map the Message level to the Functional level of representation in 3 steps: (1) Functional argument structures for propositions are determined and deep case roles are assigned to arguments. (2) That portion of the lexicon containing word meanings (the 'first lexical lookup') is accessed to find the appropriate meanings for each predicate and argument in the planned sentence. At this level of the mental dictionary, phonological form is not specified. Vocabulary words are grouped with others of similar meaning. A linking address connects the first lexical lookup to the word destined for the second lexical lookup, which selects from the lexicon where words are represented in their underlying phonological forms. (3) Selected meaning-based lexical items are assigned to the functional argument structure in a logical rather than utterance order.

With respect to earlier discussions of neologistic production, some bizarre words may be created at this level when a patient is either unable to retrieve the meaning of an intended lexical item or unable to construct the linking address. Unable to access the word's meaning, he will also be unable to subsequently retrieve its phonological form. After a period of search, this situation may trigger the lower operation of the random generator to fill the gap created by the underlying meaning based access lexical retrieval disruption.

Syntactic/phonological processes

These computations map the Functional level to the Positional level of representation. Processes at this stage of production construct matrix-like phrasal planning frames that facilitate simultaneous positioning of lexical items and phonemes into utterance order sentence slots. An empty planning frame contains slots that are coded with respect to syllabic, grammatical and phrasal stress markers. When the phonological forms for retrieved content words are accessed from the second lexical lookup (by means of the linking address system), they are assigned appropriate slots according to their respective case and surface grammatical roles. Words fill the matrix as their phonemes are positioned into segment slots. Bound and free closed class morphemes, chosen from a separate portion of the lexicon (cf. Bradley 1978), are placed into the frame after content word assignment.

The random generator is thought to operate at the Positional level of representation. If information from the second lexical lookup were unavailable, perhaps due to a disrupted linking address system, then form-based lexical retrieval would be blocked even if lexical lookup number one remained intact. Novel words created to fill anomic gaps might be characterized by the alliteration and assonance found in jargonaphasia (Brown 1972; Green 1969) and could be explained by the operation of the random generator and failure of the scan copier mechanism (Buckingham 1987). Neologisms resulting from phonemic paraphasias could also be explained at this level as resulting from breakdowns in the normal operations of the buffer, scan copier, checkoff monitor and error monitor mechanisms described below (Shattuck-Hufnagel 1979, 1983).

During normal sentence production, phonological forms for content words retrieved from the second lexical lookup are placed into a holding buffer containing space for up to one clause. An error monitor checks for unusual segment patterns such as inappropriately doubled or tripled phoneme sequences so that if suspicious patterns are detected, participating segments will be removed from the buffer. At this point, syllabic slots in the planning frame (coded with respect to onsets, peaks and codas) are filled when the scan copier selects each remaining phoneme from the buffer and places it into an appropriate onset, peak or coda position of the matrix. Ambisyllabic consonant positions are specified and syllable markedness (Clements and Keyser 1983) is represented in a hierarchy progressing from least to most marked in the following sequence: CV, V, CVC and VC. After phonemes are deposited, a checkoff monitor eliminates copied segments from the buffer to ensure that repeated copying does not occur. This process is repeated for each word of the intended sentence (Buckingham 1986).

Neologisms at the positional level

1 Errors at various points in the process described above may produce neologisms in the following ways. If meaning-based retrieval from the first lexical lookup is blocked, it will be difficult to retrieve the appropriate corresponding phonological form from the second lexical lookup. There will be no input into the buffer and no phonemes available for the positional matrix. The random generator may then produce various syllable strings that serve as alternative input to the buffer and it will be those segments that will be positioned into the frame and realized ultimately as neologisms.

2 Alternatively, even if word access from the first lexical lookup is possible, a disrupted linking address system, may prevent retrieval of any phonological form from the second lexical lookup. With no phoneme input to the buffer, the random generator may create abstruse neologisms in the same manner as described above. Either account (lexical-semantic anomia or linking address difficulty anomia) can explain neologism production only with the assumption of something like the random generator (Buckingham 1987).

3 Other characterizations of neologistic creation are definable within this model. First, correct access of an underlying word form from the first lexical lookup and also correct retrieval of the corresponding phoneme array from the second lexical lookup may be possible. This input is fed into the buffer, but as a result of severe scan copier malfunction, the phonological form

becomes so distorted (via phonemic paraphasias) that the target word is rendered neologistic. Depending on the degree of distortion, the neologism will be identifiably either target-related or abstruse. Examples of scan copier malfunctions are exemplified by the phoneme anticipations, substitutions and exchanges seen with literal paraphasias, created as the scan copier misorders information from the buffer into positional slots (see Ch. 6 above on paraphasia for more details). Thus, the random generator and scan copier mechanisms can account for both major theories of neologism production: genesis by underlying anomia with no access to correct underlying form, adumbrating the random generator and genesis from distortion by phonemic paraphasia, foreshadowing the scan copier.

4 Second, it is possible to have correct access of underlying word meaning from the first lexical lookup but then, through a disrupted linking address system, access an incorrect word, either within the semantic sphere or not. This word could be fed into the buffer, and scan copier derailment could occur, a neologism being created.

5 There may be two simultaneously selected words that share meaning – the blended form being placed in the buffer. Subsequent scanning errors here would likely lead to neology. Neologisms could result from excessive disruptions in the error monitor that functions before scan copier operation. If the error monitor were overly sensitive to repeated sequences of phonemes, i.e. those that do not represent extraneous additions but rather that are normal (in words such as *committee*, or *Tallahassee*), then it might delete desired segments from the buffer before they could be copied and placed in the positional frame. An example of this is seen with doublet pair destruction (Lecours and Lhermitte 1969). Severe hyper-sensitivity of the error monitor could severely distort correct phonological forms placed in the buffer by a here-to-fore correctly operating system. Dell (1984) has demonstrated that repeated phonemes can induce scan copier errors.

6 Combined malfunction of scan copier and checkoff monitor operations could also explain neologism creation via phonemic paraphasia distortion and can best be illustrated by doublet creation and perseverative phoneme transformation phenomena (Lecours and Lhermitte 1969). If the scan copier correctly copied a segment and placed it in the phrasal frame but then the checkoff monitor failed to delete the copied segment from the buffer, then that segment may be re-copied and doublet creation and/or other perseverative behaviours noted.

7 Perseveration as a mechanism of neology is not a new idea (Buckingham 1985; Buckingham and Kertesz 1976; Buckingham *et al.* 1978, 1979; Brown 1972; Butterworth 1979; Green 1969; Lecours and Lhermitte 1969). Green (1969), Buckingham (1985) and Buckingham *et al.* (1978) demonstrated how neologisms might be created from successive recombinations of phonological material that was itself neologistic in nature. Butterworth (1979) reported a patient whose neologisms seemed overwhelmingly characterized by phonological material related to prior neologistic productions. If perseveration occurred from reiteration by the scan copier, then repeated distortions of target phoneme arrays by literal paraphasias would be created, and the disruption would rest with the memory mechanism of the buffer – little would be checked off. Butterworth (1979) places a memory component with the

random generator, and so items held on too long would be reiteratively placed into the buffer.

Neologisms are normally inflected for the most part, the functor morphemes having their proper allomorphs. The phonetics is also intact – the phonemes having their proper allophones. All of this implies that the regular phonological processes and the motor coding processes are normal and are not involved in the genesis of neologisms.

It is evident that the additional mechanisms proposed by Butterworth and Shattuck-Hufnagel can be easily fit into Garrett's hierarchical model of sentence production and can contribute to production of neologisms in Wernicke's patients with jargonaphasia. This is not, however, the only model with explanatory power for the various phenomena under discussion. For an alternative perspective, we turn to the interactive activation model of language production.

Interactive activation model

The parallel model developed by McClelland and Rumelhart (1981), described with respect to aphasia by Stemberger (1985) and Miller and Ellis (1987) was developed, in part, to capture the simultaneous nature of cognitive processing that had not been adequately represented in so-called serial processing models. Two weaknesses of serial models were that, first, they failed to provide an account of interactions between levels in the form of feedback, and, second, they postulated that processing at one level of complexity must be completed before processing at the next level could begin (Stemberger 1985). Although Garrett's model is more serial in organization than the interactive activation model, Garrett himself acknowledges (1976: p. 236) that 'the levels of sentence planning are simultaneously active, but that each may be at different temporal stages of progress vis à vis the final articulatory level target'. His model does not necessarily rule out the possibility of feedback mechanisms, although feedback is not explicitly described in Garrett's work. Although the relative merits and weaknesses of hierarchical vs. parallel models are presently under close scrutiny, both are nevertheless able to account for some of the phenomena in neologistic production that have been the focus of discussion. The following is a general introduction to some of the concepts underlying the interactive activation model.

Within a parallel processing framework, all cognitive systems including language, are the product of the coordinated activities of an activated network composed of units whose only purpose is to collect, sum and transmit activation to each other along their interconnecting links. The analogy is drawn between units/links and neurons/synapses without any claim for isomorphism. Activation is the force that drives the system and determines which pathways will be traversed during any particular operation. System complexity is determined by the nature of the interconnections and interactions between units (Stemberger 1985).

Activation (activity) levels may vary from very low (no processing) to intermediate (partial activation) to very high (execution) for each unit. A characteristic resting level of activation (determined in part by frequency of unit use) must be exceeded before a unit can be excited and it is to this level that a unit returns afterward. Highly activated units have powerful activation and inhibition effects on other units, and vice versa, so that activation is eventually spread proportionately throughout the system along the most highly activated pathways from target node to target node. Pathway weightings mediate the strength of the effect of one particular node upon another. The patterns of weighted activating and inhibiting pathways chosen during language processing will ultimately lead to the production of different language behaviours (Stemberger 1985).

Language production results from parallel interactions among the pathways linking nodes at semantic, lexical, syntactic, segmental, featural and motoric levels of processing. The entire process originates when a speaker's communicative intents feed into the permanent memory system (where language information is stored) in chunks that may be as large as a clause or a sentence. Semantic and pragmatic units are activated, which in turn activate words at the lexical level (McClelland 1979). Once a word is selected, it passes its activation to all other units connected to it in a cascading manner such that associated phonemes and features are activated as well. Appropriate motor units will eventually be chosen to effect articulation of intended words. Activation also spreads to prior levels in the system in the form of positive feedback. This basic pattern of activity recurs for every word in the intended utterance (Stemberger 1985, Miller and Ellis 1987).

It is crucial to note that inhibition of non-target nodes is just as important as the activation of target nodes. During lexical access, for example, all words containing *any* of the intended semantic features will be activated to some degree. However, only a word containing *all* of the required semantic features will receive activation levels high enough to trigger execution. Those words will, in turn, inhibit all other partially activated words so that only intended targets will ultimately be produced (Stemberger 1985).

The level of lexical access at this point appears primarily and initially to be meaning-based. If the activation procedure were disrupted in some way, as would likely be the case with brain damage, then lexical access would be difficult or faulty. If activation pathways were destroyed or completely blocked, lexical retrieval might be impossible, at least until alternative pathways could be established. This situation resembles that of underlying anomia for meaning-based lexical retrieval. If, however, target words were able to receive activation, but at weakened levels, then they may not have sufficient activation strength to inhibit retrieval of unwanted but similar lexical items. This situation could account for the creation of semantic paraphasias (Stemberger 1985).

Analogous processes operate at the phonological level, which is composed of segmental and featural sublevels. Normally, highly activated lexical items will simultaneously activate the appropriate sets of segments, phonetic features and motor units associated with them as language production progresses. Likewise, as activation reaches the phonological level, it can flow back to the lexicon and influence word retrieval even as it is occurring. Thus, the parallel nature of the system is revealed by this interaction among levels. However, if a disrupted system prevented access from the meaning-based lexicon, then activation of phonemes, features and motor units would be disrupted for intended words. If access to the meaning-based lexicon were possible, but weak, then activated words would send weak levels of activation to segment, featural and motoric levels. In that case, two possibilities exist. The first is that correct arrays of segments and features may still be activated, in which case no error would be created. But, if weak levels of activation for phoneme targets not only reduced the accuracy with which they were selected but also reduced their ability to inhibit minimally distinct phonemes, (i.e. those that share most features with the target), then a mechanism for the creation of literal (phonemic) paraphasias would exist. Varying degrees of paraphasia could account for the creation of both target-related and abstruse neologisms.

The genesis of two-stage neologisms could be handled by this model as well. If semantic paraphasias (generated via the mechanism described above) only weakly activated associated phonological arrays, low-strength inhibition could fail to extinguish nodes for similar phonemes, and the result would be literal paraphasias transforming lexical paraphasias – the two-stage error. The degree of distortion would again render the neologism either target-relatable or abstruse.

Miller and Ellis (1987) describe neologisms as the product of difficulty activating lexical items in the speech lexicon. Reduced lexical activation levels yield weakened activations at all lower levels in the system as well. They propose that high-frequency words in the language (such as functors) can be more easily accessed and more often correctly produced than low-frequency words (such as content words) because their resting levels of activation are higher from repeated use during normal production. This, they argue, is why there are no neologistic function words.

As repeated attempts at low-frequency words are made, some phonemes in targets will be correct; proper segments having been discriminable from interfering background noise in the system. Other phoneme slots, however, will be filled with incorrect segments that could not be inhibited. According to Miller and Ellis, these substitutions will be somewhat random although consonants and vowels will remain in appropriate syllabic positions. They found that the neologisms produced by their patient, R.D., occurred most often on words he had infrequently used before his aphasia. They also discovered that there was no phonetic similarity effect conditioning the occurrence of phoneme selection errors. Phoneme transpositions were present at only a chance level of occurrence.

Miller and Ellis account for the commonly observed perseveration phenomena in jargon patients by suggesting that non-target phonemes will, once selected, acquire increasing amounts of activation and thus become dominant over other non-target phonemes in the inventory. If a patient is unable to activate phonemes for a particular word, then previously used incorrect alternatives will still have relatively high levels of activation from prior use and will most likely be repeatedly selected.

Thus far, accounts of neologisms via the interactive activation model have exclusively adopted the 'neologism as paraphasic distortion' perspective presented earlier in this chapter. Discussion has not addressed the occasion where phonological arrays are not available at all even though a lexical selection has been made. In that case, activation cascading from the lexical levels could randomly activate whichever phonemes happened to have the highest resting levels at the time of need. Initially, the phoneme strength settings would – or should – correlate directly with phoneme frequency counts of the language. But, we know from Butterworth (1979) that abstruse neologisms are comprised of phonemes that do not accord with the frequency statistics. So, interactive activation theories would have to come up with a non-phoneme frequency explanation for the segmental composition of neologisms. One thing interactive accounts could look for would be on-line momentary high levels of strength at the nodes of phonemes very recently produced, prior to the lexical (semantic) access block. Undirected vollies of activation would then find their way to these nodes (syllable structure still being controlled for), and they would reach activation – a neologism thereby unfolding. The perseverative nature of neologisms would fit this account fairly well, even more so as the jargon responding becomes increasingly alliterative and assonantial (Green 1969; Buckingham *et al.* 1978).

So, whereas in our serial view, the random generator would produce a bizarre looking string of phonemes, interactive activation models would postulate undirected or very weak vollies coming from the lexical level, which would activate sets of phoneme nodes that had high momentary resting levels – not because the required lexical node was activated – but because prior production of other lexical items in the utterance up to the lexical block had recently activated the phonemes.

Summary and conclusions

This chapter has presented some of the most commonly described clinical and linguistic features of jargonaphasia. Explanations for a most interesting and salient feature of the disorder, the production of neologisms, have depended on assumptions made about the availability of meaning-based lexical items and their associated phonological forms. Discussions have been presented both in general and in the context of two rather different models of sentence production: the hierarchical model developed by Merrill Garrett (1975, 1976, 1980, 1982, 1984) and the interactive activation model developed by McClelland and Rumelhart (1981) and extended by Stemberger (1985).

Several important differences between the two models presented here merit mention: (1) Scan copying devices, checkoff monitors, error monitors, random generators and the like create complexity, whereas with interactive activation, complexity is assumed to be inherent in the interconnections. (2) Phonological processing can interact with and influence semantic selection processes in the parallel model. The interaction is not as clear-cut in Garrett's model, since he stresses that word-meaning appreciation occurs first – phonological form being accessed subsequently. (3) There are several different levels of syntax in the Garrett model, whereas interactive activation posits basically one level. (4) Garrett's model is intentional and message driven. These factors, in the words of Fodor (1986), represent a 'nuisance' for interactive activation. (5) The mental processes of interactive activation are largely associative; Garrett's are computational. (6) Interactive activation may provide an account of the neural structures in which cognitive systems are ultimately *implemented*, but models like Garrett's work better at the cognitive level where there is a commitment to mental computations that manipulate symbols that are semantically interpretable and that have a syntax (Fodor and Pylyshyn 1988).

Despite these differences, both models in their own way have been able to offer accounts for various phenomena in neology. Further investigation of normal and abnormal language processing, and further probing of the models will undoubtedly lead to a greater understanding of the nature of language breakdown inherent in neologistic jargonaphasia.

References

Alajouanine, T. (1956) Verbal realization in aphasia. *Brain* **79**, 1–28.

Amaducci, L., Sorbi, S., Albanese, A. and Gianotti, G. (1981) Choline-acetyltransfer-ase (ChAT) activity differs in right and left human temporal lobes. *Neurology* **31**, 799–805.

Aronoff, M. (1976) *Word Formation in Generative Grammar*. Cambridge, Massachusetts: The MIT Press.

Bastian, C. (1869) On the various forms of loss of speech in cerebral disease. *British and Foreign Medical-Chirurgical Review* **45**, 158–80; 293–329.

Benson, D. F. and Geschwind, N. (1971) Aphasia and related cortical disturbances. In A. B. Baker and L. H. Baker (eds), *Clinical Neurology*. New York: Harper.

Beyn, E. S. and Vlasenko, I. T. (1974) Verbal paraphasis of aphasic patients in the course of naming actions. *British Journal of Disorders of Communication* **9**, 24–34.

Blumstein, S. E. (1973) *A Phonological Investigation of Aphasic Speech*. The Hague: Mouton.

Blumstein, S. E., Cooper, W. E., Goodglass, H., Statlender, S. and Gottlieb, J. (1980) Production deficits in aphasia: A voice onset time analysis. *Brain and Language* **9**, 153–70.

Bradley, D. B. (1978) *Computational Distinctions of Vocabulary Type*. PhD Dissertation, M.I.T., Cambridge, MA.

Brown, J. W. (1972) *Aphasia, Apraxia and Agnosia: Clinical and Theoretical Aspects*. Springfield, Illinois: Charles C. Thomas.

Brown, J. W. (1977) *Mind, Brain and Consciousness: The Neuropsychology of Cognition*. New York: Academic Press.

Brown, J. W. (1981) *Jargonaphasia*. New York: Academic Press.

Buckingham, H. W. (1977) The conduction theory and neologistic jargon. *Language and Speech* **20**, 174–84.

Buckingham, H. W. (1979). Linguistic aspects of lexical retrieval disturbances in the posterior fluent aphasias. In H. Whitaker and H. A. Whitaker (eds), *Studies in Neurolinguistics*, Vol. 4. New York: Academic Press.

Buckingham, H. W. (1981) Where do neologisms come from? In J. W. Brown (ed.), *Jargonaphasia*, pp. 39–62. New York: Academic Press.

Buckingham, H. W. (1982a) Neuropsychological models of language. In N. Lass, L. McReynolds, J. Northern and D. Yoder (eds), *Speech, Language, and Hearing: Normal Processes*, Vol. 1, pp. 323–47. Philadelphia: W. B. Saunders.

Buckingham, H. W. (1982b) Critical issues in the linguistic study of aphasia. In N. Lass (ed.), *Speech and Language: Advances in Basic Research and Practice*, Vol. 8, pp. 313–37. New York: Academic Press.

Buckingham, H. W. (1985) Perseveration in aphasia. In S. Newman and R. Epstein (eds), *Current Perspectives in Dysphasia*. Edinburgh: Churchill Livingstone.

Buckingham, H. W. (1986) The scan-copier mechanism and the positional level of language production: evidence from phonemic paraphasia. *Cognitive Science* **10**, 195–217.

Buckingham, H. W. (1987) Review: Phonemic paraphasias and psycholinguistic production models for neologistic jargon. *Aphasiology* **1**, 381–400.

Buckingham, H. W. and Kertesz, A. (1974) A linguistic analysis of fluent aphasia. *Brain and Language* **1**, 43–62.

Buckingham, H. W. and Kertesz, A. (1976) *Neologistic Jargon Aphasia*. Amsterdam: Swets & Zeitlinger.

Buckingham, H. W., Whitaker, H. and Whitaker, H. A. (1978) Alliteration and assonance in neologistic aphasia. *Cortex* **14**, 365–80.

Buckingham, H. W., Whitaker, H. and Whitaker, H. A. (1979). On linguistic perseveration. In H. Whitaker and H. A. Whitaker (eds), *Studies in Neurolinguistics*, Vol 4, pp. 329–52. New York: Academic Press.

Buckingham, H. W. and Yule, G. (1987) Phonemic false evaluation: Theoretical and clinical aspects. *Clinical Linguistic and Phonetics* **1**(2), 113–25.

Butterworth, B. (1979) Hesitation and the production of verbal paraphasias and neologisms in jargon aphasia. *Brain and Language* **18**, 133–61.

Butterworth, B. (1983) Lexical representation. In B. Butterworth (ed.), *Language Production 2: Development, Writing and Other Language Processes*. London: Academic Press.

Butterworth, B., Swallow, J. and Grimston, M. (1981) Gestures and lexical processes in jargonaphasia. In J. W. Brown (ed.), *Jargonaphasia*, pp. 113–23. New York: Academic Press.

Caplan, D., Kellar, L. and Locke, S. (1972) Inflection of neologisms in aphasia. *Brain* **95**, 169–72.

Clements, G. N. and Keyser, S. J. (1983) *CV Phonology: A Generative Theory of the Syllable*. Cambridge, Massachusetts: MIT Press.

Dell, G. (1984) Representation of serial order in speech: Evidence from the repeated phoneme effect in speech errors. *Journal of Experimental Psychology: Learning, Memory and Cognition* **10**, 222–33.

Ellis, A. W. (1985) The production of spoken words: A cognitive neuropsychological perspective. In A. W. Ellis (ed.), *Progress in the Psychology of Language*, Vol. 2. London: Lawrence Erlbaum Associates.

Ellis, A. W., Miller, D. and Sin, G. (1983) Wernicke's aphasia and normal language processing: A case study in cognitive neuropsychology. *Cognition* **15**, 111–44.

Fodor, J. A. (1986) Information and association. In M. Brand and R. M. Harnish (eds), *The Representation of Knowledge and Belief*, pp. 80–100. Tucson, Arizona: University of Arizona Press.

Fodor, J. A. and Pylyshyn, Z. W. (1988) Connectionism and cognitive architecture: A critical analysis. *Cognition* **28**, 1–72.

Fromkin, V. A. (1971) The non-anomalous nature of anomalous utterances. *Language* **47**, 27–52.

Galaburda, A. M. (1982) Histology, architectonics, and asymmetry of language areas. In M. A. Arbib, D. Caplan and J. C. Marshall (eds), *Neural Models of Language Processes*. New York: Academic Press.

Galaburda, A. M. (1984) Anatomical asymmetries. In N. Geschwind and A. M. Galaburda (eds), *Cerebral Dominance: The Biological Foundations*. Cambridge, Massachusetts: Harvard University Press.

Garrett, M. F. (1975) The analysis of sentence production. In G. Bower (ed.), *Psychology of Learning and Motivation*, Vol. 9, pp. 133–77. New York: Academic Press.

Garrett, M. F. (1976) Syntactic processes in sentence production. In R. J. Wales and E. Walker (eds), *New Approaches to Language Mechanisms*, pp. 231–56. Amsterdam: North Holland.

Garrett, M. F. (1980) Levels of processing in sentence production. In B. Butterworth (ed.), *Language Production. Vol. 1: Speech and Talk*, pp. 177–220. London: Academic Press.

Garrett, M. F. (1982) Production of speech: Observations from normal and pathological language use. In E. Ellis (ed.), *Normality and Pathology in Cognitive Functions*, pp. 19–76. London: Academic Press.

Garrett, M. F. (1984) The organization of processing structure for language production: Applications to aphasic speech. In D. Caplan, A. R. Lecours and A. Smith (eds), *Biological Perspectives on Language*, pp. 172–93. Cambridge, MA: The MIT Press.

Glick, S. D. and Shapiro, R. M. (1984) Functional and neurochemical asymmetries. In N. Geschwind and A. M. Galaburda (eds), *Cerebral Dominance: The Biological Foundations*. Cambridge, Massachusetts: Harvard University Press.

Goldman-Eisler, F. (1968) *Psycholinguistics*. London: Academic Press.

Green, E. (1969) Phonological and grammatical aspects of jargon in an aphasic patient: a case study. *Language and Speech* **12**, 103–18.

Halle, M. (1973) Prolegomena to a theory of word formation. *Linguistic Inquiry* **4**, 3–16.

Howes, D. (1964) Application of the word frequency concept to aphasia. In A. V. S. De Reuck and N. O'Connor (eds), *Disorders of Language*. London: Churchill.

Kertesz, A. and Benson, D. F. (1970) Neologistic jargon: A clinicopathological study. *Cortex* **6**, 362–86.

Lashley, K. S. (1951) The problem of serial order in behavior. In L. A. Jeffress (ed.), *Cerebral Mechanisms in Behavior*. New York: Wiley.

Lecours, A. R. (1982) On neologisms. In J. Mehler, E. C. T. Walker and M. F. Garrett (eds), *Perspectives on Mental Representation*. Hillsdale, New Jersey: Lawrence Erlbaum Associates.

Lecours, A. R. and Joanette, Y. (1980) Linguistic and other psychological aspects of paroxysmal aphasia. *Brain and Language* **10**, 1–23.

Lecours, A. R. and Lhermitte, F. (1969) Phonemic paraphasias: Linguistic structures and tentative hypotheses. *Cortex* **5**, 193–228.

Lecours, A. R. and Lhermitte, F. (1972) Recherches sur le langage des aphasiques: 4. Analyse d'un corpus de néologismes: notion de paraphasie monémique. *L'Encephale* **61**, 295–315.

Lecours, A. R. and Rouillon, F. (1976) Neurolinguistic analysis of jargonaphasia and jargonagraphia. In H. Whitaker and H. Whitaker (eds), *Studies in Neurolinguistics*, Vol. 2, pp. 95–144. New York: Academic Press.

Lesser, R. (1978) *Linguistic Investigations of Aphasia (Studies in Language Disability and Remediation 4)*. New York: Elsevier.

Luria, A. R. (1970) *Traumatic Aphasia*. The Hague: Mouton.

McClelland, J. L. (1979) On the time relations of mental processes: An examination of systems of processes in cascade. *Psychological Review* **86**, 287–330.

McClelland, J. L. and Rumelhart, D. E. (1981) An interactive activation model of context effects in letter perception. Part 1. An account of basic findings. *Psychological Review* **88**, 375–407.

MacNeilage, P. F. (1982) Speech production mechanisms in aphasia. In S. Grillner, B. Lindblom, J. Lubker and A. Persson (eds), *Speech Motor Control*. Oxford: Pergamon Press.

MacNeilage, P. F., Hutchinson, J. A. and Lasater, S. A. (1981) The production of speech: Development and dissolution of motoric and premotoric processes. In J. Long and A. Baddeley (eds), *Attention and Performance IX*. Hillsdale, New Jersey: Lawrence Erlbaum Associates.

Miller, D. and Ellis, A. W. (1987) Speech and writing errors in 'neologistic jargonaphasia': A lexical activation hypothesis. In M. Coltheart, G. Sartori and R. Job (eds), *The Cognitive Neuropsychology of Language*, pp. 253–71. London: Lawrence Erlbaum Associates.

Naeser, M. A. (1974) *The Relationship between Phoneme Discrimination, Phoneme Picture Perception and Language Comprehension in Aphasia.* Paper presented to the American Academy of Aphasia, Virginia.

Ojemann, G. A. (1983) Brain organization for language from the perspective of electrical stimulation mapping. *The Behavioral and Brain Sciences* 6, 189–230.

Perecman, E. and Brown, J. W. (1981) Phonemic jargon: A case report. In J. W. Brown (ed.), *Jargonaphasia*, pp. 177–258. New York: Academic Press.

Peuser, G. and Temp, K. (1981) The evolution of jargonaphasia. In J. W. Brown (ed.), *Jargonaphasia*, pp. 259–94. New York: Academic Press.

Pick, A. (1931) *Aphasia.* Trans. J. W. Brown. Springfield: Thomas.

Rochford, G. and Williams, M. (1962) Studies in the development and breakdown of the use of names, I: The relationship between nominal dysphasia and the acquisition of vocabulary in childhood. II. Experimental production of naming disorders in normal people. *Journal of Neurology, Neurosurgery and Psychiatry* 25, 222–33.

Rochford, G. and Williams, M. (1965) IV: The effects of word frequency. *Journal of Neurology, Neurosurgery and Psychiatry* 28, 407–13.

Schwartz, M. (1987) Patterns of speech production deficit within and across aphasia syndromes: Application of a psycholinguistic model. In N. Coltheart, G. Sartori and R. Job (eds), *The Cognitive Neuropsychology of Language*, pp. 163–99. London: Lawrence Erlbaum Associates.

Shattuck-Hufnagel, S. (1979) Speech errors as evidence for a serial-ordering mechanism in sentence production. In W. E. Cooper and E. C. T. Walker (eds), *Sentence Processing: Psycholinguistic Studies Presented to Merrill Garrett.* Hillside, New Jersey: Lawrence Erlbaum Associates.

Shattuck-Hufnagel, S. (1983) Sublexical units and suprasegmental structure in speech production planning. In P. F. MacNeilage (ed.), *The Production of Speech.* New York: Springer-Verlag.

Stemberger, J. P. (1982) *The Lexicon in a Model of Language Production.* Unpublished doctoral dissertation. University of California at San Diego, USA.

Stemberger, J. P. (1984) Structural errors in normal and agrammatic speech. *Cognitive Neuropsychology* 1, 281–313.

Stemberger, J. P. (1985) An interactive activation model of language production. In A. W. Ellis (ed.), *Progress in the Psychology of Language*, Vol. 1. London: Lawrence Erlbaum Associates.

Sussman, H. M. (1984) A neuronal model for syllable representation. *Brain and Language* 22, 167–77.

Tuller, B. (1984) On categorizing speech errors. *Neuropsychologia* 22, 547–58.

Van Lanker, D. R., Bogen, J. E. and Canter, G. J. (1983) A case report of pathological rule-governed syllable intrusion. *Brain and Language* 20, 12–20.

Vennemann, T. (1974) Words and syllables in natural generative grammar. In A. Bruck, R. Fox and M. LeGaly (eds), *Papers from the Parasession on Natural Phonology.* Chicago: Chicago Linguistic Society.

Weinstein, E. A. and Puig-Antich, J. (1974) Jargon and its analogues. *Cortex* 10, 75–83.

Wernicke, C. (1874) The aphasia symptom complex: A psychological study on an anatomical basis. Reprinted in G. H. Eggert (ed.), *Wernicke's Works on Aphasia.* The Hague: Mouton, 1977.

Chapter 8

Apraxia of Speech

Niklas Miller

Apraxia of speech is only one of a group of disorders which carry the label dyspraxia (Miller 1986). A general definition of dyspraxia is a disturbance in the programming and execution of learned volitional, purposeful movements in the presence of normal primary motor and sensory function and in the absence of any visual-perceptual, dysphasic, attentional, motivational or intellectual dysfunction. As well as diagnosis by exclusion, characteristic error patterns (see Miller 1986 for non-speech dyspraxias; Square-Storer 1989, for speech) help identify dyspraxia by inclusion. Although the label *a*praxia of speech is retained here in keeping with general usage the term *dys*praxia is preferred as being more accurate, since most patients retain some action capability, which is partially disordered, rather than have total loss of capability.

By analogy with the general criteria identifying dyspraxia, apraxia of speech has been defined as a sensorimotor impairment of the capacity to select, programme and/or execute coordination, timed sequencing and positioning of the speech musculature for the volitional production of speech sounds. Loss or impairment of phonological rules and weakened or misdirected action of specific muscle groups are not adequate to explain the disorder (Wertz *et al.* 1984).

However, clearcut as this appears, almost every word brings questions and controversies.

A brief historical note

None of these controversies is new. They have been hotly contested for over 150 years and today's questions are part of the ebb and flow of this debate. There has always been relative consensus about the description of the core features of the disorder. Challenges have concerned its underlying nature and classification.

Is it a language or a speech disorder? If it is a language, dysphasic, disorder, is it extricable from language components as a whole, as say, phonological breakdown, or is it somehow to be classed otherwise? Is it part of one of the classic dysphasic syndromes, or is it intrinsic to or co-occurrent with several? Deciding that the disorder is not dysphasic still raises problems. Should one group the breakdown with what in the Anglo-Saxon literature are termed the dysarthrias, or is it independent of dysphasia *and* dysarthria? That begs the question of why and how it is independent, and in turn relates back to the changing neurological and linguistic backgrounds that have fed over a century of debate.

Views about how the central nervous system (CNS) and its relationship to the outside world operate have swung between the early-nineteenth-century legacy of medieval notions (Buckingham 1981), through associationist, gestaltist, behaviourist and other views to more contemporary neo-associationists and interactive activationists (Rumelhart and McClelland 1986). Within these views there have existed contrasts between strict localizationists, equipotentialists, dynamic localizationists (Luria 1973), all with consequences for interpretations of speech apraxia. For instance, there are arguments concerning whether lesions causing the problem can only be cortical, even only narrowly circumscribed (left frontal operculum; insula; arcuate fasciculus have all been candidates) areas of cortex, or whether subcortical involvement is permitted or obligatory. Centre lesionists and disconnectionists (Buckingham 1979; Caplan 1987) have also been in the arena.

It is not only changing neurological fashions that have swayed thought on speech apraxia. Developments in linguistics have exerted similar influences. Earlier scholarship saw language like higher brain function, as an indivisible whole (Buckingham 1981). Subsequently there has been gradual, but varying, fractionation into subcomponents, with disagreement over where divisions occur and how components relate to one another. Parallel to this, pronouncements on dyspraxic speech have changed. For some it is a phonemic, for others a phonetic disorder; for others it arises in the interaction of the two. For some it is a disorder of phonological competence, for others of articulatory performance.

Not surprisingly the myriad permutations of neurological and linguistic interpretations have generated countless labels which attach to essentially the same surface behaviour but which betray different neurolinguistic standpoints. There have been aphemia (Broca's own term), anarthria (the preferred term in Francophone writings), efferent and afferent motor dysphasia (Luria 1973); Broca's dysphasia plus adjectives – e.g. predominantly speech versus predominantly language, big and little Brocas (Mohr 1980). Those favouring a language-based disorder have spoken of verbal aphasia or aphasic phonological disorder. Reviews of historical developments have been provided by Johns and La Pointe (1976) and Lebrun (1989); while Lesser (1978) and Rosenbek *et al.* (1984) have tackled theoretical issues.

Currently arguments for an independent, dyspraxic disorder separate from dysphasia are in the ascendency. Evidence for this is reviewed below. The definition outlined above, however, retains many contentious terms. What is programmed, where does it originate from and how is it controlled? What is the relationship between sensory and motor? Can one speak of learned for speech in the same way that it applies to walking, chewing, writing or piano-playing? Is volitional an all-or-nothing phenomenon or has it gradations, and if so, then what determines this?

Clearly this chapter cannot hope to answer all the queries raised, let alone numerous ones not even mentioned. Instead, it will firstly consider evidence for a separate disorder that is a dyspraxia and affects speech. Following that directions in answering some of the questions on underlying mechanisms are mentioned, with a final brief word connecting this to neuroanatomy.

Describing dyspraxic speech

People with apraxia of speech have been described as substituting one sound for another, and omitting, adding, transposing and distorting sounds. They do this despite on occasion demonstrating normal production of the same sounds and sound sequences. This variability is supposed to be one feature differentiating dyspraxic from dysarthric speech. These features are exemplified in the following transcription of a dyspraxic:

a) [ʔaɪ – – – ʔʌ – – – ′b′i – – ɪʔt⁷ – – ʔʌt′′ɪʰə – – ′miʰ – ′ᵐp′ti – – æ′mi – – –
æpə′tiːɪ′bi – ′b̥biʰⁱ ′biʰⁱ′biʰⁱ′bzi′biə′bi′pi ′bĭ′bĭ]

b) [wan – tssʉ – b̥ɹi – fɔɹ – ma? – faɪfs – sɪkxəs – ′e′b̥ěn′se′ben – eɪtss – naɪn
– d̥ʔtʰen ′ɪ′lɛ′vən – welz – ′ʔɜɹ′tʰin̆ – ′tɜɹ′tin]

Example 8.1
Speech apraxic producing (a) syllable [bi] and (b) counting to thirteen.

The problem is, though, that these same features characterize pronunciation breakdown that has been classified by many as other than dyspraxic. Substitutions and the like fail to distinguish different underlying aetiologies. Compare the first transcription with the second, from a patient who would normally be classified as a conduction dysphasic with literal paraphasic errors.

[. . . d̥ɹⁱsə ′phɪk⁷tʃə ɒv ə haʊs . . . . sᵗ′sɛt ɪnɪn ə ′gɑdən . . . . ehm . . . ðə ′haʊs
ɪz p′ɪtɪ ‚mɒd′n‚mɒᵈən wɪð′ə tʃɪmnɪ . . . ehm . . . ðə ′gɑdən . . . ehm . . .
ɪnɪg‚ðɛɜɹ‚ðɛə zəðɛɜɹzə ′gɑdn ðɛɜɹɪzə ′pɒnt pʰᵘᵖ.
ðɛɜɹə ′phɒnd ɪn ðə ′gɑdən . . . .]

Example 8.2

The error types stem largely from earlier reliance on ear-of-the-listener (Broad) phonetic transcriptions as bases for analysis. This meant one was making judgements on a speaker's motor control via the filter of a listener's perceptual expectations and assumptions. This particularly clouded the issues and arguments at the time (Blumstein 1973; Martin 1974) concerning whether apraxia of speech was motor, and therefore a dyspraxia, or phonological and therefore a dysphasia. The shortcoming has been acknowledged for some time. Buckingham and Yule (1987) provide more recent discussion of phonemic false evaluation of dyspraxics'/dysphasics' speech. This problem became one impetus for developing instrumental assessments giving closer access to motor activity. It is only since instrumental techniques have been used that record activity permitting more direct inferences about underlying motor activity, that issues have started to be resolved. This literature is already too large to discuss in detail in an overview chapter such as this (see Square-Storer 1989; Wertz *et al.* 1984). A summary of some techniques used, and their conclusions, illustrate the advances.

Instrumental investigations of apraxia of speech

If, as the definition above claims, dyspraxia is not a disorder of primary sensory and motor function one would expect performance in these areas to be normal – e.g. normal range of movements, attainment of normal acceleration and peak velocities, ability to exert normal force and durational values. As a disorder of motor programming and execution one would suspect that difficulties would be manifest in specifying the correct choice of space-time values, integrating these choices into a workable whole and maintaining control over their relative changes during execution of the action. Recent instrumental investigations point precisely to these areas of difficulty in dyspraxic speakers.

Fromm *et al.* (1982) carried out simultaneous EMG, force transducer (lips, mandible) and laryngeal accelerometer (for voice onset time) recordings of speech apraxic utterances. Speakers instanced examples of normal values for movement of individual articulators, and progression of multiple gestures was clearly towards intended targets. However, as exemplified by one of their subjects, despite apparently selecting the proper movement the speaker 'was unable to accomplish the multistructure, temporal-spatial programming' necessary for the closure. Instead of integrated activity, agonist-antagonist groups co-contracted in opposition, onset-offset of movement phases was discoordinated, with different articulators seemingly working independently rather than concertedly towards an overall joint goal. Importantly, Fromm *et al.*'s methods also disclosed considerable (abnormal) activity during silent pauses, and, with significant implications for programming models (see below), they found many auditorily normal productions were produced with abnormal underlying activity.

Itoh and Sasanuma (1984) in their studies of tongue velum coordination established that range and speed of movements in dyspraxics matched normals. Also, the pattern of movements when oral-nasal confusions were heard approximated normal gestures. This countered arguments that what was at fault was the initial selection of overall gestural specifications and pointed, in Itoh *et al.*'s and Sasanuma's words, to a motor impairment with faulty programming of speech musculature leading to phonetic distortion.

Ziegler and von Cramon (1985, 1986a) surmized that if apraxia of speech represents a disintegration of usually coordinated speech gestures, then dyspraxics should show a disturbance in the coarticulatory cohesion that binds groups of contiguous sounds, despite being able to achieve individual target positions. Their investigatory paradigm exploited the hypothesis that due to coarticulatory effects clues to upcoming sounds would be apparent in earlier sounds in normals, but less so in dyspraxics. Recognition judgements by listeners of spliced words confirmed this. Together with other multichannel recordings (Ziegler and von Cramon 1986b) of motor speech activity, Ziegler and co-workers were led to conclude that dyspraxics demonstrate a 'lack of organisational cohesion in the sequencing of speech movements' stemming from a 'basic problem in phasing individual speech gestures appropriately'. Similar results have been obtained by Tuller and Story (1987), and when measurement criteria are adjusted, by Katz (1987).

Several groups (Hardcastle *et al.* 1985; Sugishita *et al.* 1987; Edwards and Miller in press) have studied dyspraxics' lingual-palatal contacts using electro-palatography (EPG). Hardcastle *et al.*'s observations are typical. They found failure to attain normal values of speed and force in dysarthrics consistent with their neuromuscular weakness. While their dyspraxic subject also evidenced some undershooting and speed reduction, he primarily showed variation between under specification of target (temporal and spatial) values and over-shooting. There were examples of excessive force, gestures commenced too early, positions over-shot. Again, this pointed, for Hardcastle *et al.*, to a disorder of sequencing, selection and temporal integration. A further important finding was that abnormal articulatory patterns did not necessarily lead to perceivable speech errors.

The picture emerging is reinforced by other measures. McNeil *et al.* (1986) and Itoh and Sasanuma (1987) found achievable but variable velocities in Broca's dysphasics with apraxia of speech. On straight repetition of nonsense syllables they did not differ from normals, but in utterances beyond certain lengths control of velocity and displacement resulted in problems of phasing of individual gestures, leading to aberrant articulatory transitions, phonetic distortions and dysprosody.

Blumstein and Baum (1987) in their review of consonant production deficits in aphasia paint a similar picture. Subjects produce values (for VOT, place, manner of articulation) across the entire range of possibilities. This leads to production sometimes being perceived by listeners as normal when values fell within the desired categorical boundaries, but perceived distortions or even substitutions when performance was around or transgressed the boundaries. The difficulty does not lie in the realization of particular phonetic features, i.e. static postures, but rather in the *dynamic* aspects of speech. Crucially, they conclude that behind this problem lies a breakdown in the integration of the dynamics of multiple articulators, and control of independent parameters in transition from one segment to the next.

Other workers have interpreted this as grounded in a defect of temporal resolution. Superficially this is so. It is not absolute timing that is disordered, though, but relative timing. This does not have to be derived from a hypothetical timing device, as argued by some (contrast Keele 1987; MacKay 1987). It can arise from phasing breakdown inherent in the dynamics of movement. Blumstein and Baum (1987) point towards this, and it is supported by specific investigations reported in Kelso and Tuller (1987). There are important implications for motor planning in this assumption, a matter resumed below.

Finally, it is emphasized that impairment does not only involve consonants. Contrary to earlier claims, vowels are seen to be considerably affected. Ryalls (1987) and Ryalls and Behrens (1988) review some of the reasons why earlier beliefs might have arisen and how vowels become disordered. They suffer the same fate as consonants. Listeners perceive distortions, substitutions etc., but these can be traced back to the same underlying breakdowns outlined above. Given the right assessment techniques (naked ear transcription is not so reliable) and contexts (vowels in polysyllabic utterances are more susceptible to derailment) these vowel errors are detectable.

Kent and Rosenbek (1983) tie in vowel distortion with perceived dysprosody in apraxia of speech. Consonant and vowel distortion and abnormal pausing and prolongation while grasping for a target lead to dysprosody. Equally, though, the same *dis*-integration of control of simultaneous and sequential dynamic parameters in vocal-tract coordination that bring about vowel and consonant derailment also disrupt the control of the neuromuscular correlates of prosodic features.

All these studies have important implications for the understanding of the disorder. The speech apraxic may produce what *sound* like substitutions of oral for nasal, fricative for plosive, palatal for alveolar, but rather than these resulting from false selection of articulatory target (i.e. phonological breakdown) they can now be strongly argued to arise from disintegration or dissynchronization of the relative movement onsets and terminations of the articulators entrained, or coupled, to produce a sound. Asynchrony of voice onset time mimics substitution of voiced and voiceless segments. Disordered patterns of plosive arrest and release can sound like fricativization or affricativization.

This stresses the point that a major difficulty for people with dyspraxia is not (just) attaining isolated targets, but controlling all the transitions from one segment to the next. Much of the listener evaluation of distortions and omissions and feeling of hearing a foreign accent derive from acoustic clues in altered transitions due to underlying loss of co-articulatory cohesion. This in turn correlates not with failure to achieve absolute targets of force, velocity, acceleration and so on, but failure to achieve the fine adjustments in phasing across all values.

The phonetic-phonemic dichotomy

Of course, the above studies do not account for all pronunciation errors in the absence of primary sensory-motor defect, independent of dysphasia severity. There are classes of errors where the substitutions, additions and omissions appear to occur with normal sound spectral and motor parameters. Traditionally these have been termed literal paraphasic errors (see Buckingham, Ch. 6 above) and are assumed to point to a breakdown in linquistic, phonological programming unrelated to motor planning and therefore not dyspraxia (see Caplan 1987; and Lecours and Nespoulous 1988 for background). Within the typical speech production models exemplified in Figure 8.1 the breakdown is supposed to be at the level of phonological encoding. However, there are several objections to such a conception, on clinical and theoretical grounds.

Firstly, taking clinical objections, while patients are observed who give the impression of being pure speech apraxics or pure literal paraphasics, the vast majority of people display a mixture of both types of error. Even the selected pure speech apraxics of Fromm *et al.* (1982) had a residue of 5 per cent of errors not associated with abnormal readings on their assessments.

Further, several studies (Canter *et al.* 1985) have suggested the distinction of alleged motoric speech dyspraxia versus alleged phonological dysphasic literal paraphasia is not so razor sharp as theorists would have one believe. Blumstein *et al.* (1980) found some of their Wernicke's dysphasics had greater phonetic than phonemic errors, where listener judgement might have claimed a phonemic substitution. Tuller (1984) among her fluent dysphasics established phonetic articulatory control disruption in apparent phonemic substitutions. Kent and McNeil (1987) data challenge the justification for sharply dividing conduction dysphasic and speech dyspraxic mispronunciation. Edwards and Miller (in press), analysing EPG recordings of fluent dysphasics, found evidence of distorted temporal-spatial configurations in instances both of apparent frank substitutions and normal sounding production. Importantly, they found equivalent breakdowns in non-verbal oral tasks where linguistic arguments for error sources do not apply.

The other objection to the segregation of phonemic and phonetic derailments is a theoretical one. This division is an abstract linguistic descriptive device, a metaphor. Reconciling it with neuropsychological and neurophysiological reality would require resolution of this mental-physical leap. As it stands it transgresses the law holding that physical states in lower centres do not fine away into psychical states in higher centres. Models of speech-language production until recently failed to recognize this or attempt to resolve the dilemma. As Fowler (1985: p. 195) neatly criticized, 'Largely this difficulty is handled in language and speech production models by a kind of sleight of hand', i.e. they speak of abstract mental phonology and physical phonetics, but fail to account for the transition between them. Progress towards a unified theory and model of speech production must solve this conundrum (Bromberger and Halle 1986; Lindblom 1986).

This is not to deny that there are misarticulations which are phonetic realization breakdowns and others which are genuinely categorical selection errors. What has to be questioned is the basis for and nature of this distinction.

While paraphasic derailments may give the appearance of collapses or imbalances in individuals' phonological systems, phonological analyses indicate otherwise. Patients do not show systematic elimination or addition of a dimension (place, manner etc.), nor restructuring of the phonemic and phonetic inventory. Process analyses have fared poorly in describing pronunciation breakdown (Parsons *et al.* 1988) and even those supporting it (Wolk 1986) are open to motor interpretations. Error types are better accounted for in terms of ordering of features, contamination between features and selection, within an utterance unit. These processes occur in relation to language (lexicon, syntax . . .) functions, but are preparatory to motor behaviour. Hence, as for instance Buckingham (1979) and Tuller and Story (1987) have done, it is more accurate to speak of motoric and premotoric operations rather than linguistic versus motor. The task then is to characterize more abstract motor processes and how they relate to articulation.

There is support for this from other fields of dyspraxia. The distinction in limb dyspraxia between ideational and ideomotor is a case in point. A distinction appears between fluent ideationally dyspraxic action with anticipations, perseverations, seeming frank substitutions and other derailments similarly characteristic of literal paraphasic speech; and dysfluent ideomotor performance, with effortful, distorted segments and transitions akin to traditional accounts of speech apraxia. The suggestion is that the disruption in the motoric basis of the different phases of genesis of action responsible for the ideational-ideomotor picture is the same that underlies the difference in phonemic-phonetic pronunciation breakdown. A move towards seeing a motoric continuity between more abstract and concrete stages in the unfolding of speech production avoids the mental-physical impasse and coincides better with what is known of brain organization (see below).

Roy and Square (1985) also point to regularities of breakdown between limb and speech derailment. Edwards and Miller (in press) lend instrumental support. Poizner *et al.* (1987) offer strong evidence for this notion, showing how errors equivalent to speech arise in deaf manual signers' 'dysphasic' signing, which, of course, is acquired visually and executed according to visual-gestural coordinates, not sound phonological features.

Buckingham (1983) has worked towards a model of pronunciation breakdown along the lines of the ideational-ideomotor distinction. He argues that phonological planning is indeed a type of planning apraxia (he calls it apraxia of language) if parallels with other studies of human movement are maintained. Traditionally termed apraxia of speech he places in the category of 'execution' dyspraxias.

The suggestion that all types of non-dysarthric pronunciation breakdown could be considered one variety or another of dyspraxia is a departure from views traditionally held. In fact a lot of energy has been expended in attempts to prove that dyspraxia and literal paraphasia represent sharply demarcated disorders. However, it is felt here that understanding of these phenomena would be advanced by abandoning searches for how they differ. Speech and phonology are inextricably intertwined. Without motor speech, phonology would be mute. Without the structure provided by phonology movement would be formless. As an alternative one should be examining how they can be linked in an overall conceptualization of motor speech organization relating abstract intentions and environmentally acceptable perceptual goals. The clinical and theoretical reasons alluded to above suggest this would be a fruitful search. The next section looks at the same debate from the perspective of speech production models.

Speech production models and pronunciation breakdown

Various theorists (Mlcoch and Noll 1980; Buckingham 1986) have forwarded models of speech-language production from which the nature of normal and pathological speech (almost exclusively directed at literal paraphasic errors; few theorists have considered the traditional speech dyspraxic errors in any detail) can be deduced. Some are only *descriptive* while others try to *explain* why disordered and normal production occur. However, no overall solution yet exists that can describe, and even far less explain, all normal and pathological pronunciation. This section is thus unable to provide final answers to the countless questions that arise in considering underlying neuropsychological and physiological processes in speech production. The aim is to outline some general aspects of models that have been applied to speech production, to point out some of the problems faced by model makers and suggest some paths towards solutions.

The main division in broad model types lies between hierarchical and heterarchical models, and within the former between close-loop and open-loop schemes.

Hierarchical models

These have been compared to dictatorial political systems. Power rests at the head of a hierarchy. All subordinate levels depend on levels above to receive their orders and commands progress in a direct line, top-down, one-way. All data needed for lower levels are contained in some form in the central, superordinate programme. For this reason these models are termed address-specific, and because of the one-way flow of processing from centre to periphery without any scope for talk-back they are called linear unidirectional. Because there is no talk-back, once the cortical pianist has pressed the keys on the cortical keyboard (such is one of the analogies used), the programme is destined to run its course. Processing at one stage has to be completed before operations at the next stage commence. Hence they are described as discrete-point. Readers may be familiar with the schematic representation in Figure 8.1.

In actual fact there is a major contrast within hierarchical models between open (Figure 8.1) and closed loop approaches (Figure 8.2). Mlcoch and Noll (1980) have detailed and amalgamated these approaches in relation to speech.

Closed-loop models incorporate feedback into the system. At its crudest this is post event from the periphery to centre. More elaborate schemes contain internal feedback loops, whereby a pre-completion check can be made during productive processing on any one stage to ensure programme elaboration is proceeding correctly. Such internal comparators, or efference copies, as they have been called, check, for instance that all the abstract phoneme selections specified by the central programme have been included and that they occur in the correct slots. Probably the most sophisticated model of this type applied to speech is the scan-copier mechanism model developed by Shattuck-Hufnagel (1983), Garrett (1984) and Buckingham (1986).

Closed-loop models are still hierarchical because they depend on some central definitive specification against which stages of output are compared. They are still discrete point, requiring completed computation at one level before proceeding downwards. They are still basically top-down because the feedback, even though it superficially looks like bottom-up talk-back adds no new information of its own. Its function is essentially to edit top-down outflow.

Within these models apraxia of speech is interpreted as a fault in the programmed instructions to the neuromotor execution level situated between higher (language; phonological) and lower (primary motor and sensory; subcortical) steps in the hierarchy. As a result of this misprogramming, or the inability of this effector unit to execute the commands, it is assumed units are misordered or mistimed, and this leads to sequencing disorder, additions, substitutions and so on. In closed-loop models there exists the possibility that

Figure 8.1 Schematic of a section of a possible Open Loop hierarchical model, showing supposed disorders arising from damage to individual components

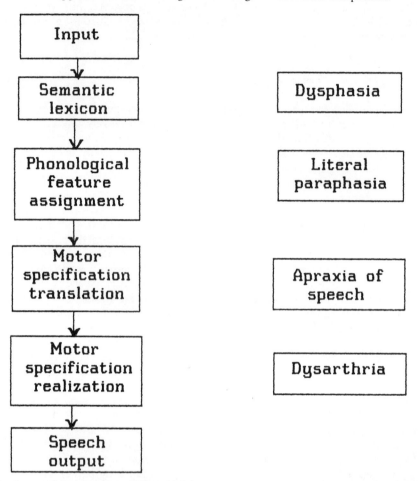

the internal comparator fails to pick up output errors and this provides the assumed sensory feedback breakdown claimed by many to characterize dyspraxia. The models mentioned previously, and others, have gone to great lengths to explain how particular errors arise. Despite plausible arguments, however, hierarchical models have limited application to speech.

Limitations of hierarchical models

Experimental studies have demonstrated that open- and closed-loop schemes provide satisfactory descriptions, even explanations, for certain motor behaviours. However, for more complex actions they suffer fundamental drawbacks. Some basic aspects of speech production mentioned here suffice to disclose the inadequacy of such models.

Figure 8.2 Schematic of a section of a Closed Loop hierarchical model incorporating internal checks on the output of each component separately, and showing sensory-feedback as an element of input information

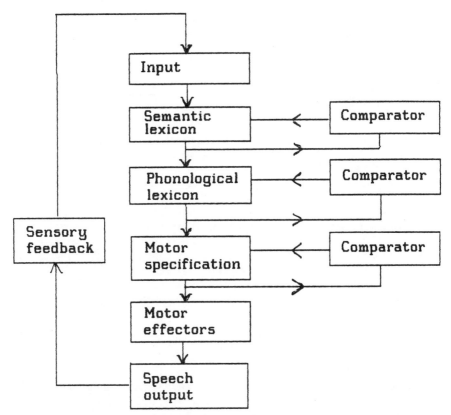

The crucial flaw lies in the assumption that there is a one-to-one correspondence between a central programme and peripheral movements. Theoretical linguistics may talk in terms of fixed feature inventories for abstract phonemes and allophones, and even link these to presumed invariant articulatory configurations. However, every attempt to identify invariant motor characteristics that directly relate to perceived acoustic outcome has failed (Perkell and Klatt 1986).

This derives from the fact that speech consists not of strings of rigidly metred leaps from one isolated, static allophone position to the next, but is a dynamic flow in a constant state of flux. Within this flow not only do neighbouring movements and their associated sounds merge into each other (as is clearly evident when trying to separate isolated 'phonemes' from EMG, sound spectrographic or other instrumental print outs), but at any moment in time features notionally belonging to individual phonemes spread over several sounds.

No address-specific model could ever hope to cope with all the separate commands that would be necessary to cover all possible combinations of all movements in all (sociolinguistic, affective etc.) contexts at every moment in time. Any kind of central command must therefore be directed towards goals other than absolute parameters of movements (force, speed etc.) or position.

Further observations render one-to-one correspondence between central specifications and peripheral results invalid. The vocal tract is capable of producing the same acoustic target via widely differing articulatory configurations. A very simple example is lengthening of the tract either by lowering the larynx or protruding the lips. Instrumental techniques like ultrasound, cinefluoroscopy and EPG have demonstrated though that multiple variations can occur throughout the tract and still produce perceptually equivalent results. The ability of the locomotor system to attain equivalent action goals by different motor means is termed motor equivalence. Address specific models do not predict this phenomenon. It appears to be an important factor in compensation for pronunciation breakdown (Edwards and Miller in press) and is the reason why people can maintain intelligibility despite radically altered oral geography (physical trauma; speaking with your mouth full; holding a cigarette in the mouth).

Hierarchical systems stipulate that there is one-to-one matching between central activation patterns and resultant movements. This does not tie in with reality. A given degree of activation will produce a different reaction according to whether a muscle starts from rest, is already contracting, is acting against antagonists, is acting with or against gravity, according to which biomechanical (elastic, viscous, inertial) forces it is subject, and so on.

Conversely, different activation patterns may be needed to produce equivalent results. Compare which muscles are involved in which ways to bring the tongue tip to the alveolar ridge while speaking with the head bowed, while out running and while lying on your back. The lesson is the same again – invariant, central, address specific, unidirectional models cannot cope with the flexibility demanded by environmental, dynamic factors.

One experimental paradigm, perturbation studies, also highlights the inadequacy of hierarchical control for complex actions and suggests directions to search for better solutions. In these studies there is controlled interference, i.e. perturbation, with execution of a movement at different times during performance, through deflection or braking. One arm might be pushed momentarily off target in a bimanual reaching task, or mandibular/lower lip closure for bilabials is arrested (Abbs 1986; Gracco and Abbs 1987). If there existed one-to-one centre to periphery address specifications one would expect correction of perturbations to take place in the muscle (group) perturbed and over a time scale commensurate with feedback from periphery to cortical keyboard and back to periphery. Neither is true. Reaction times for corrections start before central reprogramming could have taken place. More significantly recovery of the action involves not, or not just, the isolated part that has been perturbed, but takes place through reorganization of the role being played by all body parts concerned, whether anatomically related or not. Thus the upper lip performs compensatory extra lowering to meet the arrested lower lip for [pæ]. Also significant is that on-line corrections to perturbations are made for moving parts only during phases when their participation is crucial to target attainment.

Indications, then, from consideration of movements for and during speech and from perturbation studies, suggest several directions to search for how action is controlled and what disruption lies behind dyspraxia. Control cannot be the summation of discrete events that are centrally specified and operate independently of the environment. The search needs to be for systems where action goals are specified, but the specification of values in movement parameters for the means of arriving there are capable of infinite variation in reaction to changing local needs. Heterarchical models offer one solution to this.

Heterarchical models

If hierarchical models were analagous to centralized dictatorships, heterarchical schemes resemble devolved power federal unions. Hierarchical states have a central command issuing down immutable orders to lower centres which merely obey. Heterarchical systems have an overall agreement of policy and goals of action, but this is achieved by concerted working of multiple subsystems distributed throughout the organism as a whole. These subsystems are semi-autonomous, in that they are capable of achieving results and making decisions without clearing orders with central headquarters. However, generally, subsystems talk to each other on an equal footing, making action the outcome of the interactive (bottom-up, top-down, cross-talk) operation of the action system overall and not the sole decision of some central pattern generator or the like. Prime locus of control, if one can ever talk of prime in a council of equals, shifts as needs be to that part of the system most suited to achieve the current desired end. Flow and exchange of information takes place simultaneously, in parallel at all times, in all directions. This dynamic flux contrasts with the linear, serial, time dominated emergence of hierarchically programmed movement (Figure 8.3). These claims have fundamental implications for how action programming is to be viewed.

Firstly, the concept of control changes from a pattern of isolated stimuli and a simple sum of isolated responses or reactions, to one of interaction. Interaction takes place not only within the organism (i.e. between the numerous centres or levels deemed to comprise the action system), but equally importantly between the organism and the environment. A self-contained machine no longer acts on a passive environment, but an ever-changing organism is seen as trying to maintain equilibrium with equally unstable external surroundings. Because the environment is infinitely variable, predetermined movement plans have no place unless they can be constantly adjusted. Thus the target becomes not a given absolute (time, space etc.) state or progression, but the reaching of a functional action goal.

Each component of the heterarchy has in-and-outflow, not in a periphery → cortex → periphery loop, but within numbers of internal mutual interactions between components. What might traditionally be seen as afference can just as well be directly contributing to outflow. As Reed (1982) points out, the outcome of a descending impulse via the spinal cord is significantly affected by the state of activity within the cord. This activity itself is a synergistic outcome of both cortically and peripherally produced excitation. Hence the final efferent outcome is as much the product of 'ascending' information as

Figure 8.3 Schematic of a section of a possible heterarchical model demonstrating parallel input to, processing in and cross-talk between all components. Output is an aggregate of simultaneous output from all components. Lettering emphasizes the non-serial nature of processing

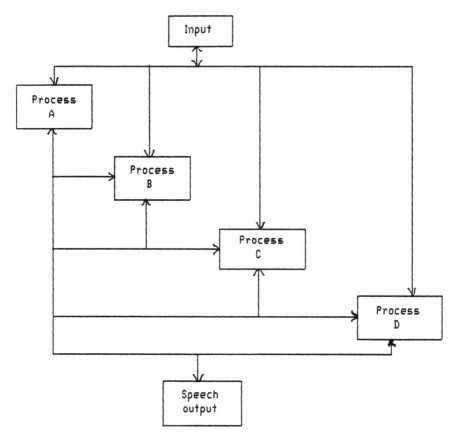

descending. This stresses a *perceptuo*-motor perspective on speech (cf. Elman and McClelland 1984; Fowler and Smith 1986).

Just as the goal of action in heterarchical systems is arrived at through a global interaction of the system, so the organism also interacts with the environment not in terms of strings of separate happenings in the environment, but as a total event. Elman and McClelland (1984) taking such an interactive view of speech perception illustrate how the listener perceives sounds not just, if at all, in terms of absolute spectral features, but in terms of the total event which includes lexicon, syntax and semantics as much as phonology. Within such a framework the search for units of control or perception is fruitless.

This changes the conception of what is controlled and what breaks down in pathological speech. It is not things (phonemes, allophones, fixed time sequences etc.), but relations, in particular the relations between postures. Reed (1982) draws a simple but excellent analogy with an aeroplane. Various mechanisms and processes play a role in action, but this does not necessarily mean they are components of this action. The plane's engines as units play a role *in* flying, but they are not the components *of* flying. The plane is a thing, but flying is a function of relations between aerodynamic factors. The plane's superstructure and mechanical components can be analysed hierarchically into parts, but none of these contains the secret of flying – this can only be deduced from the interlocking relationship of all the parts and how they interact with forces external to them.

Following this example, it can be seen why the search for properties of phonemes or phonetic features of allophones has failed to uncover the nature of speech motor control, and why segregating language from speech leads to sterile argument. There are no absolute units characterizing a sound. Sounds only become interpretable in contrast to other sounds – i.e. in their relative postures. What are important are relative timing, relative position, the overall interlocking setting of the whole vocal tract and not the isolated setting of individual articulators. As was seen above, it is exactly these relative values that appear disrupted in apraxia of speech.

Heterarchical accounts of apraxia of speech

As with hierarchical approaches, there are several types of heterarchical models (Reed 1982; Rumelhart and McClelland 1986). None of these has been used to provide a complete description nor explanation of apraxia of speech. The following draws out how some aspects of dyspraxic speech so far mentioned fit in with heterarchical models. The instrumental investigations outlined above provide converging evidence that it is relative and not absolute values that dysfunction in dyspraxia. These same studies also highlighted the difficulties experienced by dyspraxics in transitions between one setting and another of the vocal tract, and the consequences of these for listener perceptions (judged as substitutions, distortions etc.). This is exactly as predicted from models that stress relational values, as the aerodynamic factors in the plane analogy above; and that stress postures and modulations in speech as central to action control and not mechanistic components (wing flaps, engine parts, phonemes).

The same position is strengthened from evidence of normal action. Across scalar changes what remain constant are relative values in on- and off-set of movements (Harris *et al.* 1986).

Syllable segregation (Kent and Rosenbek 1983) and some of the more consistent non-normal sound productions one hears in chronic apraxia of speech can be seen as conscious or subconscious adjustments to the problem of controlling multiple relative changes, when the speaker is no longer able to cope with controlling the usual number of degrees of freedom in the system. By simplifying postures and transitions acceptable speech may be attainable.

Another major prediction of heterarchical models is that derailments will reflect breakdown in interaction between and across components in the emergence of action. Derailments will not be restricted to breakdowns at discrete points, nor to dysfunction within one traditional category of syntax, phonology, phonetics, motor, sensory and so on.

Take the following example of a patient's answer to 'what colour's the sky on a clear day?'.

['blut . . . ˌbrut . . . ˌnəʊ̆ . . . 'blrut . . . 'blaɪ̆t . . . 'waɪ̆t . . . ˌnaʊ̆ . . . bə:'r:aɪ̆t . . . naʊ̆ . . . ɪts 'blaɪ̆ut . . . naʊ̆ blɔ̆ . . . blŭu]

The paraphasias demonstrate an interaction first between blue and bright. But the near winning out of bright ([blaɪ̆t]) strengthens phonological and semantic activation of another competitor, *white*, before the speaker returns via the blue-bright struggle to success. The concurrent sound derailments, notice, are a combination of traditional literal paraphasic – [braɪt → blaɪt], [blu → blut] and what traditionally might be termed phonetic [blaɪut], [blrut] and the visible struggle with [bə:'r:aɪt].

Such multiple based errors are compatible with the data of Santo Pietro and Rigrodsky (1986) who found extensive instances of carry over of perseveratory features from e.g. semantics to phonology to produce hybrid perseveratory paraphasias. Discrete point models where operations are deemed to have been completed in one area before initiation of the next have difficulty coping with these findings.

They also have problems with out-of-plan errors where there is no apparent source of derailment within the immediate syllabic environment or across the preceding or upcoming sound context. Harley (1984) emphasized the afferent perceptual out-of-plan influences that can intrude into output. Stemberger (1984) drew parallels with lexical malapropisms where semantic paraphasias arise from preferential activation and choice of a similar sounding word. The same might happen with phonological units to produce phonological malapropisms, even when they do not occur in the planning environment. It is feasible to presume that in more local, contiguous contexts the same type of breakdown produces errors of anticipation and perseveration of single features. Buckingham and Yule (1987) add a possible non-interactive source for this error class, viz. phonemic false evaluation on the part of the listener.

The other side of the interactive coin, with derailments occurring because of dysfunction across components of the model, is that intact functioning in one locus can help correct or compensate for breakdown elsewhere. This potential for reorganization and flexibility from not having one-to-one fixed roles forms the basis of motor equivalence. It is also one reason for the struggle behaviour found in dyspraxia, when the confederation controlling output attempts to reach the action goal in the face of perturbation in the system.

The same potential for multiple loci of control provides an explanation for another source of variability in performance. If activation and control can proceed directly to and from intact components, problem areas are bypassed. This can only happen in models that are not address specific and not discrete point. A possible correlation of propositionality (see Ch. 9 below) is provided here, too. The more conscious thought/planning is required for a response, the greater is the activation across the entire system, and thereby the greater the potential for interactive breakdown to happen and the need to involve a defective component. However, this is minimized when activation can pass directly to the semi-autonomous normally functioning subsystems. Hence dyspraxics' often heard remarks that they can say a sound/word when they are not really thinking about it.

In turn the basis for this phenomenon is that heterarchical systems while flexible are constrained, through the process of acquisition of skills, to act in particular ways. The advantage of this is that possible but unwanted movements are excluded and not all aspects of movement have to be individually re-computed every time. Instead the cortical values are inherent to the organization of the system. Just how much has or has not to be re-computed each time is a matter of debate – cf. Keller 1987. A frequent analogy is the driving of a car. The driver does not need to control the speed and direction of each wheel individually because they are constrained to operate altogether. When they do need to go at different speeds (when cornering), a downstream built in component (the differential) not needing driver control, takes care of this.

This notion is similar to that claimed by Kelso and Tuller (1987) who point to intrinsic timing in coordination of movements without recourse to cortical time keepers.

No mention has been made so far of the notional units of organization and patterns of control within the models discussed. The implicit direction of thought has been that the building blocks are functional synergies (Bernstein 1967), otherwise termed coordinative structures (see e.g. Kelso 1986) and that interactive activation (McClelland 1979 for general principles; Elman and McClelland 1984 for speech perception; Stemberger 1985 for language production; Humphreys *et al.* 1988 for picture identification) brings into operation entrainments or ennestings of parent–child systems of functional synergies. A functional synergy is an interlinkage where muscles, often over several joints, are constrained to act as a single functional unit. They operate as internally coherent, self-regulatory autonomous units balancing both muscular, mechanical and inertial forces. They are context sensitive, but how far they exist as context specific preprogrammed structures is disputed (Keller 1987).

Accordingly, dyspraxia can arise from misactivation of parent structures, disruption to the entrainment (i.e. mutual synchronization) of multiple synergies and to the balance of nested, dependent values within them which are activated for arriving at desired action goals. Pronunciation breakdown can arise also from conflicts between competing activated units.

According to where in the line of entrainment or hierarchy of nestings the dissynchronization occurs, different disruption will result. If it is low in the arborization, then disruption will be relatively local, contiguous, with spread of distortion constrained by the dominance of superordinate structures. This picture compares with the local, predominantly contiguous, transitional, relative micro-value distortions arising in speech dyspraxia. It also ties in with how breakdowns in facilitation of mutual synchronization (entrainment) can spread upwards to superordinate nodes creating the impression of paraphasic errors.

The latter in their supposed purer forms can also be interpreted as arising from breakdown in entrainment or ennesting activation at higher nodes of constraint. Such breakdowns, from wrong selection or misentrainment at higher nodes, would have the effect of leaving lower branching and entrainment intact, but alter the structure of the action by more and more radical changes to its elaboration. This is because activation of certain entrainments or nested groups imply activation of given lower values. Distortion of lower branches causes only local deformation, but high branch changes alter the picture in all dependent areas. In this way transpositions, omissions, anticipations and the like arise. Context-sensitive bottom-up adjustments result then in the struggle and *conduits d'approche* (repeated run ups) and distortions as lower or ennested structures come up against misdirected higher linkages.

Within this view there is no strict phonemic–phonetic division. One grows out of the other, they are mutually interactive. No mental–physical hurdle has to be crossed as the parameters of control are the same throughout the system. All that changes is the extent of disruption caused by aberrations at different loci in the functional synergistic mutually constrained assemblage. The same conceptualization is applicable to all action whether it is speech, manual signing, typing (articles in Cooper 1983) or piano playing (Shaffer 1981; Sloboda 1983).

This brings discussion back to one of the main points of this chapter – that while a phonemic–phonetic distinction might have some abstract linguistic validity, when it comes to CNS functioning in general and speech pathology in particular a different image is required. In a simultaneous activation state all information is processed in parallel. Final outcomes are arrived at not from adding blocks or matrices fashioned at one isolated level to those of the next, but by a continuous interaction throughout the system with a gradual concurrent bringing into focus of the whole picture.

How does this view tie in with lesion studies of speech dyspraxia and knowledge of CNS functioning?

Localization and apraxia of speech

Speech is a multidimensional phenomenon not existing in a vacuum, and control is distributed throughout the CNS. These two factors alone render statements on localization problematical. What is one supposed to be localizing? Further, all such pronouncements have to be tempered by the caveat that disordered performance reflects behaviour after the whole brain has adjusted to partial loss of function. One cannot make direct inferences from observed 'loss' of a behavioural aspect to loss of specific neuronal tissue. Controversy over what precisely is being discussed under the label apraxia of speech adds another source of variability in claims regarding localization.

The main areas implicated have been, in the language-dominant hemisphere, the frontal lobe, in particular Brodmann's area 44, around the frontal operculum; the insula, or fibres deep to it (arcuate fasciculus especially); the parietal lobe and certain subcortical sites (see reviews by Abbs and Welt 1985; Square-Storer 1987; Gracco and Abbs 1987).

Such findings should not lead one to assume dyspraxia is located in any one of these sites. Rather, as implied above, the question should be what contributions to the neurological substrate of speech production a site provides and what shortfall has the rest of the system to compensate for when it is impaired?

Trends in findings suggest a role of temporal-parietal cortex in non-time dominated goal-directed selection and assembly of superordinate aspects of emerging action. Rich interconnections exist to cerebellum, basal ganglia and frontal regions where more specific dimensions are organized and tailored to the internal and external environmental demands.

Organization of neuronal pools, referring here to lateral precentral cortex (Abbs *et al.* 1985; Gracco and Abbs 1987) appears to tie in with notions of functional synergies and motor equivalence. There are extensive overlaps of cortical motor patterns. Neurons in multiple discontinuous cortical areas converge on individual motoneuron pools and some pools have multiple muscle targets, thereby facilitating synergistic coupling. From intracortical microstimulation movement in a particular muscle or joint can be elicited at multiple sites. There appears to be a contrast between precentral strip excitation which produces isolated movement around a single joint (e.g. finger extension) while stimulation rostral to the primary motor cortex elicits across-joint reactions.

From these brief observations emerges the picture of possible neuronal correlates of functional synergies, and the basis for motor equivalence compensatory behaviour. Coupled with findings from regional cerebral blood flow and brain metabolic changes (Roland 1987) there is also support for the notion of spreading activation. The possible link between neuronal excitation and inhibition and the patterns of accretion and damping in interactive activation models is a point to link up here.

A feature of many studies (Kent and Rosenbek 1982; Gillmer and van der Merwe 1983; Hardcastle *et al.* 1985) and a factor that has historically and more recently fuelled (Schiff *et al.* 1983; Schiff *et al.* 1985; Crary *et al.* 1985) argument over the nature of the underlying disorder in dyspraxia has been the presence of what are normally considered dysarthric features in dyspraxics' speech and vice versa. There are two explanations for this. Firstly, natural lesions do not respect textbook divisions, and it is quite feasible to get a combined dyspraxia–dysarthria from, for example, a lesion compromising both cortex and underlying white matter. The second explanation derives from the nature of CNS organization. This chapter has favoured a view that sees action deriving from concerted interaction of multiple structures and pathways distributed throughout the system.

Upper motor neurone lesion characteristics might combine with dyspraxic ones where primary and secondary motor cortex and their interconnections are compromised. This would presumably give the speech equivalent of limb-kinetic dyspraxia (Liepmann 1908; Miller 1986). Tone and power and primary sensation are usually normal. The defect involves loss of synergistic muscle action around one joint (e.g. wrist extension) rather than individual muscles. Difficulty increases according to fine control demands rather than psycho-motor complexity, as in true dyspraxias. The defect is uniform across contexts (sense-nonsense words; spontaneous-imitation; sounds in isolation versus in sentences).

The frontal and parietal lobes also exchange afferents and efferents with basal ganglia and cerebellum. Recent research (Gracco and Abbs 1987; Marsden 1987; Rothwell 1987; Thach 1987) has confirmed their much more active role in action planning and execution than previously acknowledged.

Marsden suggests that the basal ganglia, acting on readout of existing sensory-motor cortical activity, direct the premotor cortex in the selection of correct parameters for programming of subsequent actions. Thach emphasizes the role of the cerebellum in adjusting the magnitude of signals to optimize motor performance, and Rothwell suggests that the cerebellum acts as coordinator of parallel inputs, from multiple brain areas, for an intended movement. As example he cites a pointing task requiring integration of shoulder and elbow extension, wrist rotation and digit extension. The cerebellum is presumed to scale the amplitude of these components to bring about correct and complementary amounts of movement at each joint. The cerebellum, in this view, transforms what we want to do into how we do it.

Within the framework of functional synergies, one would envisage the role of subcortical structures as switching and tuning the coordinative structures which have been activated, and abstractly entrained by higher cortical processes. The similarity between dyspraxic distortions and dysprosody (Kent and Rosenbek 1982; Gillmer and van der Merwe 1983) and ataxic and other extrapyramidal dysarthrias can thereby be understood as not purely coincidental.

Conclusions

This chapter has argued that there does exist a disorder of speech compatible with the definition given at the outset. At the same time it has tried to indicate directions to search for establishing and substantiating what lies behind some of the controversial ambiguous terms contained in the definition. Inadequacies in past descriptive and explanatory attempts were mentioned. One of the major stumbling blocks to advancement has been the mental–physical divide, manifest in speech study in a division phonemic–phonetic, with a tendency to view apparent phonological impairment as a dysphasic disorder separate from the motor disorder of speech apraxia. While there may be differential impairment of morphology, syntax and lexico-semantics versus speech (Square-Storer and Darley 1988) it is far less clear whether a strict division exists between phonology and articulation. This chapter attempted to resolve the clinical and theoretical impasses in this area by looking to organizational and control systems that reconcile the divisions.

A common language of control was sought that could apply equally to traditional apraxia of speech and literal paraphasia. Parallels in limb dyspraxia and deaf signers after CVA, as well as studies of normal motor control in other complex activities suggested two fruitful directions; firstly towards heterarchical interactive models of action planning and organization, and secondly, within this, towards functional synergies/coordinative structures as units of control. Given this framework speech was considered specialized but not special.

Through this the search for explanations of apraxia of speech switch from examination of absolutes to studying relative values of control parameters; from looking at static targets to analysing the dynamic postures and modulations between postures in attaining functional action goals via multiple means. The revised views also emphasize how many values arise out of the nature of organization and do not always need to be individually specified. The interactive view presented stressed, too, the dual consequences of action arising out of parallel, simultaneous interactive activation across all components of the system. On the one hand it meant that derailments might arise as much out of intercomponent misactivation as intracomponent breakdown, but it also meant that self-compensation and therapy could capitalize on the fluid organization to effect acceptable speech.

Finally, it is hoped that the departure from traditional strict dichotomies that this view permits, while still laden with controversies which will require clarification and confirmation, will nevertheless free the impasse that has existed in understanding pronunciation breakdown after brain insult.

Acknowledgement The typing of this chapter was assisted by a grant, number 186, from the South West Regional Health Authority, UK.

References

Abbs, J. (1986) Invariance and variability in speech production: a distinction between linguistic intent and its neuromotor implementation. In J. Perkell and D. Klatt (eds), (op.cit.) pp. 202–25.

Abbs, J. and Welt, C. (1985) Structure and function of the lateral precentral cortex: significance for speech motor control. In R. Daniloff (ed.), *Speech Science*. London: Taylor Francis.

Allport, A., MacKay, D., Prinz, W. and Sheerer, E. (eds) (1987) *Language Perception and Production: Relationships between Listening, Speaking, Reading and Writing*. London: Academic.

Bernstein, N. (1967) *Co-ordination and Regulation of Movement*. London: Pergamon.

Blumstein, S. (1973) *A Phonological Investigation of Aphasic Speech*. Hague: Mouton.

Blumstein, S. and Baum, S. (1987) Consonant production deficits in aphasia. In J. Ryalls (ed.), (op.cit.) pp. 3–21.

Blumstein, S., Cooper, W., Goodglass, H., Statlender, S. and Gottlieb, J. (1980) Production deficits in aphasia: a voice onset time analysis. *Brain Language* 9, 153–70.

Bromberger, S. and Halle, M. (1986) On the relationship of phonology and phonetics. In J. Perkell and D. Klatt (eds) (op.cit.).

Buckingham, H. (1979) Explanation in apraxia with consequences for the concept of apraxia of speech. *Brain Language* 8, 202–26.

Buckingham, H. (1981) A pre-history of the problem of Broca's aphasia. In R. Brookshire (ed.), *Clinical Aphasiology Conference Proceedings*, pp. 3–16. Minneapolis: BRK.

Buckingham, H. (1983) Apraxia of language versus apraxia of speech. In R. Magill (ed.), *Memory and Control of Actions*. Amsterdam: Elsevier.

Buckingham, H. (1986) Scan copier mechanism and the positional level of language production. *Cognitive Science* 10, 195–217.

Buckingham, H. and Yule, G. (1987) Phonemic false evaluation: theoretical and clinical aspects. *Clinical Linguistics and Phonetics* 1, 113–25.

Canter, G., Trost, J. and Burns, M. (1985) Contrasting speech patterns in apraxia of speech and phonemic paraphasia. *Brain Language* 24, 204–22.

Caplan, D. (1987) *Neurolinguistics and Linguistic Aphasiology*. Cambridge: Cambridge University Press.

Cooper, W. (ed.) (1983) *Cognitive Aspects of Skilled Typewriting*. New York: Springer.

Crary, M., Hardy, T. and Williams, W. (1985) Aphemia with dysarthria or apraxia of speech. In R. Brookshire (ed.), *Clinical Aphasiology*. Minneapolis: BRK.

Edwards, S. and Miller, N. (in press) An electropalotographic study of dysphasic misarticulation. *Clinical Linguistics and Phonetics.*

Elman, J. and McClelland, J. (1984) Speech perception as a cognitive process: the interactive activation model. In N. Lass (ed.), *Speech and Language* 10, 337–74.

Fowler, C. (1985) Current perspectives on language and speech production – a critical review. In R. Daniloff (ed.), *Speech Science.* London: Taylor Francis.

Fowler, C. and Smith, M. (1986) Speech perception as 'vector analysis': an approach to the problems of invariance and segmentation. In J. Perkell and D. Klatt (eds), (op.cit.) pp. 123–39.

Fromm, D., Abbs, J., McNeil, M. and Rosenbek, J. (1982) Simultaneous perceptual-physiological method for studying apraxia of speech. In R. Brookshire (ed.), *Clinical Aphasiology Conference Proceedings.* Minneapolis: BRK.

Garrett, M. (1984) Organisation of processing structure for language production: application to aphasic speech. In D. Caplan *et al.* (eds), *Biological Perspectives on Language.* Cambridge, Mass.: MIT.

Gillmer, E. and van der Merwe, A. (1983) Die Stemaanvangstyd van Apraktiese en Disartriese Sprekers. *S. African J. Communication Disorders* 30, 34–9.

Gracco, V. L. and Abbs, J. H. (1987) Programming and execution processes of speech movement control: potential neural correlates. In E. Keller and M. Gopnik, pp. 163–201.

Hardcastle, W., Morgan Barry, R. A. and Clark, C. (1985) Articulatory and voicing characteristics of adult dysarthric and verbal dyspraxic speakers: an instrumental study. *Brit. J. Disorders of Communic* 20, 249–70.

Harley, T. (1984) A critique of top-down independent levels models of speech pro-duction: evidence from non-plan internal speech errors. *Cognitive Science* 8, 191–219.

Harris, K., Tuller, B. and Kelso, J. (1986) Temporal invariance in the production of speech. In J. Perkell and D. Klatt (eds), (op.cit.) pp. 243–65.

Humphreys, G., Riddoch, M. and Quinlan, P. (1988) Cascade processes in picture identification. *Cognitive Neuropsychology* 5, 67–103.

Itoh, M. and Sasanuma, S. (1984) Articulatory movements in apraxia of speech. In J. Rosenbek *et al.*, *Apraxia of Speech.* San Diego: College Hill.

Itoh, M. and Sasanuma, S. (1987) Articulatory velocities of aphasic patients. In J. Ryalls (ed.), pp. 137–61.

Johns, D. and LaPointe, L. (1976) Neurogenic disorders of output processing: apraxia of speech. In H. Whitaker *et al.* (eds), *Studies in Neurolinguistics,* Vol. 1. London: Academic.

Katz, W. (1987) Anticipatory labial and lingual coarticulation in aphasia. In J. Ryalls (ed.), (op.cit.) pp. 221–42.

Keele, S. (1987) Sequencing and timing in skilled perception and action: an overview. In A. Allport *et al.* (eds) (op.cit.).

Keller, E. (1987) The cortical representation of motor processes of speech. In E. Keller and M. Gopnik, (op.cit.) pp. 125–62.

Keller, E. and Gopnik, M. (1987) *Motor and Sensory Processes of Language.* Hillsdale: Lawrence Erlbaum.

Kelso, J. (1986) Pattern formation in speech and limb movements involving many degrees of freedom. *Experimental Brain Research* 15, 105–28.

Kelso, J. and Tuller, B. (1987) Intrinsic time in speech production: theory, method-ology and preliminary observations. In E. Keller and M. Gopnik, (op.cit.) pp. 203–22.

Kent, R. and Rosenbek, J. (1982) Prosodic disturbance and neurologic lesion. *Brain Language* 15, 259–91.

Kent, R. and Rosenbek, J. (1983) Acoustic patterns of apraxia of speech. *J. Speech Hearing Research* 26, 231–49.

Kent, R. and McNeil, M. (1987) Relative timing of sentence repetition in apraxia of speech and conduction aphasia. In J. Ryalls (ed.), pp. 181–220.

Lebrun, Y. (1989) Apraxia of speech, the history of a concept. In P. Square-Storer (ed.) (op.cit.).

Lecours, A. R. and Nespoulous, J-L. (1988) The phonetic–phonemic dichotomy in aphasiology. *Aphasiology* 2, 329–36.

Lesser, R. (1978) *Linguistic Investigations of Aphasia*. Leeds: Arnold.

Liepmann, H. (1908) *Drei Aufsaetze aus dem Apraxiegebiet*. Berlin: Karger.

Lindblom, B. (1986) On the origin and purpose of discreteness and invariance in sound patterns. In J. Perkell and D. Klatt (eds), (op.cit.) pp. 493–523.

Luria, A. (1973) *The Working Brain*. Harmondsworth: Penguin.

McClelland, J. (1979) On the time relations of mental processes: an examination of systems of processes in cascade. *Psychological Review* 86, 287–330.

MacKay, D. (1987) Constraints on theories of sequencing and timing in language perception and production. In A. Allport *et al.* (eds) (op.cit.).

McNeil, M., Caliguiri, M., Weismer, G. and Rosenbek, J. (1986) Labio-mandibular kinematic durations velocities and dysmetrias in apraxic adults. In *Annual Convention American Speech-Language and Hearing Assoc.*, Detroit.

Marsden, C. (1987) What do the basal ganglia tell premotor cortical areas. In *CIBA Foundation Symposium 132*. Chichester: Wiley.

Martin, A. D. (1974) Some objections to the term 'apraxia of speech'. *J. Speech Hearing Disorders* 39, 53–64.

Miller, N. (1986) *Dyspraxia and Its Management*. Beckenham: Croom Helm.

Mlcoch, A. and Noll, J. (1980) Speech production models as related to the concept of apraxia of speech. In N. Lass (ed.), *Speech and Language* 4, pp. 201–38.

Mohr, J. (1980) Revision of Broca aphasia and the syndrome of Broca's area infarction and its implications in aphasia theory. In R. Brookshire (ed.), *Clinical Aphasiology Conference Proceedings*. Minneapolis: BRK.

Parsons, C., Lambier, J. and Miller, A. (1988) Phonological processes and phonemic paraphasias. *Aphasiology* 2, 45–54.

Perkell, J. and Klatt, D. (eds) (1986) *Invariance and Variability in Speech Processes*. Hillsdale: Lawrence Erlbaum.

Poizner, H., Bellugi, U. and Klima, E. (1987) *What the Hands Reveal about the Brain*. Cambridge, Mass.: MIT.

Reed, E. (1982) An outline of a theory of action systems. *J. of Motor Behaviour* 14, 98–134.

Roland, P. (1987) Metabolic mapping of sensorimotor integration in the human brain. In *CIBA Foundation Symposium 132*. Chichester: Wiley.

Rosenbek, J., McNeil, M. and Aronson, A. (eds) (1984) *Apraxia of Speech*. San Diego: College Hill.

Rothwell, J. (1987) *Control of Human Voluntary Movement*. Beckenham: Croom Helm.

Roy, E. and Square, P. (1985) Common considerations in the study of limb, verbal and oral apraxia. In E. Roy (ed.), *Neuropsychological Studies of Apraxia and Related Disorders*. Amsterdam: North-Holland.

Rumelhart, D. and McClelland, J. (eds) (1986) *Parallel Distributed Processing*, Vol. 1. Cambridge, Mass.: MIT.

Ryalls, J. (1987) Vowel production in aphasia: towards an account of the consonant–vowel dissociation. In J. Ryalls (ed.), pp. 23–43.

Ryalls, J. (ed.) (1987) *Phonetic Approaches to Speech Production in Aphasia and Related Disorders*. San Diego: College Hill.

Ryalls, J. and Behrens, S. (1988) An overview of changes in fundamental frequency associated with cortical insult. *Aphasiology* 2, 107–15.

Santo Pietro, M. and Rigrodsky, S. (1986) Patterns of oral-verbal perseveration in adult aphasics. *Brain Language* **29**, 1–17.

Schiff, H., Alexander, M., Naeser, M. and Galaburda, A. (1983) Aphemia: clinical-anatomic correlations. *Archives Neurology* **40**, 720–7.

Schiff, H., Blumstein, S., Ryalls, J. and Shinn, P. (1985) Aphemia: an acoustic phonetic analysis (abstract). *Neurology* **35** (Suppl. 1), 122.

Shaffer, L. (1981) Performances of Chopin, Bach, and Bartok: studies in motor programming. *Cognitive Psychology* **13**, 327–76.

Shattuck-Hufnagel, S. (1983) Sublexical units and suprasegmental structure in speech production planning. In P. MacNeilage (ed.), *Production of Speech*. New York: Springer.

Sloboda, J. (1983) Communication of musical metre in piano performance. *Quarterly J. Experimental Psychology* **35**, 377–96.

Square-Storer, P. (1987) Acquired apraxia of speech. In H. Winitz (ed.), *Human Communication and its Disorders*. Norwood: Ablex.

Square-Storer, P. and Darley, F. (1988) Non-speech and speech processing skills in patients with aphasia and apraxia of speech. *Brain Language* **33**, 65–85.

Square-Storer, P. (ed.) (1989) *Acquired Apraxia of Speech in Aphasic Adults*. London: Taylor Francis.

Stemberger, J. (1984) Inflectional malapropisms: form based errors in English morphology. *Linguistics* **21**, 573–602.

Stemberger, J. (1985) An interactive activation model of language production. In A. Ellis (ed.), *Progress in the Psychology of Language*, Vol. 1, pp. 143–86.

Sugishita, M., Konno, K., Kabe, S., Yunoki, K., Togashi, O. and Kawamura, M. (1987) Electropalatographic analysis of apraxia of speech in a left hander and a right hander. *Brain* **110**, 1393–417.

Thach, W. (1987) Cerebellar inputs to motor cortex. In *CIBA Foundation Symposium* 132. Chichester: Wiley.

Tuller, B. (1984) On categorising aphasic speech errors. *Neuropsychologia* **22**, 547–57.

Tuller, B. and Story, R. S. (1987) Anticipatory Coarticulation in Aphasia. In J. Ryalls (ed.), (op.cit.) pp. 243–60.

Wertz, R., LaPointe, L. and Rosenbek, J. (1984) *Apraxia of Speech: The Disorder and Its Treatment*. New York: Grune Stratton.

Wolk, L. (1986) Markedness Analysis of Consonant Error Productions in Apraxia of Speech. *J. Communication Disorders* **19**, 133–60.

Ziegler, W. and von Cramon, D. (1985) Anticipatory coarticulation in a patient with apraxia of speech. *Brain Language* **26**, 117–30.

Ziegler, W. and von Cramon, D. (1986a) Disturbed coarticulation in apraxia of speech: acoustic evidence. *Brain Language* **29**, 34–47.

Ziegler, W. and von Cramon, D. (1986b) Timing deficits in apraxia of speech. *European Archives Psychiatry Neurological Sciences* **236**, 44–9.

Chapter 9

Speech Automatisms and Recurring Utterances

Chris Code

Introduction

In this chapter the pathological speech automatisms and recurrent utterances which occur with aphasia are examined. While those traditionally associated with global or severe Broca's aphasia will be of primary concern, discussion will range over other forms of pathological automatic utterance associated with neurological conditions other than aphasia where they are relevant. We shall also be concerned to examine the apparent relationships between the different kinds of speech automatisms and to ask what they can tell us about normal speech production.

One of the common effects of brain damage is a tendency to be more stereotyped in behaviour. In a variety of neurological conditions we observe that individuals can be prevented from carrying out actions and action sequences in the absence of significant muscular paralysis. In contrast, we also observe neurological conditions where individuals are stuck with a pattern of behaviour that repeats itself, so that it appears as if the individual has lost the ability to prevent the emergence of previous patterns or to generate new and original patterns. It suggests the possibility of some mechanism within the central nervous system which is responsible for initiation and termination of action, and Marshall (1977) speculates on the notion of a central *starting* and *stopping mechanism*. In addition, this mechanism, or some associated *switching mechanism*, is required to process the events which underlie our ability to move rapidly from one activity to another.

The effects on general motor activity of damage to the hypothesized stop–go mechanism are seen in such neurological conditions as Parkinson's disease, chorea and apraxia. To varying degrees, and in diverse patterns, patients are unable to initiate voluntary action or prevent involuntary action. We can view normal speech production too as under similar control (Marshall 1977), and a variety of impairments in speech production illustrate how speech initiation and termination can be effected by neurological disease. Our concern will be with pathologies of speech where the individual appears unable to generate more than one or two automatic utterances. Those conditions where patients are unable to initiate utterance include apraxia of speech (see Ch. 8 above) and akinetic mutism (Marshall 1977; Brown 1988).

We concentrate our attention in this chapter on the common characteristics of aphasia, speech automatisms and recurrent utterances. Before this we set the stage by distinguishing between language which is propositional and language which is nonpropositional or automatic, and draw some conclusions regarding the relationship between automaticity in normal language and impaired language production.

Automatic and nonpropositional language

Much of our general behaviour is routine and 'automatic'. We do not consciously guide all of our mental and motor activity. When driving a car, for instance, we do not exert conscious control over all our actions. We are able to listen to the radio, conduct a conversation or plan a chapter for a book while simultaneously engaging gears, scanning the road ahead and steering the vehicle. On a familiar route we can drive miles without remembering that we have, and we are often surprised when we suddenly realize that we are at a particular point along our route. Most of this routine activity is carried out at automatic levels that do not engage conscious control.

Despite the originality and creativity of human language, there is much that is automatic and routine in speech production. We know that thousands of muscular contractions take place during every second of speech (Lenneberg 1967; Darley *et al.* 1975) which entail complex muscular activity at respiratory, articulatory, laryngeal and pharyngeal levels. This strongly suggests that much of our speech activity is not under ongoing, moment-to-moment control, with each segment being individually planned and sequentially executed. It would be physiologically impossible for us to produce speech at the speeds and with the facility that we do if we had to plan and execute each segment individually. We can view speech as a mixture of closed-loop (feedback-controlled), segmentally planned and executed on the one hand, and open-loop (not feedback-controlled), holistically planned and automatically executed, on the other (see Ch. 8 above, for further discussion of feedback in speech production). The physiological and mechanico-inertial constraints imposed on the neuromuscular systems, set against the speed and fluency of speech production, means that a significant amount of automaticity in speech activity is highly probable.

As discussed in Chapter 1 of this volume, hierarchy is a fundamental feature of the traditional Jacksonian neurological model. The opposing forces of inhibition and facilitation or excitation are understood to operate in an hierarchically organized fashion at different anatomical, developmental and evolutionary levels in the nervous system. In the Jacksonian (Jackson 1866, 1879) concept of **levels of representation**, expression by lower levels is inhibited by higher controlling levels. In this way Jackson saw language, and other functions, as having **multiple representation** at various neural levels. On this general model language is represented at different anatomico-structural levels in the central nervous system. Cortically mediated language is expressed through formal linguistic unit-to-rule processes, and more nonpropositional language, not amenable to such analyses, achieves realization through anatomically, hierarchically and phylogenically lower levels.

The recurring utterances and speech automatisms observed in aphasia were seen by Jackson as primitive and automatic behaviour which are the expression of levels lower down the neural hierarchy which have been released from higher level inhibition through brain damage. These 'additional' features of brain damage were interpreted as 'positive' symptoms by Jackson in contrast to deficits (losses) which he saw as 'negative' symptoms. However linguistically useless the newly acquired recurrent utterance is to the individual, it represents a pattern of behaviour that the individual did not have before the brain damage occurred. It is a recognition of the possibility that brain damage does not just result in loss of function, but can produce **change** in function.

Jackson proposed the notion of propositionality in language based on his observations of aphasic individuals with speech automatisms. This notion allows us to envisage a continuum from most automatic and nonpropositional kinds of language to most original and propositional. Nonpropositional speech appears to be produced, by definition, automatically, in the sense that the individual syntactic, morphological and phonological elements are not generated individually. This contrasts with propositional language where we are converting original ideas into novel utterances.

Despite the fact that Jackson's notion of the propositionality dimension in language was formulated over a hundred years ago, it is still only on the periphery of linguistic and psycholinguistic study. It has been argued (Code 1982a, 1987; Van Lancker 1975, 1987) that nonpropositional, holistically processed, formulaic language does not entail 'straight' linguistic, unit-and-rule analysis and synthesis. However, systematic investigation of nonpropositional and automatic language has been sparse because of the failure to provide much more than a vague, indeterminate and intuitive specification of what constitutes propositionality in language. It appears to be a factor of natural language use, but it is not a variable which can be easily manipulated in the psycholinguistics laboratory.

The hallmarks of nonpropositional language are invariance and automaticity. 'Automatic' and 'nonpropositional' are often used interchangeably, but we would want to distinguish between automatic language which is low in propositionality and automatic language which is higher in propositionality. Table 9.1 shows some ways in which language can vary along the propositionality dimension. Such activities as reciting a verse, counting, listing the days of the week, the months of the year, etc. and rote repetition of arithmetic tables are low in propositionality; they do not involve the generation of new ideas and their conversion into original utterances. Such idioms, everyday phrases and 'fillers' as 'Good morning', 'How are you?', 'sort of' and 'more or less' are examples of language which is low in propositionality. Probably these expressions do not engage components of a generative grammar. Thus, for such formulaic language, a syntactic, morphological and phonological specification is not required. Such idioms as 'now and then' and 'by the way' are most probably processed as single lexical items, as a complete holistic package. Expletives, swearing and emotionally expressive utterances are perhaps higher in propositionality as, unlike serial speech, they express and communicate internal states and feelings.

Table 9.1: Some examples of non-propositional language (the non-propositionality of which probably varies between individuals and contexts)

Serial-automatic speech (e.g., counting, days of week, months of year, recited arithmetic tables)
Singing, recitation of overfamiliar verses and rhymes
Swearing, expletives, coprolalic, and emotional utterances
Conventional social greetings (e.g., good morning, good night, thank you, excuse me, nice day)
Conversational fillers (e.g. you know, sort of)
Overused phrases, idioms, clichés, and stereotyped expressions

---

Source: Adapted with permission from Code, C. (1987) *Language, Aphasia and the Right Hemisphere*. Chichester: John Wiley and Sons. Copyright (1987) John Wiley and Sons.

The lack of variability is a major feature of automatic language. Repetitions of such utterances vary very little between productions. In everyday speech, productions of 'How are you?' will vary very little. An intonation contour specification for such an utterance is capable of variability as when, with the above example, your enquiry is meant to impart some genuine sympathy for a friend who has been ill ('How *are* you'?) compared to a production of the utterance which is meant to impart enthusiasm for meeting someone whom you have heard something about (e.g. 'How are *you*'?). However, the core linguistic features have not varied: the syntax, the morphology and the segmental phonology are the same.

The characteristics of more nonpropositional and automatic language then are invariance of production and nonsegmental-holistic construction. Notwithstanding, not all such language is devoid of meaning, and is therefore perhaps inappropriately termed 'nonpropositional'; expressions of pain, emotion and feeling, for instance, are high in expressive significance. Many nonpropositional communications, such as social greetings, have a major pragmatic function. Although automatic, therefore, the degree of 'propositionality' inherent in this kind of automatically produced language must be variable and is situation-specific. But the 'semantic specification' of such a nonpropositional utterance is a complete package, a 'sealed unit' – an holistic expression of meaning which is not divisible into smaller semantic units. Much nonpropositional language may therefore be seen as evolutionarily pre-linguistic. It is concerned with social and emotional aspects of communication and expression which pre-exist the capacity to generate propositional language in human beings.

There is not space here to review in detail the mass of evidence which has accumulated in recent years which supports the view, first expressed by Jackson, that the right hemisphere has at least equal involvement in the processing of automatic and nonpropositional aspects of language. Such aspects of human communication and expression as prosody (intonation, stress, etc.), emotional language, automatic language, idioms, metaphors, and other extralinguistic features which do not engage straight linguistic processes, appear to be processed with significant right hemisphere involvement (see Code 1987, for detailed discussion).

Speech automatisms in aphasia

While often discussed together, and seemingly having much in common, speech automatisms and recurring utterances are clearly descriptively dissimilar and we consider them separately in this chapter. However, such usage is not universal, and 'recurrent utterance' and 'speech automatism' are often used interchangeably. In line with the current literature, the term *speech automatism* is used in this chapter to describe repeated and unchanging utterances made up of recognizable words which some aphasic individuals produce either every time they attempt speech, or almost every time they attempt speech. These have also been termed real-word recurrent utterances (RWRUs) (Code 1982a). However, these are not the only features which characterize these utterances: the patient with such an utterance is severely, often globally, aphasic in all modalities; although made up of recognizable words, the utterance has no apparent referential or contextual connection with the patient's world; the utterance appears to be phonologically, syntactically and semantically identical each time it is produced. In the most severely aphasic individuals, the impression the observer gets is that the patient makes no attempt to suppress the utterance, and is apparently completely unaware of the inappropriateness of the utterance. Less severely aphasic patients with recurrent utterances suggest by their behaviour and response to testing that they are clearly aware that the utterance is being produced, without their intention, in place of an intended utterance. For such patients, speech is often accompanied by great struggle and frustration in an effort to suppress the emergence of the utterance.

Often cited as the first example in the aphasiology literature is Broca's (1861) first patient Leborgne who has come down in history with the name 'Tan' as this was his speech automatism (although it is not clear whether 'tan' is a real word). However, Lebrun (1986) cites a patient with the expletive '*Sacré nom de Dieu*' described just 1 week before Broca's case at the French Anthropological Society by Aubertin. These primitive expressions have interested some aphasiologists ever since Hughlings Jackson (1874, 1879) first wrote extensively about them, and a number of terms have been used to describe them. In fact there is still little agreement on the terms used to describe and distinguish between these utterances. Jackson (1874) himself called them 'recurrent utterances' and 'recurring utterances', while 'verbal stereotypy' (Alajouanine 1956; Lebrun 1986), 'speech automatism' (Huber *et al.* 1982) and 'neologistic automatisms' (Haas *et al.* 1988) are also in current use. Much of the contemporary research in the area is being carried out in Germany where *speech automatism* is the term used for stereotyped and inappropriate utterences (real-word and non-meaningful utterances), whereas *recurring utterance* is used to refer to the non-meaningful variety made up of concatenated CV syllables. In contrast, *stereotypies* are frequently used expressions that are usually situation-specific (e.g. 'My God' used a great deal, but in appropriate situations, by a patient described by Blanken *et al.*

1988). We will adopt this usage in this chapter, but to further distinguish the types, will use the terms 'real-word' and 'non-meaningful'.

Attempts to capture some essential nature of the real-word variety include 'formula speech' and 'ready-made speech' (Jackson, 1874) 'stock utterances' and 'barrel organisms'. Marshall (1977) brings us up to date with 'pre-packed speech'.

A problem which arises when approaching the linguistic nature of real-word speech automatisms is the degree to which we can analyse what is a 'frozen' utterance – not language at all in the linguistic sense. Table 9.2 (from Code 1982a) presents probably the largest collection of real-word speech automatisms in English. Firstly, we see that there are a number of proper names, expletives, repetitions and a number beginning with 'I'. The list in Table 9.2 was compared with word frequency counts in English (Code 1982a) which showed that (with the exception of expletives and proper names which do not appear in frequency counts of normal conversational English) the words which make up these utterances are high frequency with over 86 per cent occurring more than 50 times per million in everyday English.

Many of the examples in Table 9.2 can be classified into rough intuitive

Table 9.2: Real-word speech automatism

alright	I think one two	pardon for you
away away away	I said	Parrot (proper name)
BBC	It's a pity pity pity	piano
because	I want to	Wednesday
Bill Bill	I want to	Percy's died
Billy Billy	I want to one two one	sister sister
bloody hell	two	sister
bloody hell bugger	I try one two and I can't	so and so
down	and I want to	so so
I'm a stone	John	better better
I bin to town	milk	somewhere somewhere
fuck fuck fuck	money	three three
fuck off	no	time a time
fucking fucking fucking	no	tingaling
hell cor blimey	now wait a minute wait	today
funny thing funny	a	two two two
thing	minute wait a minute	washing machine
goody goody	off	sewing machine
I can't	oh boy	well I know
I can't	oh you bugger	yep
I can talk	oil	thing
I can try	factory	thingy
I can talk and I try	policeman	yes yes yes
I did not hear	on the corner	you can't
I told you	paper and pencil	

Source: Reprinted with permission from Code, C. (1982) Neurolinguistic analysis of recurrent utterances in aphasia. *Cortex* **18**, 141–52.

types. For instance, there are 11 expletives, 5 proper names ('Parrot' is a proper name), 4 yes/no and 5 numbers. Interestingly, all the expletives were produced by males in this collection and all the proper names were relatives of the patient in question. These types are predictable and have been described in the past. However, the most common type observed in this study was the pronoun + verb type (14), a previously undescribed type. Here a pronoun (predominantly 'I') is combined with an auxiliary or modal verb, and sometimes, one or two other words. Additionally, and intriguingly, the most common word in the collection was 'I', occurring 13 times. These utterances appear as very personal and emotional expressions, often executed with great feeling and frustration and give the impression of being functionally as well as syntactically incomplete. An interesting fact is that three patients produced the same utterance ('I want to . . .') and the probability of this happening purely by chance would appear to be very low indeed. This type in particular illustrates the very restricted semantic range utilized by these utterances.

Inspection of Table 9.2 reveals that these utterances are syntactically correct structures in the overwhelming majority of cases. With the possible exception of 'pardon for you' and 'time a time', the utterances do not break the syntactic rules of English. With few exceptions the initial words in these utterances are syntactically stressed contentives. Although it is not possible to be sure of the syntactic function of words in the sample, or even if the words have a syntactic function, an analysis of their simple 'parts of speech' functions reveals that 43 (from 68) initial words are either nouns, pronouns or verbs. These are contentives in the sense that they are lexical words, high in referential meaning, as opposed to serving a grammatical function. Although data was not available in this study on stress of utterances, many of the initial words in the sample would normally be stressed. This is not always the case for the pronoun + verb examples. 'I' in initial position is sometimes unstressed (e.g. I *know*, I *want*) but in the form emphasizing that it is 'I' and not another, it is stressed (e.g. *I* know, *I* want). As noted above, some writers have considered that agrammatism (see Perlman Lorch, Ch. 5 above) emerges with recovery from recurring utterance. Goodglass (1963, 1976) has shown that it is the stressed words which are retained in agrammatic speech and has suggested that in agrammatism it is the first stressed word in a planned utterance which is focused upon by the patient, as if the stress provided the word with sufficient power to allow retrieval by the patient's severely compromised speech production system.

The frequency and distribution of the speech sounds which make up the words of these expressions have also been examined (Code 1982a). Although it is probably inappropriate to call these sounds 'phonemes', as the evidence suggests that little linguistic input goes into recurrent utterances, the phones making up the words were compared to the phoneme counts which have been conducted on normal conversational English. There was a high correlation between the frequency of occurrence of phonemes in conversational English and real-word speech automatisms. There would appear to be a greater, but statistically insignificant, use of vowel articulations in the utterances than in conversational English: according to Fry (1947) the ratio of consonants to vowels is 62.54 per cent to 37.46 per cent in normal English respectively, but in real-word speech automatisms it was found to be 56 per cent to 46 per cent.

The distribution of consonants by voice, place of articulation and manner of articulation (e.g. fricatives, plosives, nasals, etc.) was compared to normal English distribution and showed that although the distribution by voice and place in these fragments is similar to conversational English, the manner of articulation compared to normal English shows some deviation with plosives accounting for 40.25 per cent of consonant productions in these utterances (normal English = 29.21 per cent), fricatives for 16.01 per cent (normal English = 28.01 per cent), nasals for 25.10 per cent (normal English = 18.46 per cent) and sonorants for 16.45 per cent (normal English = 19.42 per cent). There is evidence for an increase in use of the motorically 'easier' articulations and a reduction of articulations which are motorically more complex and marked.

Recurring utterances

The other type of automatically produced utterance common in 'motor' aphasia is the recurring utterance (Haas *et al.* 1988) or non-meaningful recurrent utterance (NMRU) (Code 1982a). These utterances are concatenations of speech sounds which do not make up recognizable words. They consist predominantly of reiterated CV (consonant + vowel) syllables. It can be seen from Table 9.3 (Code 1982a) that the utterances make use mainly of plosive consonants coupled with pure vowels. The consonant sounds which are used in speech automatisms are drawn from the most motorically 'easy' articulations; those phones which are 'marked' for ease of speech production.

Table 9.3: Examples of non-meaningful recurring utterances

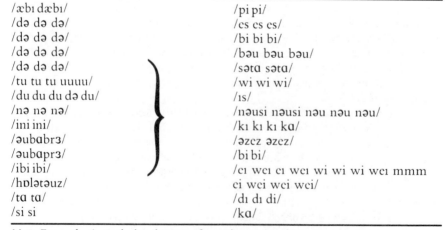

/æbɪ dæbɪ/	/pi pi/
/də də də/	/es es es/
/də də də/	/bi bi bi/
/də də də/	/bəu bəu bəu/
/də də də/	/sətɑ sətɑ/
/tu tu tu uuuu/	/wi wi wi/
/du du du də du/	/ɪs/
/nə nə nə/	/nəusi nəusi nəu nəu nəu/
/ini ini/	/kɪ kɪ kɪ kɑ/
/əubɑbrɜ/	/əzez əzez/
/əubɑprɜ/	/bi bi/
/ibi ibi/	/eɪ weɪ eɪ weɪ wi wi wi weɪ mmm
/hɒlətəuz/	eɪ weɪ weɪ weɪ/
/tɑ tɑ/	/dɪ dɪ di/
/si si	/kɑ/

Note: Examples in curly brackets are from the same subject.
Source: Reprinted with permission from Code, C. (1982) Neurolinguistic analysis of recurrent utterances in aphasia. *Cortex* **18**, 141–52.

Linguistic analysis shows a restricted use of the usual phoneme range of normal conversational English. Where the frequency of 'phonemes' used in the real-word variety correlates highly with normal English, for non-meaningful recurring utterances the frequency of occurrence does not reflect normal usage. Where /n/ and /t/ are the most common phonemes in the real-word type, and in normal English, in recurring utterances /i/, /schwa/, /b/ and /d/ are the most popular. There is also a marked increase in vowel articulations in this type: the ratio of consonants to vowels was found to be 47 per cent to 53 per cent (normal English = 62.54 per cent to 37.46 per cent). Where real-word utterances used 40 of the available 44 phonemes of English, the non-meaningful type used only 21, significantly less.

The comparison of the distribution of consonants by voice, place of articulation and manner of articulation in recurring utterances and normal English showed, like in the real-word variety, that the distribution by voice and place is similar to conversational English. However, the manner of articulation in recurring utterances shows plosives accounting for over 62 per cent of consonant productions (normal English = 29.21 per cent), fricatives for over 22 per cent (normal English = 28.01 per cent), nasals for 7.5 per cent (normal English = 18.46 per cent) and sonorants for 7.5 per cent (normal English = 19.42 per cent). In this type, therefore, there is a clear increase in use of the motorically simpler articulations with a corresponding reduction in motorically more complex articulations.

Although it has been traditionally held that patients with both types of speech automatisms are able to use normal intonation with their utterance to signify meaning, instrumental research has not been carried out to examine this question. Perceptual investigation, however, suggests a very restricted ability to vary intonation linguistically for patients with automatisms (Poeck *et al.* 1984; de Bleser and Poeck 1985). Despite this finding, recent research examined below suggests some ability to use intonation functionally.

Speech automatisms too are traditionally associated mainly with severe Broca's to global aphasia (Alajouanine 1956; Code 1982a), although there are recent findings which suggest that speech automatisms are not necessarily associated with severe Broca's to global aphasia (Blanken, personal communication). The Broca's or global patient appears to be very impaired in all areas of linguistic competence. It seems that such patients have severe deficits in their ability to utilize syntax, semantics and phonology in expression or comprehension in any modality. We might therefore conclude that the lesion has effectively destroyed most of the language system. However, recent evidence shows retention of certain language skills in some patients. There are indications that certain processes, mainly writing in the reported cases, can be partially preserved in some individuals with automatisms (Kremin 1987; Blanken *et al.* In press; Blanken *et al.* 1988). Kremin's patient could produce only the non-meaningful vowel sequence 'ah-oh-oh' (VV combinations would appear to be very rare), but produced relatively better performance on written naming, writing to dictation, repetition and reading aloud.

Blanken *et al.* (In press) describe a patient (FL) with extensive left hemisphere infarction of the area of supply of the left middle cerebral artery from a CVA in 1979, with spontaneous speech limited to the automatisms 'na-ta-ta-ta-ta', 'nau', 'ah' 'oh' and 'mhm'. The patient did not appear to be able to vary the intonation of the utterances to any extent and the utterances were produced 'fluently' with no sign of the articulatory struggle or searching characteristic of apraxia of speech. There was little spontaneous writing, though the patient was able to write his signature, address and date of birth. Speech could not be 'deblocked' through serial naming (days of week, months of year) or syntagmatic completion tasks such as completing pairs ('Night and . . .') or proverbs ('Practice makes . . .'). On tests of writing, however, the patient could insert missing letters into words, although markedly impaired at correcting single letter errors, and could convert spoken phonemes into written graphemes (phoneme-to-grapheme conversion).

On retest in 1985 there was found to be unexpectedly good written language abilities in comparison to speech. Writing concrete content words, more non–concrete words and function words to dictation produced performances between 42 to 50 per cent correct, with a slight advantage for higher-frequency content words (80 per cent correct). On oral naming the patient produced only non-meaningful recurring utterances, but was able to indicate some reliable knowledge of the correct length of one-syllable words only. On additional tests controlled for frequency, length and ambiguity, FL was able to write the names of 10 out of 30 words and write to dictation.

In a further recent study which examined the non-stereotyped features of nine severely impaired patients with automatisms, Blanken *et al.* (1988) found retained ability to differentiate question types and to complete serial sequences (e.g. counting, days of the week), and syntagmatic completion tasks such as completing pairs ('Night and . . .') and proverbs and idioms in six patients of the group. Despite their severe impairments these patients clearly had areas of retained ability. The authors point out that the patients could perform appropriate speech act decisions through language production indicating that pragmatic processing was intact and was not organized stereotypically. In addition, completion of automatic speech tasks was possible for 6 of the patients suggesting that for these patients at least the deficit underlying the generation of speech automatisms was *prearticulatory*. On the model proposed by Blanken *et al.* (1988) the ability of a patient to complete clues suggests a preserved capacity to execute phonetic sequences providing the articulatory processes can be sufficiently activated and carried through by overlearned and stereotyped sequences.

Related automatic and reiterative utterances

Other types of automatic, reiterated speech occur in neurological conditions other than aphasia, and some of these appear to be closely related to the speech automatisms produced by aphasic individuals. In individuals who suffer from anterior temporal lobe epilepsy, several types of language disturbance can occur during focal epileptic seizures. One is a kind of speech stereotype known as an *ictal speech automatism* (ISA) which is made up of recognizable words which appear to be linguistically correct, and for which the patient is amnesic following the attack. Several types have been described (Serafetinides and Falconer 1963; Falconer 1967): recurrent utterances, where the patient produces a repeated phrase (e.g. 'that is right, that is right', 'I must go, I must go'); irrelevant utterances which are almost conversational in style but not related to the immediate context; emotional utterances which may be related to an emotional and sometimes frightening hallucinatory experience where the individual appears to be talking to someone intent on doing them harm. Investigations suggest slightly more abnormal electro-encephalographic (EEG) patterns over the right hemisphere than the left during the production of these utterances (Hecaen and Angelergues 1960; Serafetinides and Falconer 1963; Kawai and Ohashi 1975; Koerner and Laxer 1988).

Chase *et al.* (1967) subjected a temporal-lobe epileptic patient to delayed auditory feedback (DAF) during the production of his ISA. Usually DAF causes an 'artificial stuttering' in a subject (increased amplitude and pitch, reduced rate of utterance, dysfluency) which is taken to indicate closed-loop auditory feedback control of speech. Chase *et al.*'s subject showed none of these effects, however, suggesting that speech during production of the automatism was under open-loop control: the automatism was produced as a single whole rather than segmentally.

The utterances observed in individuals with *Gille de la Tourette Syndrome* are of particular interest because, not only do they represent one of the only examples of spontaneous, involuntary speech produced by a conscious individual, but the *coprolalic* (obscene and sexual utterance) nature of the utterance has parallels with the expletive recurrent utterances described earlier. Tourette's syndrome afflicts mainly boys under 13 years (mean 7 yrs) and about 37 per cent of the population are either left-handed or of mixed handedness (Shapiro *et al.* 1972). Abnormalities in the EEG are found in most cases (Sweet *et al.* 1973).

The syndrome is characterized by a variety of involuntarily produced facial and body tics, barking and grunting, and, in the later stages, involuntarily produced automatic utterances which are usually coprolalic. Sometimes there may be echolalia. Although individuals with Tourette's syndrome are aware that they are producing these utterances, they appear still unable to suppress their emergence. It seems that the utterances, and other symptoms, manifest during times of stress which appears to reduce the individuals powers of suppression (Sweet *et al.* 1973). The disorder presents with limbic features, and basal ganglia lesions have been suggested as the neurological foundation (Darley *et al.* 1975; Lamandella 1977; Kent 1984).

There are clear parallels between the emotionally charged expressions and obscene language of ISAs and coprolalia and real word speech automatisms. Moreover, although ISAs and corprolalia are involuntary, ∼ll forms appear to be invariantly and holistically produced. Recurring utterances and speech automatisms are also repetitive. A patient will often repeat the utterance over and over again with some limited variation in intonation in the absence, as it were, of newly generated speech. Repetitiveness or reiteration is also a major feature of a range of behaviours which occur in aphasia and other conditions. While at the behaviourial level they appear to entail some impairment of attention and inhibition, they also seem to reflect a failure of 'the stop mechanism'.

Echolalia entails the repetition of a verbal stimulus from another person by way of response and can occur in a range of conditions. For instance, when asked 'What is your name'?, the patient with echolalia may reply 'What is your name'? It is a common observation in a range of mental and psychiatric disorders including Alzheimer's and Pick's disease and autism, as well as occurring in transcortical aphasia (Rubens and Kertesz 1983) and as part of the language impairment following thalamic haemorrhage (Mohr 1983). In mixed (motor and sensory) transcortical aphasia the echolalia appears in association with repetitive, stereotyped speech with an absence of propositional language and severely impaired comprehension. A number of studies have shown that transcortical patients can correct grammatically incorrect sentences given by an examiner (Whitaker 1976). 'This suggests that the peri-Sylvian language zone, though isolated and unable to perform semantic operations, has the capacity to recognize syntactically incorrect sentences and to change them into their correct form' (Rubens and Kertesz 1983: p. 265). As discussed in Chapter 1, the cause of transcortical sensory aphasia is either multi-focal or diffuse damage to anterior and posterior association areas which effectively isolates the peri-Sylvian language zone (Rubens and Kertesz 1983; Geschwind *et al.* 1968; Whitaker 1976). The language zone is therefore conceived as being intact though isolated from the general cognitive system.

Instead of responding to the stimulus, the patient with echolalia responds with a repetition of the stimulus. Unlike the aphasic individual with a speech automatism, the language system of the isolation patient is considered to be intact but unable to access higher cognitive centres. The lesion described by Geschwind leaves the language areas of the cortex undamaged, but results in significant damage to other higher cortical areas. While echolalia is thought to reflect basic automatic response associated with impaired comprehension, cases have been described where comprehension is good (Luria 1970; Rubens 1976).

Perseveration refers to a tendency to repeat a behaviour pattern over and over irrespective of the context or stimulus and is a common and major characteristic of brain damage manifest in all modalities (Allison 1966; Allison and Hurwitz 1967). Thus perseveration can occur on a variety of behaviours and activities, including writing, drawing, constructional tasks and speech (Helmick and Berg 1976; Sandson and Albert 1984). In writing, a patient with perseveration may write 'car' to command correctly, but when asked to write 'table' produces 'car' again. In more moderately affected cases the perseveration may be triggered by phonological similarity between stimulus items, so that the writing of 'car' and 'table' may be correct, but if asked to write 'cat' for the third item in a list, the patient may write 'car'. In severe cases the patient may be unable to write anything else but 'car' for the whole of a session. However, with a change of activity the perseverative behaviour may disappear, but only to emerge again on another task.

Sensitive tasks which detect perseveration include those which appear to require the patient to respond in the least automatic and most propositional manner, such as reversing a series in counting backwards or reciting the days of the week or months of the year backwards, drawing complex geometric designs from memory (such as the Bender-Gestalt designs used in the Wechsler Memory Scales), or having the patient write 'S' several times in series, and then to have them write it backwards (Luria 1970; Helmick and Berg 1976). If patients have a tendency towards perseverative behaviour then it is often observable in their general behaviour. Thus they may produce perseverations in spontaneous speech, in writing, comprehension, action and gesture.

Different types of perseveration have been described (Liepman 1905; Luria 1966; Helmick and Berg 1976; Sandson and Albert 1984; Santo Pietro and Rigrodsky 1986), including *continuous*, where some or all of a response is continued beyond the point of completion, and *repetitious* where some or all of a response or a previous response is repeated after an intervening event or interruption (Helmick and Berg 1976), and *semantic selection, program of action* and *phonemic carry-over* (Santo Pietro and Rigrodsky 1986). Perseveration can occur at the segmental level so producing phonemic paraphasias (see Buckingham, Ch. 6 above) and at the word level producing semantic or unrelated paraphasias (Santo Pietro and Rigrodsky 1986) as when the patient responds 'dog' correctly when shown a picture of a dog, but persists with 'dog' when shown a picture of a cup or a table.

Pallilalia is associated with Parkinson's disease, an extrapyramidal motor disorder associated with inadequate manufacture in the basal ganglia of the neurotransmitter dopamine (Boller *et al.* 1975; Darley *et al.* 1975; LaPointe and Horner 1981). Despite this, the large Mayo study of motor speech disorders (Darley *et al.* 1975) failed to find a case of extrapyramidal disease with pallilalia. The major feature of pallilalia is the tendency to repeat words and phrases during speech, mainly at the end of utterances. Examples from the case studied by LaPointe and Horner are 'from the gods to *foretell, foretell, foretell'*, 'in the air *they act, they act, they act'*, '*let me, let me, let me* keep a little of this wedding cake'. The examples from this study show that repetitions can occur at the beginning as well as at the end of utterances in some cases; propositional speech is the most vulnerable to pallilalia; in some cases reiterations can occur many times until the individual runs out of breath; repetitions tend to occur more on words with stops, nasals and affricates in initial position and less with glides, fricatives and vowels at the beginning of words. It is suggested that these utterances reflect a failure to inhibit unwanted speech (LaPointe and Horner 1981). We return to the role of the basal ganglia in motor speech programming later.

The major features of the speech automatisms of aphasia, the coprolalia of Gille de la Tourette syndrome and the ictal speech automatisms of epilepsy, are an apparent invariance and nonpropositionality; each production is linguistically the same and appears to have no referential link with the individual's present environment or state. Pallilalia and verbal perseveration appear to be unrelated to these phenomena and reiteration is their major feature. Aphasic speech automatisms are repetitive, but they do not appear to share other features. The pallilalia of Parkinson's disease appears to fit well into the general syndrome of extrapyramidal disorder – the patient can have, in addition to failure to halt an utterance, a parallel failure to halt action. As shown in an earlier section, the perseveration of the brain damaged individual manifests itself in nonverbal as well as verbal activities. Yet the mechanism which underlies speech automatisms appears to be speech-specific; there is no evidence of reiterative stereotyped behaviour in the gestural or graphic modalities of patients with speech automatisms (Blanken *et al.* In press).

Whither speech automatisms?

We have seen that linguistic analysis shows there is a preference for high-frequency words in real-word types, a much reduced range of phone use and a simplified distribution of phone use. These latter features are especially typical of the non-meaningful CV syllable type. Phoneme combinations adhere to the phonotactic constraints of the language (i.e. there are no 'foreign' or illegal phonemic combinations) and the real-word types do not break the syntactic combination rules of the language. We have also seen that many of the examples of real-word types exhibit features of 'normal' nonpropositional speech; i.e. expletives, serial speech, emotionally charged speech, 'dirty words'. Can this tell us anything about the origins of stereotyped utterances in neurological conditions and the processing of nonpropositional speech in normal speakers?

Before we look at the neural genesis of these utterances we will look at the environmental influences on their origins. When clinically observed a real-word speech automatism is nonpropositional and invariantly produced, although as indicated earlier, individuals may retain some ability to signal meaning change. But it may have been language in the full sense when first uttered and its frozen linguistic form may provide clues to the state of the language system at its origin, or clues to the nature of the language system's adaptation to insult.

A number of aphasiologists have considered that a patient's speech automatism had some special association with the actual moment of brain damage. Jackson is traditionally credited with suggesting that the utterance was a thought that the patient wished to express at the very moment of his or her stroke (this view cited by Alajouanine 1956, and Critchley 1970). An example of this provided by Jackson (1879) is the case of a man who was compiling a catalogue when his stroke occurred, and he was left with the utterance 'list complete'. A further example from Jackson is the woman whose utterance was 'gee gee', who was riding a donkey at the time of her CVA. This view is contrasted with that of Gowers (1887) who believed that the speech automatism was not a thought to be expressed, but was a thought already expressed, in fact, the last thing the patient said before the cerebral incident. Critchley (1970) favours this explanation and lists some outlandish examples. The patient with the utterance 'on the booze' had apparently had his stroke during what Critchley describes as 'a taproom brawl'. Another patient whose utterance was 'I want protection' sustained brain damage during a street fight, and an attractive woman of 'dubious marital status' (whatever that means) following a cerebral haemorrhage 'could say nothing but the revealing words "Not tonight, I'm tired" '. Yet another of Critchley's low-life patients who is said to have sustained a CVA while making love in the early hours was left with the utterance 'good morning' (p. 207). Alajouanine proposed an explanation somewhere between these two which considers a real-word utterance to have been a thought in the process of being organized into an utterance at the time of the cerebral incident.

In fact the contrast between these two explanations may be more apparent than real, especially as Jackson may have been misquoted. What he actually said regarding these utterances was 'I believe them to represent what was, or to represent part of what was, the last proposition the patient uttered *or was about to utter* (my emphasis) when taken ill' (Jackson 1879: p. 178); so it appears that Jackson did include the possibility that words were not actually uttered.

Whatever is the case these explanations emphasize a semantic, pragmatic or illocutionary connection between the utterance and an activity being pursued at the time of onset of brain damage, and all assume that the utterance has its origin at this moment. These explanations do not extend to the non-meaning-ful type, but conceivably these might be accommodated by an explanation which proposes that they are neologistic distortions of real words that were either spoken or about to be spoken before the CVA.

There are problems with these accounts for many of the speech automatisms described earlier, especially as patients can have more than one utterance (Code 1982a). Table 9.4 shows 14 patients (from 75 subjects) who presented with more than one utterance. In more than half there is a clear phonological, syntactic or semantic relationship between the utterances the patient produces. Also worth noting is that real-word and nonmeaningful types are rarely mixed (but see Blanken *et al.* In press, who describe two patients who mix the types). Additionally, it appears that in a number of cases individuals developed the second and subsequent utterances, and in six of the cases there was clear knowledge that one utterance existed independently before a second or third was added to the repertoire. There are also cases reported where a patient has acquired a new speech automatism (Lebrun 1986).

Those utterances which are second speech automatisms cannot be accounted for by the traditional explanations: they clearly emerged *following* the original neurological incident. Moreover, if we were to entertain the view that the second or third utterance to emerge might be linked to some pathological neurological incident, then we would have to explain how this could be given that the emergence of additional utterance in a patient is generally seen as a good sign of recovery. It would appear more parsimonious to suggest that the emergence of additional utterances is linked to some recovery of the underlying impairment where the individual can gain sufficient control to allow some variation in the single utterance they have been left with, and this is why subsequent utterances are often linguistically similar to the original. Moreover, analysis has made clear that a large proportion of these utterances represent a remarkably restricted semantic range. For this reason the common pronoun + verb type, in particular, is unlikely to have had its origin at the time of the stroke. The odds on 3 separate individuals engaged in identical pragmatic situations and all about to say 'I want to . . .' (see p. 160) at the moment of their stroke is unlikely, to say the least. It seems improbable that an individual's unexpressed or just about to be expressed thought at the precise time of the CVA should fall within the limited semantic range expressed by these utterances.

I have argued that many distinguishable speech automatisms could have there origin during the very early recovery of the patient (Code 1982b). Thus such utterances as 'BBC', 'sister, sister' and the serial type can be accounted for as originating in response to stimuli since the stroke. There are two broad possibilities: speech automatisms observed in clinic may be (a) related to the first utterance the patient produced post-onset of their stroke or (b) the first utterance the patient *heard* post-onset.

Table 9.4: Fourteen subjects presenting with more than one speech automatism

Subject	Speech Automatism	
1	I can talk	
	I can try	
	I can talk and try	
2	tu tu tu	
	du du du də du	
	dədədə	
	nə nə	
3	fucking fucking fucking hell cor blimey	1st
	funny thing funny thing	
4	bi bi bi	
	bəu bəu bəu	
5	washing machine	1st
	sewing machine	
6	I did not hear	
	I told you	
7	əzez əzez	1st
	piano	
	Wednesday	
8	oil	
	factory	
	policeman	
9	ini	
	əubɑbrɜ	
	əubɑprɜ	
	ibi ibi	
10	yep	
	thing	
	thingy	
11	down	1st
	I'm a stone	
	I bin to town	
12	so so	1st
	better better	
13	sister sister	1st
	Percy's died	
14	I want to one two one two	
	I try one two and I can't and I want to	

Note: Where known the first utterance is marked '1st'.
Source: Reprinted with permission from Code, C. (1982) Neurolinguistic analysis of recurrent utterance in aphasia. *Cortex* **18**, 141–52.

Therapeutic intervention from therapists, ward staff and relatives might account for some. It is possible that the serial-number type could originate through the initial interview with the therapist. It is common practice for the therapist on first seeing a severely aphasic patient on the ward to attempt to deblock speech through serial speech tasks, and it is often the only kind of speech severe patients can produce. Such residual abilities are often intensively drilled by ward staff and relatives. Lebrun (1986) cites Alajouanine's patient who managed to exclaim 'Telephone!' when hearing the bell ring, after which 'telephone' replaced the existing utterance. Environmental factors may be involved in the origin of expletives and many of the emotionally charged pronoun + noun types could be linked to initial frustration post-onset. The examples given by Jackson and Critchley could be seen as attempts to explain what was going on at the time of the incident. Some utterances could be related to the first utterance the patient heard post-onset. For example, the first thing heard by the patient with 'BBC' could have been a radio or television announcement, 'It's a pity' might have been expressed by a sympathetic nurse or relative, 'sister, sister' (two examples) is commonly heard in hospital wards and 'wee' is a common euphemism used with elderly patients. It is also possible that the 'I want to . . .' utterances could have originated through therapeutic intervention or adoption of a strategy by the patient (Wallesch, personal communication).

Involuntary utterances are possible from the brain under certain neurophysiological conditions, as during epileptic seizure and Gille de la Tourette syndrome. It is also the case that recognizable speech has never been elicited from the cerebral cortex with electrical stimulation (Penfield and Roberts 1959), but has been evoked during subcortical electrical stimulation (Ojemann 1983; Code 1987). It may be possible that some speech automatisms have their origins at the time of the cerebral incident due to some electro-chemical activity in subcortical mechanisms and others have their origins following the stroke and are the result of initial interactions with the environment. Examination of the limited linguistic qualities of speech automatisms suggests a range of different origins. Worth stating is that the restricted semantic range of the utterances shows that these are by no means arbitrary, randomly selected, expressions. Consequently it is unlikely to be the case that the majority of utterances have no connection at all with either pre- or post-CVA factors and that they never in their history had any illocutionary intention.

The pathogenesis of speech automatisms

Using the information we have on these expressions, what are the possible neurogenic mechanisms which underlie their origins and perpetuate their production? A range of recent studies have examined the neuropathology of aphasic speech automatisms. Blunk *et al.* (1981) found that globally aphasic patients with speech automatisms had large anterior lesions, whereas globally affected patients without such utterances had a more posterior pattern of damage. This suggests that speech automatisms occur with lesions of the 'greater' Broca's area, and are associated with severe aphasia and apraxia of speech. Subcortical and limbic structures have been implicated in automatism production, and the basal ganglia of the extrapyramidal system have received particular attention. The structure is seen as the site of a motor program generator (Kornhuber 1977; Darley *et al.* 1975), and damage here has been implicated in the production of recurring utterances, speech automatisms, coprolalia and pallilalia.

The results of Brunner *et al.* (1982) suggest that basal ganglia damage is essential for the production of speech automatisms. Of 40 subjects with CT-scan verified lesions of the left hemisphere, 26 had basal ganglia involvement. Twelve of the 26 had either recurring utterance or automatism. In this sample, neither recurring utterances nor automatisms occurred in patients without basal ganglia damage and these utterances did not occur in patients who had *only* subcortical (including the basal ganglia) damage. This latter group suffered only transient aphasia. In other words, a large left hemisphere lesion incorporating both the cortex and basal ganglia is required to cause these utterances. Of these 12 patients, 9 had both anterior and posterior damage involving the basal ganglia and 3 had just anterior damage involving the basal ganglia.

The CT study of 8 patients with exclusively CV recurring utterances by Poeck *et al.* (1984) was unable to verify the importance of the basal ganglia. They found also that there were no significant differences in lesion patterns for global patients with and without automatisms. However, as Haas *et al.* (1988) have pointed out, Poeck *et al.* designated as damaged structures where more than 30 per cent was included in the CT scan. In addition, patients of less than 2 months onset were included in the Poeck *et al.* study who must be considered unstabilized. Haas *et al.* (1988) conducted a recent CT study on 49 aphasic patients with damage including more than 2 per cent of forebrain volume who were more than four months post-onset. Sixteen of the group had non-meaningful utterances and two real-word speech automatisms and all 18 had lesions in the deep fronto-parietal white matter of the left hemisphere. The detailed analysis suggested a relationship between recurring utterance production and structures in the depth of the area of supply of the middle cerebral artery.

There is known to be an association between age and aphasia (Obler *et al.* 1978; De Renzi *et al.* 1980; Kertesz and Sheppard 1981; Brown and Grober 1983; Code and Rowley 1987) which may reflect *continuing lateralization* where hemispheric specialization develops through life from infancy to late adulthood (Brown and Jaffe 1975). This continuing lateralization hypothesis proposes that aphasia type can be predicted as a function of age because a different neural substrate for language exists at different ages. Hass *et al.* found that recurring utterances were associated with older patients suggesting that recurring utterances could be due to continuing left lateralization or degenerative damage not visible on the CT scan associated with advancing age, or some diffuse and progressive vascular pathology. Current evidence therefore suggests that the pathogenesis of recurring utterances is not unifactorial – diffuse brain damage associated with advancing age or progressive vascular insufficiency combined with subcortical (including basal ganglia) damage may interact to leave a globally aphasic individual with a recurring utterance.

Our general neurolinguistic perspectives have been widened in recent years, directly related to the development of more sophisticated imaging techniques, and we now appreciate the fuller involvement of the whole brain in communication. There is more to language than is covered by a generative model and more to brain than the neocortex. Apart from the specific roles of the subcortical structures and the right hemisphere already alluded to, the contribution made to human communication by the complex network of cortical and subcortical structures of the forebrain known as *the limbic system* has been emphasized (Lamendella 1977).

In all mammals this ancient system is implicated in the expression of emotional and affective processing in automatic signals of rage, fear, surprise (as it is in humans) and social expressions of dominance, submission and aggression, as well as male–female and mother–child relationships. It is suggested that the right hemisphere has a special relationship with the affective subsystems of the limbic system, a relationship that the left hemisphere does not enjoy. For Lamendella the limbic system is 'the obvious candidate for the level of brain activity likely to be responsible for the bulk of nonpropositional human communication' (p. 159) and 'the "homebase" for communication functions in primates even though both higher and lower levels of brain organization are involved in the overall behaviour complex in which limbic activity plays the dominant role' (p. 188). In temporal lobe epilepsy it is areas of the limbic system which 'trigger' the seizure which produce the ISAs discussed earlier and Tourette's syndrome presents with limbic features.

It has been argued that some real-word utterances fit well with what we know of right hemisphere-limbic interactions (Code 1987). The emotionally charged, obscene and expletive utterances are favourite candidates, being holistically produced without formal linguistic input. 'Assuming that the limbic system has no linguistic or phonetic programming capability, but is simply the motivational force behind the utterance, then the right hemisphere, through its capacity to provide a motor Gestalt, controls the actual motor speech activity of the phonoarticulatory mechanisms' (Code 1987: p. 73). The same arguments can be applied to coprolalia and ictal speech automatisms. Here too the fragment of emotionally charged, holistically structured and invariantly produced language implicates a limbic–right hemisphere interaction.

Concatenated CV syllables, although clearly nonpropositional, have no 'words' to implicate affective-emotional processing, they do not appear to be produced holistically and prosody is also impaired. These utterances appear to be produced segmentally and are not arbitrary CV syllables but concatenations governed by phonological constraints. The utterances appear to reflect a simplification process where only high frequency and motorically 'easy' articulations taken from the phonetic inventory of the speaker's language are produced to conform to phonotactic rules. For these reasons it has been suggested (Code 1987) that the initial production of a non-meaningful type of CV syllable automatism is by a severely compromised left hemisphere phonological system without subcortical-right hemisphere input. The finding that damage is in the deep fronto-parietal white matter disconnecting right hemisphere and subcortical systems from left cortical areas is compatible with this hypothesis.

Conclusions

Real-word speech automatisms may originate as holistically created products of a right hemisphere–limbic system mechanism. If they do then the linguistic system of the left hemisphere is not engaged during their genesis. In the case of the non-meaningful variety, almost by default as they showed little evidence of right hemisphere language structure, it was suggested that these utterances might be the product of severely compromised left hemisphere mechanisms disconnected from subcortical and right hemisphere mechanisms. This might suggest that access to the phonology was so impaired that only very primitive CV syllables (usually one repeated syllable) were produced. The continuing failure on the part of the individual to produce more than the automatism will only be frustrated by an almost total apraxia of phonoarticulatory mechanisms.

The real-word variety have an adequate, if limited, syntactic structure. Some carry a restricted range of semantic reference while a large group appear semantically bizarre with no apparent reference to objects or experience in the individual utterer's world. This could suggest that different processing mechanisms may be responsible for the production of different types. It may be, for instance, that expletives, pronoun + modal auxiliaries, real name types, bizarre – all have different underlying mechanisms. In terms of modular access non-meaningful types may fail to access phonological modules, semantically bizarre fail to access semantic or lexical output modules, and the pronoun + verb types fail to complete because of an inadequate lexical specification. A further important dimension is the apparent chronically impaired phonoarticulatory mechanism where these utterances are, in many patients, the complete extent of the individual's speech repertoire. The invariant nature of both types of automatism implies no access to linguistic components at all, at least following the first utterance of the expression, although recent research suggests significant individual variability in severity. More detailed investigation of small groups shows a variety of retained expressive and receptive abilities in some patients.

In speech automatisms we see, especially in the case of automatically reiterated CV syllables, perhaps the most primitive capability of the fragmented expressive speech mechanism. Despite the primeval nature of some real-word utterances, they perhaps express fundamental emotional reactions to a devastating and cataclysmic circumstance. Investigation of the variety of utterances suggests that what we may also be observing is the fractionated output of different sub-systems reflecting contributions from neuronal structures and mechanisms at different organizational and representational levels throughout the brain.

Acknowledgements I am grateful to Claus Wallesch and Gerhard Blanken for insightful comments on an earlier draft of this chapter.

References

Alajouanine, T. (1956) Verbal realization in aphasia. *Brain* **79**, 1–28.

Allison, R. S. (1966) Perseveration as a sign of diffuse and focal brain damage-1. *British Medical Journal* **2**, 1027–32.

Allison, R. S. and Hurwitz, L. J. (1967) On perseveration in aphasics. *Brain* **90**, 429–48.

Blanken, G., Dittmann, J., Haas, J-C. and Wallesch, C-W. (1988) Producing speech automatisms (recurring utterances): looking for what is left. *Aphasiology* **2**, 545–56.

Blanken, G., De Langen, E. G., Dittmann, J. and Wallesch, C-W. (Submitted) Implications of preserved written language abilities for the functional basis of speech automatisms (recurring utterances): A single case study.

Blanken, G., Papagno, C., Wallesch, C-W., Mezger, G. and Dittmann, J. (In press) Varieties of linguistic performance in aphasics with speech automatisms (recurring utterances).

Bleser, R. de and Poeck, K. (1985) Analysis of prosody in the spontaneous speech of patients with CV-recurring utterances. *Cortex* **21**, 405–16.

Blunk, R., De Bleser, R., Willmes, K. and Zeumer, H. (1981) A refined method to relate morphological and functional aspects of aphasia. *European Neurology* **30**, 68–79.

Boller, F., Albert, M. and Denes, F. (1975) Pallilalia. *British Journal of Disorders of Communication* **10**, 92–7.

Broca, P. (1861) Remarques sur le siege de la faculté du langage articule suivies d'une observation d'aphemie (perte de la parole). *Paris Bulletin de la Societe d'Anatomie* **36**, 330–57.

Brown, J. W. (1988) *The Life of the Mind*. Hillsdale, New Jersey: Lawrence Erlbaum Associates.

Brown, J. W. and Grober, E. (1983) Age, sex, and aphasia type: evidence for a regional cerebral growth process underlying lateralization. *The Journal of Nervous and Mental Disease* **171**, 431–4.

Brown, J. and Jaffe, J. (1975) Hypothesis on cerebral dominance. *Neuropsychologia* **13**, 107–10.

Brunner, R. J., Kornhuber, H. H., Seemuller, E., Suger, G. and Wallesch, C-W. (1982) Basal ganglia participation in language pathology. *Brain and Language* **16**, 281–99.

Chase, R. A., Cullen, J. K., Niedermeyer, E. F., Stark, R. E. and Blumer, D. P. (1967) Ictal speech automatisms and swearing: studies on the auditory feedback control of speech. *The Journal of Nervous and Mental Disease* **144**, 406–20.

Code, C. (1982a) Neurolinguistic analyais of recurrent utterance in aphasia. *Cortex* **18**, 141–52.

Code, C. (1982b) On the origins of recurrent utterances in aphasia. *Cortex* **18**, 161–4.

Code, C. (1987) *Language, Aphasia, and the Right Hemisphere*. Chichester: John Wiley & Sons.

Code, C. and Rowley, D. (1987) Age and aphasia type: the interaction of sex, time since onset and handedness. *Aphasiology* **1**, 339–45.

Critchley, M. (1970) *Aphasiology and Other Aspects of Language*. London: Edward Arnold.

Darley, F. L., Aronson, A. E. and Brown, J. R. (1975). *Motor Speech Disorders*. Philadelphia: Saunders.

Falconer, M. A. (1967) Brain mechanisms suggested by neurophysiologic studies. In C. H. Millikan and F. L. Darley (eds), *Brain Mechanisms Underlying Speech and Language*. New York: Grune and Stratton.

Fry, D. B. (1947) The frequency of occurrence of speech in Southern English. *Arch. Neerlandaises de Phonetique Experimentale* **20**, 103–6.

Geschwind, N., Quadfasel, F. and Segarra, J. (1968) Isolation of the speech area. *Neuropsychologia* **6**, 327–40.

Goodglass, H. (1963) Redefining the concept of agrammatism in aphasia. In L. Croatto and C. Croatto-Martinolli (eds) *Proceeding of the 12th. International Speech and Voice Therapy Conference of the International Association of Logopedics and Phoniatrics*. Padua, 108–16.

Goodglass, H. (1976) Agrammatism. In H. Whitaker and H. A. Whitaker (eds) *Studies in Neurolinguistics*, Vol. I. New York: Academic Press.

Gowers, W. R. (1887) *Lectures in the Diagnosis of Diseases of the Brain*. Philadelphia: P. Blakiston.

Haas, J. C., Blanken, G., Mezger, G. and Wallesch, C-W. (1988) Is there an anatomical basis for the production of speech automatisms? *Aphasiology* **2**, 552–65.

Hecaen, H. and Angelergues, R. (1960) Epilepsie et troubles de langage. *Encephale* **49**, 138–69.

Helmick, J. W. and Berg, C. B. (1976) Perseveration in brain-injured adults. *Journal of Communication Disorders* **9**, 143–56.

Huber, W., Poeck, K. and Weniger, D. (1982) Aphasie. In K. Poeck (ed.), *Klinische Neuropsychologie*. Stuttgart: Thieme.

Jackson, J. H. (1866) Notes on the physiology and pathology of language. In J. Taylor (ed.) (1958) *Selected Writings of John Hughlings Jackson*, Vol. II. London: Staples Press.

Jackson, J. H. (1874) On the nature of the duality of the brain. In J. Taylor (ed.) *Selected Writings of John Hughlings Jackson*, Vol. II. London: Staples Press.

Jackson, J. H. (1879) On affections of speech from disease of the brain. In J. Taylor (ed.) *Selected Writings of John Hughlings Jackson*, Vol. II. London: Staples Press.

Kawai, I. and Ohashi, H. (1975) Ictal speech disturbance and cerebral dominance. *Studia Phonologica* **9**, 40–4.

Kent, R. D. (1984) Brain mechanisms of speech and language with special reference to emotional interactions. In R. C. Naremore (ed.), *Language Science*. San Diego: College-Hill Press.

Kertesz, A. (1979) *Aphasia and Associated Disorders*. New York: Grune & Stratton.

Kertesz, A. and Sheppard, A. (1981) The epidemiology of aphasic and cognitive impairment in stroke: age, sex, aphasia type and laterality differences. *Brain* **104**, 117–28.

Koerner, M. and Laxer, K. D. (1988) Ictal speech, postictal language dysfunction, and seizure lateralization. *Neurology* **38**, 634–6.

Kornhuber, H. H. (1977) A reconstruction of the cortical and subcortical mechanisms involved in speech and aphasia. In J. E. Desmedt (ed.) *Language and Hemispheric Specialization in Man: Cerebral ERPs*. Basel: Karger.

Kremin, H. (1987) Is there more than ah-oh-ah? Alternative strategies for writing and repeating lexically. In M. Coltheart, R. Job and G. Sartori (eds) *The Cognitive Neuropsychology of Language*. London: Lawrence Erlbaum Associates.

Lamendella, J. T. (1977) The limbic system in human communication. In H. Whitaker and H. A. Whitaker (eds), *Studies in Neurolinguistics*, Vol. III. London: Academic Press.

LaPointe, L. L. and Horner, J. (1981) Pallilalia: a descriptive study of pathological reiterative utterances. *Journal of Speech and Hearing Disorders* **46**, 90–105.

Lebrun, Y. (1986) Aphasia with recurrent utterances: A review. *British Journal of Disorders of Communication* **21**, 3–10.

Lenneberg, E. (1967) *The Biological Foundations of Language*. New York: John Wiley and Sons.

Liepmann, H. (1905) *Ueber storungen des handlens bei gehirnkranken*. Berlin: Karger.

Luria, A. R. (1966) *Human Brain and Psychological Processes*. New York: Harper and Row.

Luria, A. R. (1970) *Traumatic Aphasia*. The Hague: Mouton.

Marshall, J. (1977) Disorders in the expression of language. In J. Morton and J. C. Marshall (eds), *Psycholinguistics Series-1: Developmental and Pathological*. London: Elek Science.

Mohr, J. P. (1983) Thalamic lesions and syndromes. In A. Kertesz (ed.) *Localization in Neuropsychology*. New York: Academic Press.

Obler, L., Albert, M., Goodglass, H. and Benson, D. F. (1978) Aphasia type and aging. *Brain and Language* **6**, 318–22.

Ojemann, G. A. (1983) Brain organization for language from the perspective of electrical stimulation mapping. *The Behavioral and Brain Sciences* **2**, 189–230.

Penfield, W. and Roberts, L. (1959) *Speech and Brain Mechanisms*. Princeton: Princeton University Press.

Poeck, K., De Bleser, R. and Von Keyserlingk, D. (1984) Neurolinguistic status and localization of lesion in aphasic patients with exclusively consonant-vowel (CV)-recurring utterances. *Brain* **107**, 199–217.

Renzi, E. de, Faglioni, P. and Ferrari, P. (1980) The influence of sex and age on the incidence and type of aphasia. *Cortex* **16**, 627–30.

Rubens, A. B. (1976) Transcortical motor aphasia. In H. Whitaker and H. A. Whitaker (eds), *Studies in Neurolinguistics*, Vol. 1. New York: Academic Press.

Rubens, A. B. and Kertesz, A. (1983) The localization of lesions in transcortical aphasias. In A. Kertesz (ed.), *Localization in Neuropsychology*. New York: Academic Press.

Sandson, J. and Albert, M. L. (1984) Varieties of perseveration. *Neuropsychologia* **22**, 715–32.

Santo Pietro, M. J. and Rigrodsky, S. (1986) Patterns of oral-verbal perseveration in adult aphasics. *Brain and Language* **29**, 1–17.

Serafetinides, E. A. and Falconer, M. A. (1963) Speech disturbances in temporal lobe seizures: a study of 100 epileptic patients submitted to anterior temporal lobectomy. *Brain* **86**, 333–46.

Shapiro, A. K., Shapiro, E. and Wayne, H. (1972) Birth, developmental, and family histories and demographic information in Tourette's syndrome. *Journal of Nervous and Mental Disease* **155**, 335–44.

Sweet, R. D., Solomon, G., Wayne, H., Shapiro, E. and Shapiro, A. (1973) Neurological features of Gilles de la Tourette's syndrome. *Journal of Neurology, Neurosurgery and Psychiatry* **36**, 1–9.

Van Lancker, D. (1975) Heterogeneity in language and speech. *UCLA Working Papers in Phonetics* 29.

Van Lancker, D. (1987) Nonpropositional speech: neurolinguistic studies. In A. W. Ellis (ed.) *Progress in the Psychology of Language*, Vol. III. London: Lawrence Erlbaum Associates.

Whitaker, H. (1976) A case of isolation of the language function. In H. Whitaker and H. A. Whitaker (eds) *Studies in Neurolinguistics*, Vol. I. New York: Academic Press.

Chapter 10

Acquired Disorders of Reading and Spelling: A Cognitive Neuropsychological Perspective

Christopher Barry

Psychologists researching the mechanisms and processes underlying normal cognitive functions have become increasingly interested in the study of how these may break-down in patients with acquired neurological damage. In this chapter, I shall give an introduction to how cognitive psychologists have interpreted the varieties of disorders of reading and spelling that follow brain damage and which are often concomitant features of aphasia. Such disorders are *acquired* dyslexias and dysgraphias, because they occur as a result of neurological damage in adults in whom reading and spelling were premorbidly normal. As such, they are to be distinguished from *developmental* disorders of literacy (to which the blanket term *dyslexia* is commonly applied). This chapter will review a number of the major varieties of these acquired disorders of literacy. My approach throughout the chapter will be a *cognitive neuropsychological* one (see Ch. 1). Although not to the taste of all *neuro*psychologists, this has been the approach within which much of the recent detailed empirical characterization of acquired dyslexia and dysgraphia has taken place. Cognitive neuropsychology entails a reciprocal relationship between theories of normal cognitive processes and investigations of acquired disorders of those processes. On the one hand, data from neurological patients are used to illuminate theories of normal processing. On the other hand, patterns of specific impaired and preserved abilities of particular neurological patients are interpreted within models of normal processing: the performance observed is presumed to reflect selective breakdown of (or functional dissociation between) separable, normal processing systems. In this chapter I will focus on this second, interpretative aim of cognitive neuropsychology and so, before my descriptive account of reading and spelling disorders, I will need to discuss briefly the general theoretical framework within which one may attempt to understand *normal* visual word recognition and production. I shall first consider reading. I shall discuss the construction of a model of the oral reading of single words (and nonwords such as *MANT*) and show how predictions concerning acquired disorders of reading may be derived from it. These hypothetical disorders will be used to structure a discussion and evaluation of different varieties of acquired dyslexia. Varieties of acquired dysgraphia will then be described and interpreted within a structurally similar model of spelling production. It will then be necessary to consider the heterogeneity within these varieties of reading and spelling disorders and to consider the utility of analyses based upon clinical syndromes. Finally, I shall offer a brief discussion of the relationship between reading and spelling disorders.

A model of oral reading

In order to be a skilled, competent language-user, one must possess (and be able to operate upon) stored information concerning the meaning, sound and spelling of all the words one knows. How is this information stored? And, how do we move from one domain of information to another? In attempting to illuminate some of the theoretical issues underlying language use, cognitive psychologists have advanced the notion of an internal lexicon and an obvious place to begin a discussion of the organization of such an internal lexicon is to consider a word's representation in an external lexicon. In my pocket dictionary, the entry for the word 'mauve' is given as follows:

mauve (mōv) n. pale purple colour. -a. of this colour.

In this entry, the following domains of information (or codes) are represented: orthography (the spelling of the word, represented here in the word's 'heading' of the entry), phonology (a guide to the word's pronunciation), syntax (indicating the word's grammatical classes) and semantics (definitions of the word). From this simple dictionary entry, we can also see how we may move from one domain to another; for example, it is possible to obtain the word's pronunciation without actually consulting the word's semantics. This entry may be represented diagrammatically as in Figure 10.1, which shows the three domains of information and some connections between them.

The word 'mauve' has been artfully chosen. In fact, I selected this example for two reasons. First, 'mauve' is a word with an irregular spelling-to-sound correspondence and in my pocket dictionary (as in others) only such irregular or exception words are given a specific pronunciation guide. For the majority of words, pronunciations may be generated from general rules (that may be listed elsewhere). However, I selected 'mauve' to show that word phonology can be stored in dictionary entries (and could, in principle, be stored for all words). Second, the semantic code for this colour word refers to conceptual knowledge: aspects of the 'definition' of the word refer to other entries (e.g., to the meaning of the word 'pale') and to referential systems not represented in words (experiences of perceived and labelled colours for this example).

As a model of the internal lexicon, Figure 10.1 is clearly incomplete. For example, there must be some connection from the semantic domain to word phonology to permit spontaneous speaking. In fact, Figure 10.1 is incomplete even for those limited components and connections which are necessary to permit the full range of normal oral reading skills: there are other functions we can perform, such as reading aloud a nonword such as *POG*. We also require an input system to allow us to recognize that **cat**, CAT, *cat* and **cat** are all instances of the same word and an output system to permit us to hold

Figure 10.1 The informational domains of a dictionary entry (for the word 'mauve')

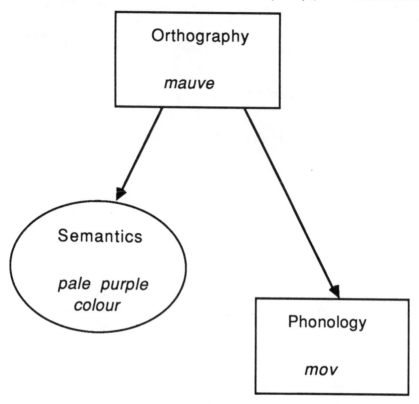

phonological forms, such as /cæt/, while we get our articulators working, as we may want to produce words in a variety of different contexts, intonations, etc. Figure 10.2 therefore shows a number of these necessary additions: a visual (and/or graphemic) input analysis system; a phonological output buffer system (which temporarily holds phonological codes); a system permitting assembled phonological recoding (necessary for reading nonwords); and also a connection from the semantic system to word phonology.

Essentially identical models to that represented in Figure 10.2 have been advanced by many authors (e.g. Ellis 1983; Coltheart 1985) and a prototype of this type of model may be found in Morton and Patterson (1980). Although the model as shown in Figure 10.2 has been motivated here solely by logical linguistic and intuitive *psycho*-linguistic reasoning, there exists a range of experimental data from normal readers that is broadly consistent with such a model.

I have labelled a number of 'routes' in Figure 10.2. These 'routes' are not to be seen as the specified neural pathways that the nineteenth-century 'diagram-makers' such as Wernicke attempted to delineate. Rather, they are functional, information processing channels; i.e. sequences of processing components and the connections between them. Route **A** is the process by which we implement 'phonic' reading: it assembles phonological codes from orthographic ones. It

Figure 10.2 A model of the component processes underlying oral reading

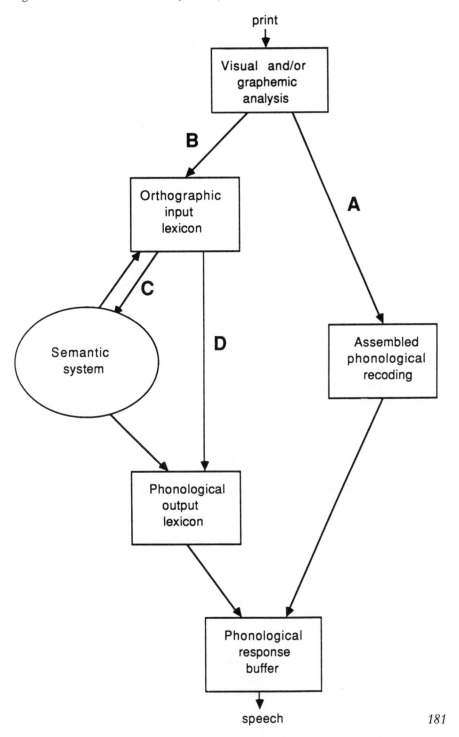

is often conceived as a set of grapheme-to-phoneme correspondence (or GPC) rules. However, there is increasing evidence that the phonological correspondences of orthographic units larger than graphemes (e.g. terminal vowel+consonant 'bodies' such as -*EAD*, as in *bead* and *head*; Patterson and Morton 1985) may also be used in the recoding process. Indeed, some authors (e.g. Marcel 1980) have gone further and have suggested that assembled phonological recoding operates by a process of lexical analogy. The operation of route **A** enables us to read aloud nonwords (and all words which have no representation in our internal lexicons). Route **A** would also correctly read aloud words with regular spelling-to-sound correspondences, but would falter over irregular words such as *YACHT* (which would be pronounced 'regularly' but incorrectly as /jætʃt/).

Route **B** may be seen as the access route to our 'sight vocabulary'. The orthographic input lexicon contains the 'dictionary headings' for all words we know (irrespective of their spelling-to-sound regularity) and activation of these representations permits us to recognize words. Route **C** enables us to access the meanings (and syntactic information) of recognized words. Figure 10.2 shows reciprocal connections between the semantic system and the orthographic input lexicon and this is to permit context effects in word recognition. It is a reliable effect in experimental psychology that the recognition of a word is facilitated by the presentation of prior semantic context. This is achieved by activation of semantic information (from the context) which is fed-back to the units of predictable words in the input lexicon. Note also that there is a connection from the semantic system to the phonological output lexicon (which contains representations of the phonological forms of words) to permit semantically mediated reading. Route **D** is a direct (i.e. non-semantically mediated) and lexically-specific set of connections between recognized words and their stored phonological representations. The model shown in Figure 10.2 is essentially the popular 'dual route' model of oral reading (as championed by Coltheart 1980a), with route **A** being the 'non-lexical' route and route **B** being the lexical access route (with routes **C** and **D** being subdivisions within lexically specific reading processes).

Theoretical dyslexias from model lesions

Having advanced the model presented in Figure 10.2, we are now in a position to predict what would happen if particular functional routes were rendered inoperative (or were severely damaged). That is, we can make hypothetical 'lesions' in the model. This exercise should be useful for a number of reasons. First, it tests our understanding of the details of the operation of the model. Second, it should also serve to examine how we may devise psycholinguistic tests to evaluate components of the model. In fact, once someone appreciates the general logic of how particular tasks are used to 'tap' the functional integrity of components of the model (and how particular types of reading errors implicate impairments of components), then the activity of cognitive neuropsychology becomes considerably easier to follow. Third, predicted patterns of impaired and preserved functions should enable us to structure a discussion of the varieties of acquired dyslexia observed in brain-damaged patients. Finally, it should also illuminate some shortcomings of the model and the problems of the general approach.

If route **A** was not working, one would predict that nonwords could not be read aloud. Further, it should not be possible to decide that *FID* and *PHID* (but not *FID* and *PRID*) sound the same and nonwords which sound like words (such as *WURD*) would not be appreciated as such. In short, there would be no phonics. If word reading necessarily requires phonics then it too would be abolished. If word reading does not require obligatory phonological recoding, then it would be unaffected. Thus, the existence of patients who could not read nonwords represents an important testing case for theories of the role of phonological recoding in word reading.

If route **B** was not working, one would predict that there should be no visual recognition of words (i.e. no 'sight vocabulary' recognition). All oral reading should be entirely and solely phonic and no comprehension could occur prior to phonological recoding. Everything would be treated as if it were a nonword until it reaches the response buffer. Note that the model has no direct connection from assembled phonological codes to any lexical or semantic information. It is assumed that information held in the response buffer may be both rehearsed and fed-back to systems responsible for auditory word recognition (not shown in Figure 10.2). Thus, the word *PINT* would be pronounced to rhyme with 'mint' and the nonword *BURD* would be understood (as soon as its phonology is assembled) as 'bird'. Also, irregular words should be misclassified as nonwords (because, when regularized, they sound like nonsense). Further, one would expect a number of problems with distinguishing between the meanings of homophones (as in the same way if I asked someone to define /rein/, they might select 'rain', 'reign' or 'rein', or even all three).

If route **C** was not working (or there was central damage to the semantic system), then the oral reading of all words should be preserved (as route **D** could do it), but there should be no comprehension.

If route **D** was not working, then nonword reading should be preserved, as should the reading of words with regular spelling-to-sound correspondences (as the assembled phonological recoding component could handle them). All words should be correctly comprehended, as there is intact access to the semantic system. If one assumed (as may seem uncontentious) that the semantic system contains representations which are sufficiently precise never to confuse synonyms (such as *small* and *little*) or highly related words (such as *greyhound* and *whippet*) in oral reading, then all words should be read correctly. However, if the semantic representations of some words were not normally sufficiently precise to uniquely specify only one representation in the phonological output lexicon, then one might expect some difficulty (especially for words with overlapping or impoverished semantics, such as abstract words like *idea* and *the*). However, if only route **D** were inoperative, one might expect that the intact operation of route **A** would prevent the production of semantic errors. Thus, even for 'mauve', whose semantic representation might activate the phonological forms of 'mauve', 'violet' and 'purple' (via route **C**), the phonological recoding system (route **A**) should be able to supply sufficient information (such as that the word begins with /m/), to distinguish between these alternatives. (Note that in normal readers, all routes are assumed to operate in parallel.)

The final pattern of predicted reading impairment follows from some of this discussion of the nature of the semantically mediated route. If both routes **A** and **D** were to be abolished, then no nonwords could be read (as there is no phonics) and all word reading would be semantically mediated (as there is no lexically specific route). Whether reading (especially semantic) errors should be produced depends upon one's conception of the normal operation of route **C** and whether one also supposes that this too might be impaired. This highlights a particular difficulty for cognitive neuropsychological research: if one assumes that a particular pattern of dyslexic performance reflects an isolated processing component (because, by exclusion, other components can be proved to be inoperative), then it cannot be certain whether reading errors reflect either an impaired or a normally imprecise system. (This problem is made worse by the fact that one cannot really study the precise operation of these parallel reading routes in isolation in the normal system.) In this particular instance, the difficulty is compounded by the fact that the defining symptom of the variety of acquired dyslexia which corresponds most to this theoretical pattern (called *deep dyslexia*) is the presence of semantic errors to single words (such as reading VODKA as 'schnapps').

These are predicted patterns of reading impairment and we shall now see how these might correspond to the observed reading disorders found in some brain-damaged patients. Although there are many means of testing reading skills (such as semantic comprehension tasks, spoken and visual word matching tasks, lexical decision tasks, investigations of reading latency, etc.), cognitive neuropsychologists have typically primarily analysed the effects of various psycholinguistic dimensions on oral reading accuracy and the nature of any reading errors produced. Comparisons have been made between a patient's reading performance of (among others): words and nonwords; words with regular vs. irregular spelling-to-sound correspondences; concrete (and highly imageable) words (e.g. *DOG*) vs. abstract (and difficult to image) words (e.g. *IDEA*); function words (such as *THE, AND*) vs. content words; common words vs. rare words; words with one vs. many meanings (e.g. *PALM*); homophones (such as *SAIL, SALE*) vs. nonhomophones; etc. We have already discussed how some of these variables would be expected to differentiate between the functional integrity of particular reading routes and Table 10.1 shows the predicted effects upon reading accuracy of three of these word dimensions for the theoretical dyslexias discussed above. The analysis of the nature (and relative frequency and consistency) of any reading errors is also an important and illuminating source of information. We have already mentioned the possibility of both phonological 'regularization' (e.g. *YACHT* read as /jætʃt/) and semantic (e.g. *YACHT* read as 'boat') errors, the presence of which may be taken to implicate the particular involvement of particular reading routes (phonologically and semantically mediated, respectively) and, because they lead to inaccurate performance, suggest that other, normally available routes are *not* functional.

Table 10.1: Predicted presence (+) or absence (−) of effect of three psycholinguistic dimensions on reading performance

| | *Routes impaired in Figure 10.2* | | | | |
	A	**B**	**C**	**D**	**A + D**
Lexicality:	+	−	−	−	+
(+ = problems on nonwords)					
Spelling-to-sound regularity:	−	+	−	−	−
(+ = problems on irregular words)					
Concreteness or imageability:	−	−	−	+?	+
(+ = problems on abstract words)					
Actual dyslexia approximating to predicted form	Phonological	Surface	'Direct'	Not discovered	Deep

Varieties of acquired dyslexia

I shall now describe the major varieties of acquired dyslexia. (Other reviews can be found in Coltheart 1981; Patterson 1981; and Shallice 1981a.) I shall restrict the body of this review to what may be called the 'central' dyslexias (Shallice and Warrington 1980). These are acquired dyslexias arising from deficits of the major (central) reading 'routes' (as labelled in Figure 10.2) and which have been interpreted as supporting (and have been interpreted within) the model of *normal* oral reading. However, brain damage can also produce both 'global alexia' (a total abolition of reading) and a variety of 'peripheral' dyslexias, many of which appear to be due to deficits at the early visual/ graphemic processing of printed input. These disorders are difficult to relate to (i.e. interpret in terms of) normal reading processes as they manifest in performance which is both quantitatively and qualitatively abnormal. Perhaps the most commonly known of these peripheral dyslexias is **'letter–by–letter' reading** (see Patterson and Kay 1982), also known as 'pure' alexia, 'word-form' dyslexia, or alexia without agraphia. These patients often name letters (either vocally or 'under their breath') before reading a word (e.g. *CAT* → 'cee, ay, tee, cat'); they use letter names and not the sounds of the letters. The reading latencies of these patients are slow and generally reflect a linear function of the number of letters in the word. This kind of reading, which may reflect compensatory strategies, is unlikely to reflect the operation of any normally used reading process. **Neglect** dyslexia (see Shallice 1981a) is a reading disorder in which patients make frequent (essentially visual) errors which are restricted to one half (either the beginning or the end) of the stimulus word, e.g. *SIT* → 'bit', *MILK* → 'yolk', (errors at the beginning of words) and *STRONG* → 'stroke' and *RELATE* → 'relays' (errors at the end of words). In **attentional** (or 'literal') dyslexia (Shallice and Warrington 1977), patients may be able to read words presented individually but flounder when more than one word is presented and are worse in naming letters presented in words than when presented individually.

Phonological dyslexia This is a reading disorder which has been 'discovered' only relatively recently, not, presumably, because it is a new affliction, but because it has been only recently that cognitive psychologists have been theoretically motivated to include in their assessment procedure tests of the oral reading of nonsense. Its distinguishing feature is a selective impairment of reading aloud nonwords, which co-exists with the relatively intact reading of words. It was first reported by Beauvois and Dérouesné (1979), whose French patient R.G. was able to read 82 per cent of words correctly but only 10 per cent of nonwords, such as *DIRMA* (which, I beg you to believe me, is a nonword in French). The English patient A.M. reported by Patterson (1982) could read about 90 per cent of words but only 12 per cent of non-words. Although A.M. could read aloud nonwords which were homophonic (i.e. sound identical) to real words, such as *BURD*, slightly more accurately than other nonwords, he appeared to be assisted by their visual similarity to words: he read 58 per cent of those with high visual similarity to words (such as *TOUN* → town), but only 32 per cent with low visual similarity (such as *PHUDE* → food). A.M. performed quite well on a (silent) task of deciding whether two visually presented words were pronounced in an identical way (e.g. *LACKS* & *LAX* and *SEW* & *SO*) or not (e.g. *LACES* & *LAX* and *NEW* & *NO*) and for both regular and irregular words, but was selectively impaired when nonwords were used (e.g. *PHUD* and *FUD*, vs. *PRUD* and *FUD*).

A.M.'s word reading was not perfect: he made some visual errors (e.g. *BIBLIOGRAPHY* → 'biography'), some errors classed as 'derivational', in that the response shared the same root morpheme as the stimulus (e.g. *THINK* → 'thinking' and *APPLAUD* → 'applause') and some 'function word substitution' errors (e.g. *THE* → 'when' and *IN* → 'an'). This association of deficits lead Patterson to consider tentatively the theoretical possibility that the processes underlying the production of such errors and an impairment of assembled phonological recoding may be functionally linked. The reasoning behind such a hypothesis was as follows: if phonological recoding is normally involved in the reading of affixes and function words, then an impairment of such recoding (as evidenced by a deficit of reading aloud nonwords) would result in a necessary deficit in reading function words and affixed words. However, a subsequent report of a phonological dyslexic patient by Funnell (1983) showed that this hypothesis could not be true. Funnell's patient W.B. could only read one of the 30 nonwords presented to him, but on a large sample of words was able to correctly read at least 85 per cent. However, W.B. was no worse reading words with affixes than without and was no worse reading function words than content words. W.B. did make occasional 'derivational' errors (e.g. *AGAIN* → 'against'), but he made more visual errors (e.g. *THEME* → 'scheme'), some of which were also semantically related (e.g. *ARM* → 'armchair'), which may suggest that his 'derivational' errors were not necessarily (or specifically) the result of any impaired linguistic or morphological process. This shows that in cognitive neuropsychology *patterns of dissociations* (of impaired and preserved skills) are theoretically more pertinent (i.e. provide stronger evidence) than *associations of deficits*, which may result from anatomical proximity of lesions rather than functionally necessary relationships.

It would therefore appear that phonological dyslexia corresponds quite closely with the predictions made from the model (as shown in Figure 10.2) with route **A** abolished. Although the dissociation between word and non-word reading is not absolute (i.e. 100 per cent correct for words and 0 per cent for nonwords), this may not be too surprising given that the neural mechanisms supporting the various reading routes are likely to be anatomically adjacent, at least with respect to how rather gross brain injuries (such as strokes) are likely to effect their devastation: it is rare that a stroke could completely abolish one complex cognitive system while leaving another completely intact.

Surface dyslexia This variety of acquired dyslexia was first reported (and named as such) by Marshall and Newcombe (1973) whose patient J.C. made the often quoted error of reading LISTEN as 'Lis-ton, that's the boxer'. This error suggests that J.C. both read by phonological recoding and comprehended what he said rather than what he saw written. However, J.C.'s dyslexia did not correspond perfectly to that predicted if all reading reflected a normally functional route **A**: (1) he could correctly read some irregular words; (2) not all of his reading errors to irregular words were unambiguous regularizations; (3) he made various visual errors to both regular and irregular words, which complicates a straightforward interpretation of his apparently phonologically mediated reading errors (in that if he read *INSECT* as 'insist', his error *LISTEN* → 'Liston' might actually be due to visual confusion); and (4) as Marcel (1980) has pointed out, there were far more 'lexicalization' errors made (in which the response was a word rather than a regularized neologism) than would be expected by a purely nonlexical reading process. These features (which can also be found in other patients) are embarrassing for an interpretation of surface dyslexia in terms of a single functional impairment (to route **B** in Figure 10.2). As patients produce many letter deletion, substitution, addition and order errors (e.g. A.B.'s *FROG* → 'fog', *LIFE* → 'lift', *AN* → 'and' and *SIGN* → 'sing'; Coltheart *et al.* 1983), it would appear that they may have impairments to the early visual processing stage and/or that their assembled phonological systems are not working without error.

Surface dyslexia is an extremely complex and rather variable reading disorder. However, it is probably fair to say that it can be described as an over-reliance upon phonological recoding in reading. Surface dyslexics are more accurate reading words with regular than with irregular spelling-to-sound correspondences and produce regularization errors. For example, the fairly 'pure' surface dyslexic patient M.P. (Bub *et al.* 1985) correctly read almost all regular words but only about 40 per cent of irregular words. M.P. misread *HAVE* to rhyme with 'cave' and *BROAD* to rhyme with 'road'. Surface dyslexics may also have problems deciding that homophones with irregular spellings (such as *SEW* and *SO*) sound identical and defining the meaning of homophones. Coltheart *et al.*'s patient A.B. produced homophone confusion errors in a task which required him to define and then pronounce a printed word: shown *PANE*, he said 'something which hurts, pain'. Although A.B.

generally comprehended what he pronounced rather than what was printed (e.g. *SCARCE* → 'fairly serious cut, scar'), not all his errors reflected regularizations. Further, A.B. occasionally produced homophone confusion errors to homophones with irregular spelling-to-sound correspondences (e.g. *BURY* → 'a fruit on a tree, berry'), which, if only route **A** were functional, should not be 'pronounced' correctly. Coltheart *et al.* offered the following, rather ingenious, interpretation of this unexpected performance. They proposed that some words (including some irregular homophones) can access their (correct) representations in the orthographic input lexicon, but not their representations in the semantic system; that is, for some words, route **B** is intact but route **C** is not. However, these words can use route **D** to access their phonological representations in the output lexicon and that these phonological codes are then fed-back (presumably via the auditory word recognition system) to the semantic system. This indirect process would occasionally produce homophone confusions, as the phonological codes will be semantically ambiguous for homophones.

However, it now appears that some surface dyslexic patients (e.g. E.S.T.; Kay and Patterson 1985) can correctly comprehend words to which they produce regularization errors. This suggests that, for some patients, the over-reliance upon phonological recoding for oral reading is not due to an impairment of route **B** but may result from an impairment of access to the phonological output lexicon. It would appear that there can be different functional impairments that 'cause' surface dyslexic oral reading (i.e. result in an over-reliance on route **A**).

'Direct' dyslexia   W.L.P. was a patient with a progressive pre-senile dementia reported by Schwartz *et al.* (1980). She could correctly read aloud nonwords, regular words and irregular words, but had vast problems with comprehension. A revealing (and often quoted) example of W.L.P.'s reading performance is the following: *HYENA* → 'hyena . . . hyena . . . what in the heck is that?' In fact, W.L.P. appeared to be able to read aloud almost everything, but understood very little. Further, W.L.P.'s comprehension problems were the same for all modalities, which suggests that, in terms of Figure 10.2, she had central damage to the semantic system, rather than only an impairment of (the reading specific) route **C**. The fact that W.L.P. could correctly read frankly irregular words (which, presumably, could not be read via the assembled phonological recoding route) without any apparent semantic mediation, suggests that she read words using direct (and lexically specific) connections between representations in the orthographic input and phonological output lexicons (i.e. route **D**).

Deep dyslexia   In many respects, the study of this variety of acquired dyslexia marked the emergence of cognitive neuropsychology as both an important contribution to cognitive psychology and as a 'new wave' within neuropsychology. The important book on deep dyslexia, edited by Coltheart *et al.* (1980), both stimulated and, in many ways, set the tone for subsequent cognitive neuropsychological research.

Deep dyslexia is a complex set of reading impairments, which may be considered to have three main characteristics. First, there is a complete abolition of assembled phonological recoding. Deep dyslexic patients are completely unable to read aloud nonwords, or, indeed, to perform reliably any task which requires the assembly of nonlexical phonology (such as matching a spoken with a printed nonword). Second, the patients make a variety of oral reading errors to individually presented words, the most striking of which are semantic errors (such as reading *CITY* as 'town', *LITTLE* as 'small', *BITTER* as 'pints'). However, there are also visual errors (such as *DEEP* → 'deer'), which tend to involve the production of responses which are more concrete than the stimuli, 'derivational' errors (such as *FARMING* → 'farmer') and some 'function word substitutions' (e.g. *HIS* → 'she'). Third, there is a clear effect of word concreteness on reading accuracy, with concrete words being more often read than abstract words. Some accounts of deep dyslexia have claimed that, in addition to this concreteness effect, there is also an effect of syntactic class, with reading accuracy reflecting the following order: nouns > adjectives > verbs > function words. However, it now seems likely that, at least for content words, the apparent syntactic class effect is due to variations of concreteness and frequency between words of different classes (Allport and Funnell 1981; Barry and Richardson 1988). However, it remains an open question whether the severe problems deep dyslexics have with function words may be reducible to a more general impairment in the processing of abstract words (as function words are extremely abstract), or whether this reflects an additional impairment of syntactic processing within reading.

Following Morton and Patterson (1980), this complex set of symptoms may be interpreted in terms of the model shown in Figure 10.2 as follows. Route **A** is assumed to be completely abolished and route **D** is also assumed to be inoperative. All deep dyslexic reading is assumed to rely exclusively upon the semantically mediated route, although this may not be working perfectly efficiently, in two major ways. First, the process by which semantic representations activate entries in the phonological output lexicon is prone to error, which leads to the production of semantic errors. However, it is unclear whether this reflects normal instability, or is pathological. Second, that the representations of concrete and abstract words are differentiated within the semantic system and that those for abstract words are rendered less accessible, which results in the concreteness effect upon reading accuracy. Such a possibility may also offer an explanation for the production of the particular form of visual errors made by deep dyslexics (which tend to involve the production of words which are more concrete than the stimulus): these may be seen as second attempts (by the orthographic input lexicon) to activate a semantic representation (which will be more likely for a concrete word) which will be able to access an entry in the phonological output lexicon. In addition to these two main theoretical interpretations, it is also possible that there exists an additional syntactic processing impairment, which may offer an explanation of the severe difficulty with reading function words and for the production of derivational errors, although it is possible, as Funnell (1987) has recently shown, that such errors in acquired dyslexia may be due to variations of the relative concreteness value of affixed words and their constituent root morphemes.

The above (and admittedly complex) interpretation of deep dyslexia is essentially one in which components of a normal reading system are assumed to have been 'lesioned' or functionally 'subtracted' (the general theoretical attempt of cognitive neuropsychology). In contrast, Coltheart (1980b) has suggested that deep dyslexic reading reflects a reading system (located in the right cerebral hemisphere) which is not used to support normal reading competence. Although there are similarities between deep dyslexic reading and the putative (but limited) linguistic competence of the right hemisphere (as revealed by studies of split-brain patients and visual half-field asymmetries in normals), there are serious problems for this anatomically based 'right hemisphere hypothesis' (see Patterson and Besner 1984; Barry and Richardson 1988).

Other dyslexias Although the preceding varieties of acquired dyslexia have attracted the most interest, a number of other types have been reported, although (at least so far) represented by only one patient. I shall briefly describe only three.

(1) Warrington and Shallice (1979) described a patient (A.R.) with what they call 'semantic-access' dyslexia. This is similar to deep dyslexia, in that A.R. produced some semantic errors (e.g. *MONTH* → 'week') and had an impairment of nonword reading (although this was not as severe as most deep dyslexics). However, it differed from deep dyslexia in that A.R. showed no effect on concreteness upon his reading accuracy. It would appear that A.R. had an impairment in generally accessing semantic information.

(2) Warrington (1981) reported a patient (C.A.V.) with what she described as 'concrete word' dyslexia. Nonword reading was impaired in C.A.V., but the most striking aspect of his performance was the fact that (unlike deep dyslexics) he read abstract words more successfully than concrete words. C.A.V. produced numerous visual word reading errors, but (and again showing almost the converse pattern to that of deep dyslexia) his erroneous responses tended to be more abstract than the stimulus words (e.g. *MOON* → 'mood'). This (theoretically important, but as yet unsupported) pattern of results is consistent with the notion that the representations of concrete and abstract words are differentiated in the semantic system and can be independently impaired by brain damage.

(3) Coslett *et al.* (1985) have reported a patient with a rather unusual combination of disordered reading (and reading related) skills. The patient was a deep dyslexic reader: he was unable to read aloud printed nonwords, could read only 30 per cent of function words, showed a concreteness effect on word reading accuracy (but absolutely no effect of spelling-to-sound regularity) and produced semantic errors (e.g. *SHOE* → 'boot'). However, when he was asked to name words which were spelled to him orally (like 'tea, haitch, eye, ess'), he correctly named half of all nonwords, was no worse on function words than on nouns, showed no concreteness effect, produced no semantic errors at all and was much worse naming irregular words (20 per cent correct) than regular words (70 per cent)! This combination of deep dyslexia in oral reading and something like surface dyslexia in recognizing orally spelled words suggests that the two tasks (despite their intuitive association) do not necessarily share common, identical functional processes and are in fact separable.

Spelling production and the central dysgraphias

The 1980s have seen the adoption, development and increasing application of models of spelling production which are similar to (and often directly adapted from) those advanced to account for normal and disordered reading, such as that shown in Figure 10.2. The dominant *dual route* model of spelling production posits that there exist two distinct sets of processes (or functional routes), which may operate in parallel: a lexical (or word-specific) route operates by retrieving the spellings of known words from an orthographic output lexicon; and a nonlexical route operates by assembling spellings using a sound-to-spelling conversion process applied to segmented phonological codes. All known words could be spelled by the lexical route (indicated by **B** in Figure 10.3), Words with regular (predictable or 'transparent') sound-to-spelling correspondences could be, and all nonwords must be, spelled by the nonlexical route (indicated by **A** in Figure 10.3). (Once spellings are either assembled or retrieved, they are deposited in a 'graphemic output buffer' while output handwriting, typing or oral spelling processes are implemented). There exist numerous theorists who support versions of this general framework, including Ellis (1984), Hatfield and Patterson (1984), and Margolin (1984), who also provide reviews of acquired dysgraphia.

Models of spelling production have been most persuasively supported by cognitive neuropsychological investigations of neurological patients with acquired disorders of spelling competence (patients with central dysgraphias). In fact, given the paucity of research into normal, correct spelling production, these models have been almost entirely motivated by such data. In particular, the separability of the dual routes of spelling has been supported by the dissociations observed within (and the claimed double dissociation between) patients with phonological and 'surface' dysgraphia.

Phonological dysgraphia Like phonological dyslexia, this has also been described only relatively recently. Its major characteristic is a selective impairment of the ability to spell nonwords to dictation, although word spelling is well preserved. Phonological dysgraphia may be interpreted as a deficit of the assembled spelling route coupled with an intact lexical route. The first systematic report of such a phonological dysgraphic patient was by Shallice (1981b), whose patient (P.R.) was able to correctly spell 94 per cent of words, but only 18 per cent of nonwords (e.g. /uːk/ → UKE). For word spelling, P.R. was less accurate spelling function words than other words and for nonword spelling he was less accurate on longer than on short nonwords. Bub and Kertesz (1982a) report the case of M.H. who could spell 79 per cent of words but only one of a list of 29 nonwords. (M.H. was also more accurate at written than spoken naming, which might be seen as another example of non-phonological spelling.)

Surface dysgraphia Patients whose spelling appears to rely mainly upon the operation of the postulated phonologically mediated, assembled spelling route to spell words, have been termed cases of 'surface' dysgraphia (which has also been called 'lexical' agraphia and 'phonological spelling'). Beauvois and Dérouesné (1981) found that their French patient (R.G.) was able to correctly spell nonwords and, indeed, in the majority of cases, he produced the most economical orthographic renderings in French of particular phonemes (e.g. O and not EAU for /o/). However, R.G. also tended to spell words in the same, phonologically plausible fashion and as a consequence, produced many errors on words with ambiguous and irregular sound-to-spelling correspondences. When spelling words, R.G. often omitted silent letters (e.g. 'habile' → HABIL) and substituted graphemes with identical phonemic realizations (e.g. 'souk' → SOUC) and he was particularly poor spelling words with very rare (i.e. frankly irregular or exceptional) correspondences (e.g. 'monsieur' → MESSIEU). Hatfield and Patterson (1983) report an English patient (T.P.) who also spelled regular words more successfully than irregular words and who produced very many phonologically plausible (but, for English, seldom necessarily correct) spellings (e.g. 'flood' → FLUD, 'answer' → ANSER, 'mortgage' → MORGAGE). T.P. also produced homophone confusion errors, despite the fact that the homophones were presented in a sentence which clearly indicated which spelling was required (e.g. 'The man turned pale at the news' → PAIL), which is another example of 'phonological spelling'. Roeltgen and Heilman (1984) have reported four English speaking patients who could spell regular words more successfully than irregular words and who could also spell nonwords appropriately. Recently, Baxter and Warrington (1987) have presented a detailed and elegant investigation of a very clear case of a surface dysgraphic speller.

Patients with surface dysgraphia have an impairment in the retrieval of lexical (i.e. word-specific) orthography, which forces reliance upon the assembled spelling route. For languages with irregular orthographies such as English and French, such reliance would frequently produce incorrect but phonologically plausible spellings for irregular words. However, there are two complicating findings for this simple view. First, all the surface dysgraphic patients so far reported were able to correctly spell at least some irregular words. This suggests that not all lexical orthographic representations are rendered inaccessible in surface dysgraphia. Goodman and Caramazza (1986) report a patient M.W. who could spell high frequency regular and irregular words with equal (and almost perfect) levels of accuracy but had a selective impairment in spelling low frequency irregular words. This suggests that the representations of low frequency words in the orthographic output lexicon are somehow more vulnerable to impairment. Second, not all surface dysgraphic spelling errors are phonologically plausible; some appear to reflect what Ellis (1984) calls 'partial lexical knowledge', such as T.P.'s errors 'yacht' → YHAGT and 'sword' → SWARD. These errors suggest that some, although incomplete, lexical orthographic information may be available (for example, that the word 'yacht' contains the letter H somewhere and that its vowel is spelled, irregularly, as A), which is then incorporated into information supplied by the assembled spelling route. Other phonologically implausible errors in surface dysgraphia, such as letter substitution errors (as in T.P.'s 'town' → TOMN and M.W.'s 'pierce' → TIERCE), may be akin to normal 'slips of the pen' (see Ellis 1982) or reflect impairments of processes subserving writing production which are implemented after a spelling has been assembled (or retrieved).

Figure 10.3 presents a model of spelling production which embodies the major dual routes. The assembled spelling system is indicated by route **A** and

Figure 10.3 A model of the component processes underlying spelling production

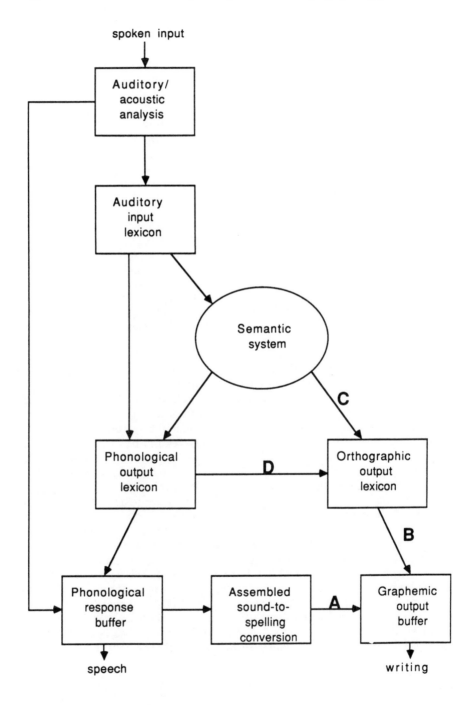

the lexically specific route is indicated by **B**. However, Figure 10.3 also contains a number of other connections which are motivated by different varieties of dysgraphic patient (most of which are fractionations of 'addressed' or lexically retrieved spelling).

(1) The existence of a semantically mediated addressed spelling route (indicated by route **C** in Figure 10.3) is supported by the pattern of spelling performance shown in **deep dysgraphia** (Newcombe and Marshall 1980; Bub and Kertesz 1982b; Nolan and Caramazza 1983). These patients are unable to spell nonwords, produce semantic errors to words in dictation tasks (e.g. 'sentence' → TRIAL and 'time' → CLOCK) and spell concrete words more accurately than abstract words. (Further, deep dysgraphic patients may be particularly impaired spelling function words.) The received interpretation of deep dysgraphia is that the assembled spelling route is abolished and that all word spelling reflects the following processing sequence: auditory word recognition to semantic comprehension to orthographic output lexicon. Semantic errors and the concreteness effect in spelling accuracy are assumed to reflect either a partially impaired semantic system or imprecision in the semantic specification of orthographic lexical representations (a similar explanation to that offered for the qualitatively similar pattern of reading impairments shown in deep dyslexia).

(2) The existence of a direct lexical (but nonsemantic) addressed spelling route (indicated by route **D** in Figure 10.3 as the connection from the phonological output lexicon to the orthographic output lexicon) is supported by the production of homophone substitution errors which involve the production of words with irregular spelling patterns (e.g. 'write' → RIGHT). Such errors are occasionally made by normals in spontaneous writing (Ellis 1984) and by some surface dysgraphics (e.g. T.P., Hatfield and Patterson 1983). Roeltgen *et al.* (1986) have recently reported five dysgraphic patients who although neither phonological nor surface dysgraphic, often produced the incorrect and sometimes irregular spelling of homophones in a dictation task, despite the fact that the words were disambiguated by semantic context (e.g. 'led' → LEAD and 'doe' → DOUGH). Such errors would be explicable if one assumed that the lexical phonological representation of a homophone directly addressed all its orthographic forms (e.g. /rein/ = RAIN, REIN and REIGN). Semantic (contextual) information is obviously required to select the appropriate spelling and Roeltgen *et al.*'s data show that the lexical system can be dissociated from semantic influence. Homophone substitution errors would then result from the (unguided) selection from alternative spellings.

The foregoing has concerned *spelling* disorders. However, brain damage may also cause impairments to stages of processing which are implemented after a spelling representation has been either retrieved or assembled and deposited in the graphemic output buffer (as shown in Figure 10.3). Such impairments would produce *writing* (or oral spelling or typing) disorders, or what could be considered to be 'peripheral' dysgraphias, such as '*apraxic*' agraphia, in which letters are very poorly formed in writing (see Ellis 1982), and '*afferent*' dysgraphia, in which strokes within letters may be omitted or repeated (Ellis *et al.* 1987).

Syndromes of dyslexia and dysgraphia?

The varieties of acquired dyslexias described above broadly correspond to the theoretical dyslexias predicted from a conceptual analysis of the model presented in Figure 10.2 and so increase confidence in its general framework. The varieties of the acquired dysgraphias are similarly explicable in terms of dissociations within a modular, information processing model (as presented in Figure 10.3). Such correspondences between data and theory are indeed impressive and this bodes well for further cognitive neuropsychological research.

However, despite these broad correspondences, the situation is more complex at a finer-grained level of analysis. The functional routes depicted in Figures 10.2 and 10.3 represent extremely complex sets of intricate psycholinguistic mechanisms. The components (represented by boxes) implement complex information processing functions and will undoubtedly need to be considerably 'unpacked' before a detailed and complete computational understanding of their operation is to be achieved. As one example of such computational 'unpacking' (and probably only a relatively minor one), consider the system underlying assembled spelling. This would appear to involve at least three component processing 'stages': phonological segmentation; the application of some conversion process which assigns spelling patterns to phonological segments; and the graphemic assembly of spelling patterns. An impairment of any of these three sub-processes would result in disturbed nonword spelling. It is therefore possible that there could exist at least three sub-varieties of phonological dysgraphia, each arising from damage to different separable processing systems. Patients who show a gross deficit of nonword spelling would not necessarily be homogeneous.

It is almost certain that as future research increases our detailed understanding of the mechanisms subserving reading and spelling, then *all* the components which constitute the routes shown in Figures 10.2 and 10.3 will probably fractionate (i.e. become computationally divisible). Fine-grained analyses of individual patients suggest that those who share a grossly defined impairment of a particular route may differ in functionally important ways from each other. It will not, then, be legitimate to assume that all patients within a broad descriptive 'syndrome' (e.g. surface dyslexia, etc.) will be homogeneous with respect to the microstructure of the processes underlying their performance. Consider deep dyslexia, a disorder with many reported 'exemplars'. Barry and Richardson (1988) discussed the many differences among deep dyslexic patients, in terms of both associated symptoms (such as levels of intact oral repetition) and characteristics more central to theoretical interpretations of semantically mediated reading (such as the relative rates of semantic and visual errors, awareness of semantic errors and lexical decision and comprehension performance with words that cannot be read). Indeed, patients would appear to make semantic errors (the cardinal symptom of deep dyslexia) for quite different reasons, including central damage within the semantic system (as indicated by impaired performance in word-to-picture matching tasks) and disturbances of the selection of entries in the phonological output lexicon. As Coltheart (1987) argues, if there is no single cause of semantic errors, then there can be no justification for using any one deep dyslexic patient to study (and hope to interpret or treat) the 'deep dyslexia syndrome' (scare quotes!), 'since there will be no guarantee that any one patient will be representative of all' (p. 3). We have also seen that there exists considerable (and theoretically pertinent) heterogeneity among cases of surface dyslexia. An over-reliance upon phonic reading, that results in the production of regularization errors, can result from impairments to the lexical reading system at any of the following loci: access to the orthographic input lexicon, access to the semantic system, or access to the phonological output lexicon. As Ellis (1987) says: 'the "syndrome" of "surface dyslexia" is dissolving before our eyes' (p. 401).

Given these behavioural demonstrations (and theoretical interpretation) of considerable heterogeneity, it is time to seriously reconsider the utility of the traditional neuropsychological methodology that (1) seeks to classify patients into syndromes on the basis of a few (usually rather grossly defined) symptoms and (2) attempts to offer accounts of the syndromes rather than the complete pattern of preserved and impaired abilities as found in *individual* patients. The actual *description* of symptoms is becoming a complex but a necessarily meticulous task; analysis needs to be detailed and alternative accounts of particular phenomena need to be carefully explored. The subsequent classification of patients into syndromes (and, inevitably, subsyndromes) will probably prove to range from needlessly troublesome to potentially misleading. Any gross impairment of a particular psycholinguistic function (such as nonword spelling) could not on its own be sufficient to warrant a classification of a patient into a functionally homogeneous syndrome (such as phonological dysgraphia). Further, it is difficult to see what explanatory power could be gained from such an explosion of sub-groups of syndromes, or how this exercise would benefit the interests of either neuroanatomists or speech therapists.

Neuropsychology therefore faces a dilemma concerning both explanatory accounts of syndromes and the status of taxonomies of acquired disorders of cognitive functions based upon syndromes. Ellis (1987), taking the dilemma firmly by its horns, has trumpeted the call to totally abandon the methodology of assigning patients to syndromes. He argues that precise empirical descriptions of the patterns of preserved and impaired functions (the 'symptoms') shown by individual patients should be treated as one would treat the results of single experiments within psychology (namely as the data-base to evaluate theories of normal functioning). My own view is that, at a broad level, syndrome labels will retain only descriptive utility (in that, for example, a patient with an impaired route X will differ from one with an impaired route Y), but that detailed and informative interpretations of reading and spelling impairments must operate solely at the level of data from individual patients rather than syndromes. Further, I would argue that speech therapy (as well as cognitive neuropsychology) must operate at the level of individual case studies. If therapy is to be directed to functionally overcoming, circumventing, or somehow adjusting to any particular 'problem', then therapeutic approaches (however subtle) will need to be tailored to individuals, taking full (but theoretically informed) cognizance of the particular set of problems with which each individual presents.

Reading and spelling disorders: two sides of the same damaged coin?

When introducing and discussing the model of oral reading earlier in this chapter, I advanced (but did not support) the claim that there exist separate orthographic input and output lexicons and so reading and spelling cannot be seen as being simply different 'routes' into and out from a common orthographic word store. The claim that the systems underlying reading and spelling are essentially independent permits the possibilities that brain damage might both (1) selectively impair reading but leave spelling intact (and vice versa) and (2) produce different forms of reading and spelling impairments. In fact, both of these two possibilities seem to be the case. First, many letter-by-letter readers have unimpaired spelling and the deep dysgraphic patient reported by Bub and Kertesz (1982b) had no detectable reading impairment. Second, qualitatively different patterns of dyslexia and dysgraphia can exist in the same patient. The clearest case to show this is the French patient R.G. (Beauvois and Dérouesné 1979, 1981) who was phonological dyslexic but surface dysgraphic. Additionally, the surface dysgraphic patient T.P. (Hatfield and Patterson 1983) appeared to read in a letter-by-letter fashion.

Although most patients appear to have qualitatively similar forms of dyslexia and dysgraphia, the existence of those with different patterns of impairments suggests that these result from different (i.e. multiple) functional disturbances to separable reading and spelling systems. Reading and spelling do not seem to be two sides of the same coin; they deal with units of the same currency of literacy in different ways and impairments of these complex skills require separate theoretical analyses (and probably separate therapeutic intervention also).

References

Allport, D. A. and Funnell, E. (1981) Components of the mental lexicon. *Philosophical Transactions of the Royal Society of London* **B295**, 397–410.

Barry, C. and Richardson, J. T. E. (1988) Accounts of oral reading in deep dyslexia. In H. A. Whitaker (ed.), *Phonological Processes and Brain Mechanisms*. New York: Springer.

Baxter, D. M. and Warrington, E. K. (1987) Transcoding sound to spelling: single or multiple sound unit correspondence? *Cortex* **23**, 11–28.

Beauvois, M.-F. and Dérouesné, J. (1979) Phonological alexia: three dissociations. *Journal of Neurology, Neurosurgery and Psychiatry* **42**, 1115–24.

Beauvois, M.-F. and Dérouesné, J. (1981) Lexical or orthographic agraphia. *Brain* **104**, 21–49.

Bub, D., Cancelliere, A. and Kertesz, A. (1985) Whole-word and analytic translation of spelling to sound in a non-semantic reader. In K. E. Patterson, J. C. Marshall and M. Coltheart (eds), *Surface Dyslexia: Neuropsychological and Cognitive Studies of Phonological Reading*. London: L. Erlbaum.

Bub, D. and Kertesz, A. (1982a) Evidence for lexicographic processing in a patient with preserved written over oral single word naming. *Brain* **105**, 697–717.

Bub, D. and Kertesz, A. (1982b) Deep agraphia. *Brain and Language* **17**, 146–65.

Coltheart, M. (1980a) Reading, phonological recoding, and deep dyslexia. In M.

Coltheart, K. Patterson and J. C. Marshall (eds), *Deep Dyslexia*. London: Routledge and Kegan Paul.

Coltheart, M. (1980b) Deep dyslexia: a right hemisphere hypothesis. In M. Coltheart, K. Patterson and J. C. Marshall (eds), *Deep Dyslexia*. London: Routledge and Kegan Paul.

Coltheart, M. (1981) Disorders of reading and their implications for models of normal reading. *Visible Language* **15**, 245–86.

Coltheart, M. (1985) Cognitive neuropsychology and the study of reading. In M. I. Posner and O. S. M. Marin (eds), *Attention and Performance XI*. Hillsdale, New Jersey: L. Erlbaum.

Coltheart, M. (1987) Functional architecture of the language-processing system. In M. Coltheart, G. Sartori and R. Job (eds), *The Cognitive Neuropsychology of Language*. London: L. Erlbaum.

Coltheart, M., Masterson, J., Byng, S., Prior, M. and Riddoch, J. (1983) Surface dyslexia. *Quarterly Journal of Experimental Psychology* **35A**, 469–95.

Coltheart, M., Patterson, K. and Marshall, J. C. (1980) *Deep Dyslexia*. London: Routledge and Kegan Paul.

Coslett, H. B., Rothi, L. G. and Heilman, K. M. (1985) Reading: dissociation of the lexical and phonologic mechanisms. *Brain and Language* **24**, 20–35.

Ellis, A. W. (1982) Spelling and writing (and reading and speaking). In A. W. Ellis (ed.), *Normality and Pathology in Cognitive Functions*. London: Academic Press.

Ellis, A. W. (1984) *Reading, Writing and Dyslexia: A Cognitive Analysis*. London: L. Erlbaum.

Ellis, A. W. (1987) Intimations of modularity, or, the modularity of mind: doing cognitive neuropsychology without syndromes. In M. Coltheart, G. Sartori and R. Job (eds), *The Cognitive Neuropsychology of Language*. London: L. Erlbaum.

Ellis, A. W., Young, A. W. and Flude, B. M. (1987) 'Afferent dysgraphia' in a patient and in normal subjects. *Cognitive Neuropsychology* **4**, 465–86.

Funnell, E. (1983) Phonological processes in reading: new evidence from acquired dyslexia. *British Journal of Psychology* **74**, 159–80.

Funnell, E. (1987) Morphological errors in acquired dyslexia: a case of mistaken identity. *Quarterly Journal of Experimental Psychology* **39A**, 497–539.

Goodman, R. A. and Caramazza, A. (1986) Dissociation of spelling errors in written and oral spelling: the role of allographic conversion in writing. *Cognitive Neuropsychology* **3**, 179–206.

Hatfield, F. M. and Patterson, K. E. (1983) Phonological spelling. *Quarterly Journal of Experimental Psychology* **35A**, 451–68.

Hatfield, F. M. and Patterson, K. E. (1984) Interpretation of spelling disorders in aphasia: impact of recent developments in cognitive psychology. In F. C. Rose (ed.), *Advances in Neurology, Vol. 42: Progress in Aphasiology*. New York: Raven Press.

Kay, J. and Patterson, K. E. (1985) Routes to meaning in surface dyslexia. In K. E. Patterson, J. C. Marshall and M. Coltheart (eds), *Surface Dyslexia: Neuropsychological and Cognitive Studies of Phonological Reading*. London: L. Erlbaum.

Marcel, T. (1980) Surface dyslexia and beginning reading: a revised hypothesis of the pronunciation of print and its impairments. In M. Coltheart, K. Patterson and J. C. Marshall (eds), *Deep Dyslexia*. London: Routledge and Kegan Paul.

Margolin, D. I. (1984) The neuropsychology of writing and spelling: semantic, phonological, motor, and perceptual processes. *Quarterly Journal of Experimental Psychology* **36A**, 459–89.

Marshall, J. C. and Newcombe, F. (1973) Patterns of paralexia. *Journal of Psycholinguistic Research* **2**, 175–99.

Morton, J. and Patterson, K. (1980) A new attempt at an interpretation, or, an attempt at a new interpretation. In M. Coltheart, K. Patterson and J. C. Marshall (eds), *Deep Dyslexia*. London: Routledge and Kegan Paul.

Newcombe, F. and Marshall, J. C. (1980) Transcoding and lexical stabilization in deep dyslexia. In M. Coltheart, K. Patterson and J. C. Marshall (eds) *Deep Dyslexia*. London: Routledge and Kegan Paul.

Nolan, K. and Caramazza, A. (1983) An analysis of writing in a case of deep dyslexia. *Brain and Language* 20, 305–28.

Patterson, K. E. (1981) Neuropsychological approaches to the study of reading. *British Journal of Psychology* 72, 151–74.

Patterson, K. E. (1982) The relationship between reading and phonological coding: further neuropsychological observations. In A. W. Ellis (ed.), *Normality and Pathology in Cognitive Functions*. London: Academic Press.

Patterson, K. E. and Besner, D. (1984) Is the right hemisphere literate? *Cognitive Neuropsychology* 1, 315–41.

Patterson, K. and Kay, J. (1982) Letter-by-letter reading: psychological descriptions of a neurological syndrome. *Quarterly Journal of Experimental Psychology* 34A, 411–41.

Patterson, K. E. and Morton, J. (1985) From orthography to phonology: an attempt at an old interpretation. In K. E. Patterson, J. C. Marshall and M. Coltheart (eds), *Surface Dyslexia: Neuropsychological and Cognitive Studies of Phonological Reading*. London: L. Erlbaum.

Roeltgen, D. P. and Heilman, K. M. (1984) Lexical agraphia: further support for the two system hypothesis of linguistic agraphia. *Brain* 107, 811–27.

Roeltgen, D. P., Rothi, L. G. and Heilman, K. M. (1986) Linguistic semantic agraphia: a dissociation of the lexical spelling system from semantics. *Brain and Language* 27, 257–80.

Schwartz, M. F., Saffran, E. M. and Marin, O. S. M. (1980) Fractionating the reading process in dementia: evidence for word-specific print-to-sound associations. In M. Coltheart, K. Patterson and J. C. Marshall (eds), *Deep Dyslexia*. London: Routledge and Kegan Paul.

Shallice, T. (1981a) Neurological impairment of cognitive processes. *British Medical Bulletin* 37, 187–92.

Shallice, T. (1981b) Phonological agraphia and the lexical route in writing. *Brain* 104, 412–29.

Shallice, T. and Warrington, E. K. (1977) The possible role of selective attention in acquired dyslexia. *Neuropsychologia* 15, 31–41.

Shallice, T. and Warrington, E. K. (1980) Single and multiple component central dyslexic syndromes. In M. Coltheart, K. Patterson and J. C. Marshall (eds), *Deep Dyslexia*. London: Routledge and Kegan Paul.

Warrington, E. K. (1981) Concrete word dyslexia. *British Journal of Psychology* 72, 175–96.

Warrington, E. K. and Shallice, T. (1979) Semantic access dyslexia. *Brain* 102, 43–63.

Index

28   5

Coventry University